SPIRALGUIDE

Travel With Someone You Trust®

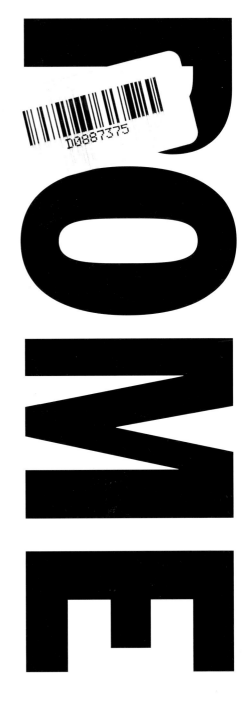

D0887375

Contents

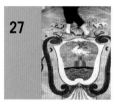

Original text by Tim Jepson
Updated by Sally Roy

Edited, designed and produced by AA Publishing, a trading name
of AA Media Limited, whose registered office is Fanum House,
Basing View, Basingstoke, Hampshire RG21 4EA. Registered
number 06112600.

Published in the United States by AAA Publishing,
1000 AAA Drive, Heathrow, Florida 32746-5063.
Published in the United Kingdom by AA Publishing.

ISBN 978-1-59508-505-4

Cover design and binding style by permission of AA Publishing
Color separation by AA Digital Department
Printed and bound in China by Leo Paper Products

A04749
Maps in this title produced from mapping © MAIRDUMONT/Falk
Verlag 2012
Transport map © Communicarta Ltd, UK

The Magazine

A great holiday is more than just lying on a beach or shopping till you drop – to really get the most from your trip you need to know what makes the place tick. The Magazine provides an entertaining overview to some of the social, cultural and natural elements that make up the unique quality of this engaging city.

V·BVRGHESIV

The
ETERNAL CITY

The first glimpse of Rome is bewildering – massive ruins, crumbling walls, stately palazzi, towers and domes are all jumbled together. Buildings of every epoch jostle side by side. The 3,000-odd years of the city's history lie all around.

The history of Rome may be long, but at least it has a shape, falling neatly into four eras: the 1,200 years of classical Rome with its mythical origins and Republican virtues, and the subsequent long, steady decline of the Empire; the chaotic years of medieval Rome, as the papacy emerged as a temporal, as well as a religious, supreme power; papal Rome, from the 15th to the late 19th century, when Rome became the capital of united Italy; and modern Rome, the capital as it is today, having withstood two world wars.

Classical Rome

Legend assigns a precise date to Rome's beginning: 21 April 753BC, when Romulus, famously suckled, along with his brother, Remus, by a she-wolf, founded the city. Fact confirms that there was a ninth-century BC settlement on the Palatine, controlled by the Etruscans, who drained the marshy ground where the Forum was to be created. By the fifth century BC the Roman Republic had been established, the ruling Senate instituted, and the Romans were busy expanding their territory. This set them against the other superpowers of Carthage and Greece, both of whom were defeated by the ever-growing Roman armies.

By 100BC these armies were more powerful than the Senate, leaving the way open for the emergence of single rulers such as Julius Caesar, Mark Anthony and then Augustus, who became the first Emperor. His empire stretched from Egypt and Asia Minor in the east to Gaul and Spain in the west. In AD68, this power passed to Vespasian, head of the Flavian family. This was the start of a golden age, with peace throughout Rome's territories and wealth flowing into the city. Rome was huge, with magnificent buildings and a population of one and a half million.

It couldn't last, and, following the death of Marcus Aurelius in AD180, the Empire started to crumble. The costs of protecting the Empire escalated, and by the reign of Constantine (303–367), the emperors were concentrating their energies on the Empire's boundaries, leaving the city increasingly undefended. The way was open for the barbarians, and in 410 the Visigoths sacked Rome. In 476 the last emperor was deposed by a German chieftain.

Medieval Rome

Surrounded by the vestiges of past glory, the dwindling sixth-century population cowered behind the remains of the Roman fortifications. The government ceased to exist, leaving a vacuum to be filled by the Popes, the sole figures of authority in these dark times. Pope Stephen II allied

Page 5: The magnificent dome of the Basilica di San Pietro (St Peter's Basilica)
Below: The atmospheric ruins of the Colosseo (Colosseum) floodlit at night; it is the largest surviving monument of Roman antiquity

Reclining statue, one of two representing the Nile and the Tiber, at the Palazzo Nuovo

himself with Charlemagne and his Franks, making Charlemagne the first Holy Roman Emperor. This seemed a canny move, but it was one that brought nothing but trouble over the following centuries, as popes, monarchs and powerful families struggled for the upper hand. This came to a head in 1084, when Pope Gregory VII took on the powerful Emperor Henry IV, who marched on Rome and looted and burned the city. The papacy had taken a major knock, exacerbated 300 years later, when the French declared their own candidate pope, and the papacy moved to

THE FIRST EMPEROR

In 31BC, Octavian, nephew of Julius Caesar, defeated his rival Mark Anthony, lover of the Egyptian queen Cleopatra, at the Battle of Actium. He was proclaimed Emperor, taking the name Augustus, "favoured by the gods", and brought peace to the Roman world. The beautiful Ara Pacis Augustae (► 102), decorated with family portraits, was erected as a reminder of this, and statues of him sprang up all over the Empire. A mixture of modesty and arrogance, he lived in a simple house on the Palatine, while making the city splendid, saying, "I found Rome built of brick, I leave it clothed in marble."

THE PRISONER OF THE VATICAN

In 1870, Pius IX retreated to the Vatican, leaving Rome to become Italy's capital. Here he, and three succeeding popes, remained, refusing to recognize the Italian state. The situation was finally sorted out by Mussolini in 1929, when a deal was hammered out that made Vatican City an independent sovereign state and the world's smallest "country".

Avignon in France for 69 years. Stability was only gained in 1417, when Pope Martin V declared that the papacy would henceforth control the city council. Rome and its papal ruler were restored, paving the way for the great days of papal power.

Papal Rome

Nicholas V (1447–55) was the first Renaissance pope, a ruler who started the transformation of Rome into a great and beautiful city. Under his successors, artists, sculptors and architects transfigured the face of the city, while the papal armies carved out ever-growing territories for the papacy. This brought them up against the French and Spanish, Europe's leading powers, and in 1527 the French sacked the city, looting, burning and killing.

> "...party-loving Rome was an essential stop on the Grand Tour"

The popes thereafter turned their energies to fighting Protestantism and transforming Rome into one of Europe's most spectacular metropolises. The first tourists, rather than pilgrims, arrived, and by the 18th century hedonistic, party-loving Rome was an essential stop on the Grand Tour.

In 1798, Napoleon invaded, and made Rome a Republic, which was only returned to Pope Pius VII in 1814. The spirit of nationalism was born, culminating in the 1860 establishment of the Kingdom of Italy. Rome held out as an independent papal state until 1870 when it became part of a united Italy. Pius IX fled to the Vatican, declaring himself a prisoner; between 1870 and 1929 no pope set foot outside the Vatican.

Modern Rome

Rome was now Italy's capital and underwent a huge building programme that created the government buildings and wide thoroughfares needed for a capital city. World War I had little impact, but Mussolini and his Fascists left their mark, though Rome was declared an open city during World War II and suffered virtually no damage. Post-1945, Rome benefited from Italy's economic boom and the main problem today is balancing the preservation of Rome's ancient monuments and historic buildings against 21st-century development.

SECRETS
AND ODDITIES

Rome is a city fuller than most of the weird and wonderful. Many of its more unusual sights are connected with death – notably the catacombs – or are the strange consequences of religion. Others are secret places seen by few visitors.

A Way with Bones

One of the city's most bizarre sights lurks deep underneath the 17th-century church of Santa Maria della Concezione (Via Vittorio Veneto 27, tel: 06 487 1185, Mon–Sat 9–12, 3–6, Sun 3–7, donation). In its crypt lie the skeletons and loose bones of some 4,000 Capuchin monks. Stranger still is the way many of the bones have been used to create chandeliers and beautifully crafted decorative patterns. Monks were originally buried here in soil brought from Jerusalem. When this ran out, they were left in the open, a practice that continued until as recently as 1870.

Secret Keyhole

Rome's most charming view can be enjoyed from Piazza dei Cavalieri di Malta – a square designed by Giovanni Piranesi – on the

Skeleton in Cripta dei Teschi, Capuchin Cemetery

Aventine Hill southwest of the Colosseo. To find it, walk to the left of the church of Santa Sabina as you face it (the church and the gardens are also lovely places). Continue to the end of the piazza and look through the keyhole of the huge door of the Priory of the Knights of Malta (No 3). Through the tiny hole you see a secret garden and an avenue of trees cleverly framing…but let's not spoil the surprise: see for yourself.

Wall of Horrors

Here's a departure from the mosaics and refined paintings of many of Rome's churches. Frescoes in the church of Santo Stefano Rotondo (Via di Santo Stefano Rotondo 7, tel: 06 481 9333) portray all manner of grisly martyrdoms, their subjects described by an enthralled Charles Dickens

during a visit in the 19th century: "Grey-bearded men being boiled, fried, grilled, crimped, singed, eaten by wild beasts, worried by dogs, buried alive, torn asunder by horses…these are among the mildest subjects."

Going Underground

Burial within the city limits was forbidden to all but emperors in ancient Rome. As a result the city has 300km (186 miles) of catacombs; these were the burial place of pagans, Jews and early Christians. Most date from between the fourth century BC and first century AD, and consist of long passages and chambers filled with niches used to inter the linen-wrapped bodies. Some have larger chambers, often the resting places of saints or martyrs. Many were cleared when the long-forgotten catacombs were rediscovered in the ninth century. The majority of the relics were removed to the Basilica di San Pietro and other churches, but it was not until the 16th century that the catacombs' full extent was realized.

The most visited catacombs lie near the Via Appia Antica: the catacombs of Domitilla, San Sebastiano and San Callisto. Other catacombs are less well known but often more atmospheric: try the Catacombe di Priscilla on the city's northern fringes, or the smaller catacombs below the church of Sant'Agnese fuori le Mura, a short way southeast of the Catacombe di Priscilla. The church and its near neighbour, Santa Costanza, are worth a visit for their superb early mosaics. (For opening times and admission prices visit www.catacombe.roma.it; see separate website, www.santagnese.org, for the Catacombe di Sant'Agnese.)

> "men being boiled, fried, grilled… singed, eaten by wild beasts"

Above: Grisly remains in Capuchin Cemetery, church of Santa Maria della Concezione

ART IN ROME

3,000 Years of Creativity

In Rome, man-made beauty is everywhere. Like some magnet composed of stone and paint, Rome's art has been pulling in crowds from around the world for centuries, making the city an essential destination for culture. Architecture, sculpture or painting, art is all around you, an integral part of the physical city that covers 3,000 years of artistic development and represents astounding creativity.

It can be overwhelming; Rome has no "one-stop" museum covering a comprehensive survey of its art. Instead, art is scattered all over the city, much of it still in the buildings and settings for which it was created. It's this that adds an extra dimension to what's on offer, and there's a sense of serendipity to tracking down art in Rome. Of course, you don't want to miss must-sees such as Vatican City (➤ 143–165), Palazzo Altemps (➤ 86–89) and the Borghese galleries (➤ 128–131), but there are many gems off the beaten track where you may find yourself alone with a great statue or picture.

Detail of a battle on the Colonna Traiana in Trajan's Forum

The Classical Ideal

The Romans inherited their concept of the beauty of the human form from the Greeks, and museums still display supreme examples of this ideal, often in the form of Roman copies of long-lost Greek originals. Head for Palazzo Altemps and the Vatican's Pio-Clementino (➤ 148–149) to see some of the best, or take in the Etruscan art at the Villa Giulia (➤ 135).

For home-produced classical art, there's the choice of architecture, sculpture and painting: Roman buildings surviving virtually intact, such as the Pantheon (➤ 90–94) and Colosseo (➤ 56–60), monumental forms that marry architecture to sculpture such as the triumphal arches of Septimius Severus (➤ 52) and Constantine (➤ 58), and Colonna Traiana (➤ 67–68).

> "there's a sense of serendipity to tracking down art in Rome"

For Roman sculpture, take in works such as the *Dying Gaul* in the Capitoline Museums (➤ 66–67) or the iconic *Laocoön* in the Vatican (➤ 148), one of the world's most dynamic pieces of sculpture; while painting is represented by the beautiful and decorative wall frescoes in the Palazzo Massimo alle Terme (➤ 120–123).

The Dark Ages and Beyond

Christian art made its appearance in Rome in the fourth century, when the Emperor Constantine decriminalized the new religion. Though few paintings remain, Rome boasts a clutch of early churches, many decorated with mosaics. These feature Byzantine, hieratic figures on gold ground, but are often also full of charming detail of everyday life, such as

Looking up at the magnificent dome of the Basilica di San Pietro from below

those in San Clemente (▶ 61–63) and Santa Prassede (▶ 132). Later medieval art includes Arnolfo di Cambio's ciborium, a stone altar canopy in Santa Cecilia in Trastevere (▶ 105–106) and the city's only Gothic church, Santa Maria sopra Minerva (▶ 94).

Choir stall in Basilica di San Clemente

Renaissance to Neoclassicism

By the 15th century the Renaissance, that great rebirth of artistic and intellectual expression, was well underway, and the following 400 years were the zenith of artistic productivity. With the popes and the great Roman aristocratic families as patrons, just about any noteworthy artist worked in Rome.

The result was an astounding variety of art. Head for the Musei Vaticani (Vatican Museums, ▶ 148–155, 162–164) to see work by early Renaissance artists such as Fra Angelico, Botticelli, Perugino and Pinturicchio, then take in Basilica di San Pietro itself (▶ 156–161), a triumph of the High Renaissance, whose design was influenced by superstars such as Michelangelo. His most monumental work, in the form of the astonishing frescoes he painted in the Cappella Sistina (Sistine Chapel, ▶ 152–154) is also in the Vatican, where it contrasts with Raphael's gentle and luminous frescoes. There's contrast too, in the shape of Caravaggio's (▶ 24–25) dramatic output, scattered in churches and galleries throughout the city.

Drama and energy are the keynotes of Bernini's sculptural work, which you can see in the Borghese as well as magnificent churches such as Santa Maria della Vittoria (▶ 116). Baroque architecture combined with a touch of rococo in the 18th century, producing ensembles such as the Fontana di Trevi (▶ 124–125) and the Spanish Steps (▶ 126–127), until neoclassicism brought a more restrained note, personified by the slick marble perfection of Canova's sculpture.

Into the Modern Age

From the 19th century, it is planning and architecture that have taken centre stage, with great piazzas laid out and boulevards carved through medieval areas. Mussolini was a prime mover here, creating the Via della Conciliazione as an approach to the Basilica di San Pietro and the Via dei Fori Imperiali, as well as entire new districts and buildings such as Termini station, with its undulating canopy, which was finished in the 1950s.

This trend has continued into the 21st century with the construction of some truly innovative complexes, such as Richard Meier's Ara Pacis

HOW TO PAINT THE SISTINE CEILING

Open-mouthed in the Cappella Sistina, forget the art for a moment and think about the sheer practicalities of painting a ceiling on this sort of scale. Virtually every day for four years, Michelangelo climbed the 18m (60ft) high scaffolding and stood all day, painting with his arm and hand above his head with paint and plaster dripping in his eyes. As fresco involves applying pigment to an incised outline on wet plaster, he had first to plaster the area, then get the paint on at a speed that enabled him to cover the prepared surface in the course of a single day. He wrote plaintively to his brother: "I wish simply to eat a hot meal in peace."

building (➤ 102), Renzo Piano's magnificently modern Auditorium-Parco della Musica, and the transformation of the Scuderie Quirinale into one of Rome's most exciting and modern exhibition spaces.

A Touch of Recycling

If you're wondering why quite so many classical buildings in Rome are so comprehensively ruined, you've only got to look about you. For centuries after the fall of Rome, palaces, temples and public buildings provided a handy source of ready-dressed building material, which medieval and Renaissance builders cheerfully plundered. Stone, columns and pillars from the Colosseum, Forum and countless other ancient structures were re-used in new buildings – just go to 12th-century Santa Maria in Trastevere and take in the 22 granite columns that line its nave – all purloined from the third-century Baths of Caracalla (➤ 96).

Auditorium-Parco della Musica, redeveloped from one of the 2006 Olympic stadiums

Buon APPETITO

As everywhere, Roman eating habits are changing. The cliché of pasta served up in family-run trattorias now vies with new-style restaurants, which have kept the best of traditional Roman cuisine but added a 21st-century twist.

The changes have definitely been for the better. Twenty years ago, the options were limited – glitzy expense-account slanted restaurants, humble trattorias or a rough-and-ready pizza dive, and that was about it. Nowadays, you can eat in wine bars, salad bars, gastropubs and decent ethnic restaurants, in surroundings where traditional fusty decor has given way to light and air and stone, steel and glass.

> ## "unfussy ingredients and dishes but served with a new oomph"

Rome does still offer wonderful family-run restaurants, where tables spill onto sun-dappled piazzas and the menu features all the classic Roman specialities. Even here, though, times are changing, with the rise of the *nuova trattoria*, eating houses retaining the traditional, unfussy dishes and ingredients but served with a new oomph. This is mainly due to young creative chefs in the kitchen, and greatly improved wine lists. Such places pride themselves on the supreme freshness of their ingredients and their provenance, with menus and

Freshly made pizza from a traditional pizzeria is one of the culinary delights of Rome

attentive waiters proudly detailing the sources of the meat, fish and vegetables. This is a direct result of the Slow Food movement, which originated in Italy and has spread worldwide, and emphasizes the importance of local producers and organic produce.

On the Menu

As with almost any Italian city or region, Rome has a plethora of culinary specialities unique to the city. Among these are the widely available *saltimbocca alla Romana* (ham-wrapped veal flavoured with sage) and *bucatini all'Amatriciana* (pasta with a fiery chilli-hot tomato and pancetta (Italian bacon) sauce).

Other culinary influences include those introduced over the centuries by the city's Jewish population – restaurants in the old Ghetto and elsewhere serve wonderful and otherwise little-known dishes such as deep-fried artichokes (*carciofi all giudia*), pasta and chickpea broth, and *minestra d'arzilla* (ray

Produce at the Campo dei Fiori market

PIZZA, PIZZA, PIZZA

Pizza is taken pretty seriously in Rome and the city's *pizzaioli* have always taken pride in their thin, flat and crisp *pizza romana*, cooked in five minutes in a blisteringly hot wood-fired oven. *Pizzerie* are normally open during the evening and very few places serve pizza at lunchtime – if they do, they could be aiming squarely for the tourist market. Come dinnertime, make sure you head for one that specifies it's got a *forno a legna* (wood-fired brick oven); *pizze* aren't the same from an electric number. Toppings are pretty limited and the staples you can expect to find include *margherita* (tomato and mozzarella), *napoli* (tomatoes, anchovy and mozzarella), *funghi* (mushroom) and *quattro formaggi* (four cheeses). Variations on the theme include *calzone* (pizza dough sealed around a filling) and *pizza bianca ripiena* (a thick pizza base split and filled with ham, cheese and vegetables).

GELATI TO GO

The best gelato (ice cream) should be labelled *produzione artigianale* (home-made): that means a choice of *crema* (creamy) or *frutta* (lighter fruit ices) made from seasonal fruit flavours and no bright chemical colourings or artificial flavourings. You can have a *cono* (cone) or *coppa* (tub), and expect to choose at least two flavours, even for the smallest size. You'll be asked if you want *panna* (whipped cream), which will be dolloped on top. Il Gelato di San Crispino (► 138), I Tre Scalini (► 108), and Ciuri Ciuri (► 72–73) are among the best of Rome's *gelaterie*.

Inside Il Gelato di San Crispino

fish soup). Traditional trattorias will often feature a help-yourself antipasto buffet, a wonderful selection of seasonal vegetable and fish dishes, all cooked and seasoned *alla Romana*. This range of starters is great for vegetarians, who otherwise, like everywhere else in Italy, are pretty badly served, more because of a lack of comprehension than anything else. If you don't eat meat, don't despair; there's plenty to try.

Waste Not, Want Not Cuisine
Some of Rome's most typical specialities however, might not be high on your list of "must tries". Traditional cooking is based on the *quinto quarto* – the so-called "fifth quarter", or what is left of an animal when everything that would normally be considered edible has been stripped from the carcass. This penchant for the obscure originally had little to do with taste, and everything to do with poverty, long the culinary mother of invention.

In practice this meant – and still means – menus filled with items that might startle even the most adventurous diner. The most traditional Roman specialities include tripe *(trippa)*, oxtail braised in celery broth *(coda alla vaccinara)*, strips of cartilage *(nervetti)*, brain *(cervello)* – delicious with peas – the pancreas and thyroid glands *(animelle)*, and *pajata*: baby veal's intestines with the mother's milk still inside (cooked in lard for added effect). And how about *lingua* (tongue), *guanciale* (pig's cheek) and *insalata di zampa* (hoof jelly salad)?

A State Within a State

Step into the Piazza di San Pietro and you leave Italy. This is the Vatican State, a tiny enclave in the heart of Rome, from where the Pope rules the world's billion-plus Catholics, and whose clout equals that of any of the world's heads of state.

Background to the Church

The first head of the Christian church was St Peter the Apostle, traditionally thought to have been executed for his faith in the circus built across the Tiber, on the spot now occupied by the Vatican, by the Emperor Caligula. Successive popes, following Peter's footsteps, based themselves in Rome, acquiring land all over central Italy. These territories, known as the Papal States, meant the popes combined their roles as religious leaders with that of temporal monarchs, and all that entails.

For over a thousand years all went well, but in 1870 Italy was united, the papacy lost its lands and the pope retreated into self-imposed imprisonment inside the Vatican. Here, successive pontiffs railed against the Italian state, declaring it illegal and its elections meaningless. The situation was finally resolved in 1929, when Mussolini signed a treaty of reconciliation, establishing the Vatican as an independent state, but one whose power henceforth would be purely spiritual. In return for this, the Vatican got a huge cash payment, tax-free status and a role as a moral influence in Italian legislation. This state of affairs continues today, with modern popes focusing on the spiritual affairs of their worldwide flock.

Left: Ceiling of the Sala delle Muse in the Musei Vaticani; centre: View of the basilica from the Priory of the Knights of Malta; right: Swiss Guard on duty in Vatican City

DESIGNED BY MICHELANGELO – THE SWISS GUARD

The Pope may have lost most of his territory, but he still has an army, the Swiss Guard. You can't miss them in and around the Vatican, mostly wearing their usual dark blue uniform, but transformed for special occasions. The dashing red, yellow and blue uniforms, the colours of the Medici popes, are said to have been designed by Michelangelo, and help make these men the most photographed young people in Rome. The 110-strong Guard, founded in 1506, is drawn from Switzerland's four Catholic cantons; between 19 and 30 years of age, underneath the fancy dress they are highly trained modern soldiers, ready to protect the Pope at all times.

Who and What's Inside the Vatican

Vatican City covers an area of less than half a square kilometre, most of which is occupied by the Basilica di San Pietro and palace buildings. These house the museums, and are also home to the Curia, the papal civil service who are responsible for the day-to-day running of the church. They're aided by the papal ambassadors, the nuncios, who represent the Vatican all over the world; in return, many major powers have their own ambassador at the Vatican. The Pope is guarded by his own Swiss Guard (see panel above) and his representative retains observer status at the UN

The tiny resident population – around 800 – shops in the Vatican supermarket, buys its medicine in the Vatican pharmacy, and uses the Vatican post office and bank, which issue their own stamps and currency. There's a heliport and railway station, a publishing house, responsible for the daily newspaper, the *Osservatore Romano*, and a radio and TV station.

Giuseppe Momo's spectacular spiral staircase (1932) in the Musei Vaticani

Greek and Roman busts and statuary in Museo Chiaramonti in the Musei Vaticani

A Treasure House of Art

Most visitors come to the Vatican to see the art, a heritage which encompasses the very fabric of the Vatican buildings as well as the huge collection of painting, sculpture, manuscripts, reliefs, tapestries and books that's housed within the Vatican and Basilica di San Pietro. The basilica (► 156–161) is home to some great art, including Michelangelo's Pietà (► 159–160). But the wow factor reaches its zenith in the Musei Vaticani (► 148–155), which house some of the world's greatest works of art.

A Spiritual Powerhouse

For many visitors to the Vatican, however, the art is utterly peripheral. For 2,000 years, pilgrims have journeyed to Rome, to pray at the tomb of St Peter, Christ's first appointed head of the church, and catch a glimpse of his successor, the Pope. They come from all over the world on what, even today, is the journey of a lifetime. Watch them; sure they're enthralled by the beauty of St Peter's Basilica, but they've really come to touch base with the roots of their faith. So make way for the true pilgrims – those who throng the Piazza for a sight of the Pope and queue to pray at the tombs.

SEEING THE POPE

When the Pope is in Rome he makes an appearance at the window of his study overlooking the Piazza every Sunday at noon. There are also weekly general audiences on Wednesdays, for which you need a ticket. They're free, but you will need to apply well in advance to the Prefettura della Casa Pontifica, 00120 Vatican City, then collect your ticket when you arrive in Rome. There's more information on the Vatican website (www.vatican.va). The Prefettura also issues tickets for the pontifical ceremonies, such as celebratory masses and canonizations.

Life Inside Rome in the 21st Century

In the second decade of the 21st century, Rome is learning to balance its role as a historic city and one of the world's most popular tourist destinations with that of being a modern capital, providing employment, housing and an infrastructure that will carry its inhabitants through changing times.

Left: Italian haute-couture on the runway; right: Busy shopping street in the city centre

The Challenges

Rome's problems mirror those of many historic European cities – and then some. This is a city whose population leapt by 68 per cent in the 20 years between 1951 and 1971, and it is still growing. The *centro storico* (historic centre) is ringed with sprawling suburbs of high-rise apartment blocks, *periferie*, which unsurprisingly fail to give their inhabitants any pride.

Congestion is another factor; with more than 900 cars per 1,000 Romans, traffic is still grid-locked on the cobbled and pot-holed streets in the old city, pollution levels are high and public transport leaves much to be desired. As elsewhere in Italy, the cost of living is soaring and unemployment is up. Locals have to contend with year-round hordes of visitors descending on a city centre that can barely cope with its own population. And yet, despite all, these challenges are being addressed, with improved infrastructure and better housing and facilities for citizens.

Movers and Shakers

The Holy Year of 2000 saw 3 million visitors to Rome and the government allocated large sums for improvements. These were used by the mayor, Francesco Rutelli, to spruce up historic buildings and museums and to create parks; consequently new business and employment rose. His successor, Walter Veltroni continued the good work, and by 2008, when Gianni Alemanno became mayor, cultural life had been revitalized with the opening of the Auditorium-Parco della Musica. By 2011 one new section of the Metro system was under construction while tourist numbers continued to rise.

Romani

Gli Romani, the Romans themselves, are the key to the city's future. Disliked by other Italians, they're perceived as essentially southerners – a bit lazy, a touch chaotic, and too inclined to let things ride. But it's this relaxed approach to life that endears Rome and its people to visitors.

Left: The Metro; right: Piazza Rotonda, perfect for a *passeggiata* – evening stroll

What the city lacks in style it makes up for with its *joie de vivre*. Romans are proud of their city, heading into town to shop, eat or simply throng the piazzas for the *passeggiata*. Their style is laid-back, the emphasis on relationships and contacts. They can be aggressively offhand and rude, and then they'll melt your heart with a kind act or graceful gesture.

Getting the Balance Right

For its citizens, as well as its visitors, Rome has to tread the line between being the capital of a modern, thriving Italy and one of the world's most important tourist destinations. It must keep its soul – the essence that makes it Rome – and challenge the sort of modernization that might destroy its traditional charms. It's a case of balancing 21st-century demands against its heritage, and hanging on to its sense of continuity in the face of global consumerism and development. Time will tell.

CARAVAGGIO
ART'S BAD BOY

Fashions in art come and go; the big boys, the Michelangelos, Leonardos, Raphaels and Berninis, are a constant, but every age rediscovers the genius of some less stellar figure, and Caravaggio is the new darling of the 21st century.

The Man

Born in Milan in *c.*1571, Michelangelo Merisi moved to the town of Caravaggio (after which he is known) with his family in 1576. Aged 21, and already quarrelsome and aggressive, he travelled to Rome, arriving with no money and nowhere to live. He found work as a hack artist,

producing secular, often almost homoerotic, pictures that attracted the attention of Cardinal del Conte, who soon commissioned Caravaggio to decorate the Contarelli chapel in the church of San Luigi dei Francesi (▶ 101).

It was his big break. Caravaggio's marvellous paintings of St Matthew, with their intense naturalism and supreme handling of light and shade, caused a sensation, and a string of prestigious commissions followed.

On the Run

However, his artistic development went hand in hand with a reputation for bad behaviour, heavy drinking, arrogance and brawling. In 1606 he killed a young man in a street fight and was

St Matthew and the Angel (1602) in the San Luigi dei Francesi church

WHERE TO SEE THE BEST

Pinacoteca, Musei Vaticani:
The Entombment
Cappella Cerasi, Santa Maria del Popolo:
Conversion of St Paul, Crucifixion of St Peter
Cappella Contarelli, San Luigi dei Francesi:
Calling of St Matthew, Martyrdom of St Matthew, St Matthew and the Angel
Galleria Borghese: *Boy with a Basket of Fruit, David with the Head of Goliath, Madonna dei Palafrenieri, St Jerome, St John the Baptist, Bacchus*
Galleria Doria Pamphilj: *Penitent Magdalen, Rest on the Flight into Egypt*
Palazzo Barberini: *Judith and Holofernes, Narcissus, St Francis*
Pinacoteca Capitolina: *The Fortune Teller, St John the Baptist*

For more information about Caravaggio and his art visit:
www.caravaggio-foundation.org

forced to flee for Naples. The rest of his short life is the story of incredible artistic production, flight and violence. After a few months in Naples, he fled to Malta, then Sicily, each time leaving a string of offences behind him and the law hot on his heels. In 1609 he returned to Naples, hoping to receive a papal pardon that would enable him to return to Rome.

In the meantime, he was injured in yet another street brawl and left Naples not long after to head north, carrying with him his three last pictures. His ship sailed without him after a stop on the malaria-ridden coast of Tuscany, where Caravaggio caught a fever and died, alone, at Porto Ercole on 18 July 1610. His body was never found.

Caravaggio: the First Baroque Artist

Caravaggio's work stands out for several reasons: the extreme realism of his paintings – he used the poor as his models and painted from life; his handling of light; and the dramatic intensity of his work. Many of his contemporaries branded his work as vulgar, lacking any sense of the ideal or sacred, and the drama too high. The irony is, that it's precisely these traits that make him a painter for modern times. Contemporary audiences love the dark and shade, the shafts of light, the dirty, scruffy models and the edgy undertones of his work. He was among the first truly baroque artists, but it took 20th-century critics to rediscover his genius.

Above: *Madonna di Loreto* (*c.*1606) in the Cavalletti Chapel, church of Sant'Agostino

ACQUA VITAE

Rise early, before the traffic builds up, to hear one of Rome's most quintessential sounds – the gentle splash and gurgle of water. No other city has more fountains than Rome.

Every piazza has its own, ranging from the monumental to the homely, and modern Romans have inherited the classical delight in living in a city where the sight and sound of falling water forms the backdrop to life. Classical Romans took access to clean running water for granted, and it's estimated that Imperial Rome provided around 250 gallons of water per capita per day to every citizen. A network of aqueducts brought water from the hills to the city – you can still see the arches around the city outskirts.

Incredibly, much of Rome's water still comes from these ancient sources, notably the Acqua Vergine, the Acqua Paola and the Acqua Felice. The supply failed during the chaos of the post-Roman era, but by the 15th to 16th centuries the Popes restored the supply and built new fountains. The nobility vied with the Popes to make them works of art; tritons, nymphs, dolphins, gods and goddesses abound, along with quirkier embellishments that range from recycled Egyptian obelisks and Roman sarcophagi to stone tortoises, books and wine barrels.

THE TOP TEN

Fontana di Trevi (➤ 124–125)
Fontana del Tritone, Piazza Barberini:
dolphins supporting a Triton (1643)
Fontana delle Tartarughe, Piazza Mattei:
built in the 1580s with boys hoisting
tortoises up to the waters (➤ 178)
Fontana dell'Acqua Paola, Via Garibaldi:
built between 1610 and 1612 (➤ 96)
Fontana dell Naiadi, Piazza della Repubblica:
modern fountain built in 1901
Fontana dei Quattro Fiumi (➤ 85)
Fontana della Barcaccia (➤ 127)
Fontane di Piazza San Pietro (➤ 158)
Fontane Piazza Farnese (➤ 99)
Quattro Fontane, Via Quattro Fontane: a
baroque fountain built in the 1640s

Fontana del Tritone, like all of Rome's fountains, is powered by hydraulic pressure

Finding Your Feet

First Two Hours

There are two international airports in Rome, but Fiumicino Airport has better links to the city centre and more tourist facilities.

Arriving at Fiumicino Airport

Scheduled international and internal flights land at Rome's main airport, Leonardo da Vinci (main line and international flight information, tel: 06 65951, www.adr.it), more usually known as Fiumicino after its nearest village. The airport lies 36km (22 miles) southwest of the city centre.

- The airport (open daily 24 hours) has **four terminals**. Terminal 1 handles domestic flights; 2, flights from the European Schengen countries; 3, international flights from countries outside the Schengen area and some intercontinental flights; 4, flights operated by American Airlines, United Airlines, Continental, Delta, US Airways and El Al. The terminals are on two levels; arrivals are on the lower floors, departures on the floor above.
- Facilities in arrivals include foreign exchange desks *(cambio)*, automated exchange and cash machines, bars, chemists, post offices, tourist and general information points.
- Avoid taxi and hotel touts in the airport, even those who appear simply to be offering general help. Keep a close watch on your luggage at all times.

Getting to Central Rome by Public Transport

- The easiest and fastest way to get from the airport to the city centre is the **express rail service** to Rome's main railway station, Stazione Centrale Giovanni Paolo II, more commonly known by its former name "Termini". For information on onward travel from Termini, ➤ 31–33. Trains depart from a dedicated rail terminal close to the main international terminal – look for the raised covered walkway from the main terminal building. It can also be reached via an underpass from the arrivals hall or by walking across the road and coach parking area from outside the arrivals terminal.
- **Tickets** (€14) for the express rail service can be bought from automatic machines in the arrivals terminal and on the station concourse, or from a small ticket office (daily 7:48–2:30, 2:48–9:30) and adjoining "Tabacchi & Giornali" newsagents on the right of the station as you face the platforms. Consider buying a second ticket for your return journey, as there can be long queues at Stazione Termini.
- Tickets must be **validated** at Fiumicino in the machines at the entrances to the platforms before boarding the train. On your return from Rome you must stamp your ticket in the yellow or gold machines on each platform immediately before travelling. Failure to validate your ticket may result in a heavy fine.
- **Express trains** depart at regular intervals between 6:38am and 11:38pm with departures at 8 and 38 minutes past the hour. The journey time to Termini is just over 30 minutes. Be sure to board the right train, as departures from the airport station also link (roughly every 20 minutes) to four other Rome stations: Ostiense, Tuscolana, Tiburtina and Trastevere. The journey time is longer, around 50 minutes, but costs about half the price of the express train. Tickets can be bought from the same sources as tickets for the express trains (see above).
- During and outside express train hours, a **bus service** runs approximately every 30 minutes (5:40am–9:45pm) from outside the arrivals hall to

Page 27: The superb inlaid coat of arms at the Basilica of Santa Maria Maggiore

Tiburtina station and Termini; there are four services between 1:15am and 5am. Journey time is about 70 minutes with four stops; tickets (€6) can be bought on-board or online (www.terravision.it or www.cotralspa.it).

Getting to Central Rome by Taxi

Taxis from the airport to the city centre are expensive, costing €48. Journey times to the centre are around 40 minutes, but often take considerably longer because of heavy traffic.

- Check the **meter** is set and running before you depart, and note that special supplements are payable for taxis between Fiumicino and Rome (higher from Rome to the airport), as well as for items of luggage placed in the boot, journeys on Sunday, and journeys at night. By law, all surcharges must be clearly displayed inside the taxi.
- Only take rides in **licensed cabs** (generally white or yellow), which wait in a line just outside the arrivals hall. Never accept the offer of a taxi from touts, even those who seem to have an "official" badge and uniform.
- **Prepaid taxis** and limousine services can be booked at dedicated desks in the arrivals hall. These cost about the same or a little more than taxis that wait outside, and have the advantage that you know exactly how much you're paying before setting off. They are also usually more comfortable.

Car Rental

Driving into the city centre is not advised as traffic and parking presents difficulties. Visit www.theaa.com/motoring_advice/overseas for further advice if you do need to drive. The car rental desks at Fiumicino are not in the main arrivals hall, but are located in the same complex as the airport train station (► 28).

Arriving at Ciampino Airport

Many charter flights and a few European low-cost scheduled flights use Ciampino, Rome's second airport (tel: 06 65951, www.adr.it), which lies about 15km (9 miles) southeast of the centre. There are few tourist facilities at the airport, so it is a good idea to get some euros before you arrive.

Getting to the City Centre

- Ciampino has no rail links with central Rome and the easiest way into the city is by **taxi**, which costs €35 for up to four people.
- By public transport, there is a choice of bus services, which leave from outside the terminal. **Buses** are operated by Cotral (www.cotralspa.it), Atral-Lazio (www.atral-lazio.com), Terravision (www.terravision.eu) and SIT (www.sitbusshuttle.it); between them, they offer half-hourly departures. You can buy tickets online, inside the arrivals terminal or on-board.
- Easyjet and Ryanair operate their own **shuttle service** from Ciampino to Termini. Passengers can buy return tickets (€4) for this coach service at the exit from arrivals (tel: 06 9761 0632, www.terravision.eu).

Arriving by Train

- Most national and international train services arrive at **Stazione Centrale Giovanni Paolo II (Termini)** railway station (5am–midnight. Information, tel: 06 892 021 or 06 4847 5475 from outside Italy, www.trenitalia.com).
- Some long-distance services, and services arriving at night, terminate at **Ostiense** or **Tiburtina** stations, from where the best way into the city centre at night is by taxi (► 33). During the day, you can take a Metro train from Piramide station close to Ostiense station.

From the Station to Your Hotel

Termini lies on the eastern side of central Rome and it is too far to walk with luggage from here to the heart of the old city or to most central hotels. Money lavished on a taxi at this point will be well spent.

The station is a haven for pickpockets, so it is vital to keep a close watch on your luggage and valuables at all times. Never accept offers from any hotel, taxi or other touts who approach you.

■ **Taxis** depart from immediately outside the front of the station building – do not exit using the side entrances off the central concourse and walkway. Be aware that queues for taxis are often long.

■ The open area that serves as central Rome's main **bus terminal** spreads out beyond the taxis. Finding your bus in the big and busy area can be an intimidating prospect on a first visit. If you do decide to take a bus, however, note that you must buy tickets before boarding (➤ 32). You will also have to pay a supplement for pieces of luggage over a certain (small) size; taking cumbersome luggage on buses is frowned upon and difficult as they get very crowded.

■ Depending on where in the city your hotel is situated, you may be able to take advantage of the two **Metro** lines that run from Termini (➤ 32). These present a less intimidating prospect than the buses. Follow signs from the main station concourse for the relevant platforms. The Metro is especially useful for hotels north of the Vatican or in the area around Piazza di Spagna.

Tourist Information

■ The best source of tourist information is via the **tourist information website** (www.060608.it). This has replaced the main tourist office and also operates a multi-lingual information line (tel: 06 0608).

■ There are also 10 **Tourist Information Points** (PIT) at the airports and key tourist locations around the city. All are open daily 9:30–7 (except Termini, which may open longer hours). The locations are as follows:
Aeroporto Ciampino, Arrivi Internazionale (inside baggage collection area)
Aeroporto Fiumicino, Arrivi Internazionale Terminal 3
Ostia, Lungomare Paolo Toscanelli, corner of Piazza Anco Marzio
Castel Sant'Angelo, Piazza Pia
Minghetti, Via Marco Minghetti
Navona, Piazza delle Cinque Lune
Nazionale, Via Nazionale, Palazzo delle Esposizione
Santa Maria Maggiore, Via dell'Olmata
Sonnino (Trastevere), Piazza Sidney Sonnino
Termini, Via Giovanni Giolotti 34 and opposite platform 24

■ **Archeologia Card** (valid for 7 days, €27.50) gives admission to Palazzo Massimo, Palazzo Altemps, Crypta Balbi, Terme di Diocleziano, Colosseo, Foro Romano and Palatino, Terme di Caracalla, Villa dei Quintili and Mausoleo di Cecilia Metella, and offers considerable reductions on individual prices.

Websites

The following websites are useful sources of general tourist information about Rome:
■ **www.romaturismo.it**
■ **www.vatican.va** is the official site of the Vatican
■ **www.060608.it** is an excellent and comprehensive information site, which covers every aspect of tourist information about Rome
■ **www.capitolium.org** is the official site of the Forums

Getting Around

Much of central Rome is small enough to explore on foot and it is the easiest way to get around to most of the sights, but you will probably need to use taxis or public transport at some point during your visit, especially to reach the more interesting outlying sights and for excursions from the city.

The city's transport system, run by various operators, is co-ordinated by **ATAC**. City-centre and inner-suburban destinations are served by the **Metrebus** and **Metro** services, and regional destinations by **COTRAL** blue buses. **Trenitalia**, operating from Termini and four other stations, are useful for out-of-town excursions.

The network is generally safe, reliable and inexpensive, although Rome's heavy traffic can make travel by bus frustratingly slow. Buses and Metro trains are often crowded, especially at **peak times** – roughly 7:30–9am, 12:30–1:45pm and 7:30–8:30pm. Trains and buses are also uncomfortably hot in high summer.

It is essential to be on your guard against **pickpockets on crowded buses**; the popular 64 bus between Termini and St Peter's is notorious for this.

Buses and Trams

ATAC's red-grey, orange or green buses and trams run on a web of routes across the city. The main terminus is outside Termini railway station, which is where you'll find the main **ATAC office** at Via Ostiense 131L (1st floor, tel: 06 57003, 06 4782 4044, toll-free 800 431 784, Mon–Fri 9–5). ATAC have introduced the **Roma Pass**, a three-day combined transport ticket and city map. This pass gives two free entries to museums, reductions on others, and discounts on restaurants and attractions, and is on sale at Tourist Information Points or via the website (www.romapass.it); price €25 (► 190).

Bus Routes

Relevant bus **route numbers** are given alongside individual sights throughout the book but these may be subject to change. The free *Charta Roma: The Official City-Map* contains up-to-date bus-tram-Metro information for key sights. It is available from visitor centres and tourist information points throughout the city (► 30). Alternatively, buy a *Lozzi* transport map (€10), available from newspaper stands. ATAC's website (www.atac.roma.it) has a useful journey planner and maps available to download.

Useful bus services in the city include:
23 San Paolo–Ostiense–Piazza Risorgimento (for the Vatican Museums)
40 Termini–St Peter's. Express with fewer stops than 64
64 Termini–Piazza Venezia–Corso Vittorio Emanuele II–St Peter's
75 Termini–Foro Romano–Colosseo
81 Piazza Venezia–St Peter's–Piazza Risorgimento (for Vatican Museums)
◀ **16** Via Veneto–Campo dei Fiori–Piazza Navona
◀ **17** San Giovanni in Laterano–Colosseo–Piazza di Spagna–Piazza del Popolo
◀ **19** Circular minibus service in the historic centre: Piazza Augusto Imperatore–Piazza della Rotonda (Pantheon–Via del Corso–Piazza di Spagna)

Bus Essentials

◼ Tickets must be bought before boarding a bus or tram (► 32, Tickets).
◼ You should always **board a bus** by the rear doors *(Salita)* and exit by the central doors *(Uscita)*. If you have a validated ticket, you may enter at the

front doors by the driver. Often buses are too crowded to reach the central doors, in which case it is acceptable – if sometimes difficult – to leave by front or rear doors.

- Route numbers, headstops *(capolinea)* and intermediate stops are listed at each bus stop *(una fermata)* for the direction of travel. Note that the city's one-way system means that outward and return routes may differ.
- **Night buses** operate after the main bus, Metro and tram services cease after about midnight. Most have conductors, and here you are permitted to buy tickets on-board.

Tickets

- A ticket *(un biglietto)* for buses and trams must always be bought in advance of your journey. Inspectors board buses frequently and at random: travelling without a valid ticket incurs a heavy automatic fine. Tickets are sold from automated ATAC machines around the city, and from shops, newsstands, tobacconists *(tabacchi)* and bars displaying an ATAC sticker.
- Tickets must be **validated** immediately you enter the bus by stamping them in the small orange or yellow boxes at the rear of buses.
- The basic ticket (€1) is a timed ticket known as the **Biglietto Integrato a Tempo** (BIT). Ask for "*un biglietto per l'autobus per favore*" (a ticket for the bus please) and this is what you will be given. It is valid for 75 minutes from the time of validation for any number of bus journeys and one Metro journey.
- The integrated ticket (€4), the **Biglietto Integrato Giornaliero** (BIG), is valid until midnight on the day of first validation across the ATAC and COTRAL network and FS suburban services, except the Fiumicino airport express train. It need only be validated once, on your first journey.
- Also available are integrated three-day (€11) tickets (BTI) and weekly (CIS) and monthly (**Abbonamento Mensile**) tickets (€16 and €30), but these last two are unlikely to be useful for most casual visitors.

Metro

Rome's simple underground system, known as *la Metropolitana*, or Metro for short, consists of just two lines, A and B, which intersect at Stazione di Papa Giovanni (Termini). The primarily commuter service serves several key sites in the city centre and provides fast trans-city journeys. Extensions to the system are under construction – though the wealth of archaeological treasures that lie beneath the city's streets inevitably make the process slow.

- Station entrances are marked by a white M on a red background.
- Services run daily about every five to ten minutes from 5:30am to 11:30pm, except Saturday when they stop at 12:30am.
- Buy standard **BIT tickets** from the usual sources (see above) for use on the Metro. Tickets (€1) valid for a single Metro journey are also available from machines at Metro stations.
- **Line A** is the most useful for the majority of visitors, linking Termini with stations near Piazza Barberini (Barberini), Piazza di Spagna (Spagna), Piazza del Popolo (Flaminio), the Vatican Museums (Ottaviano–San Pietro and San Giovanni in Laterano (San Giovanni).
- **Line B**, which also runs through Termini, has a useful station (Colosseo) immediately opposite the Colosseum.

Taxis

Licensed Roman taxis generally are white (or very occasionally yellow) and are identified by a name and number, usually on the outside of the rear door and/or a plaque inside the car.

- Go to a **taxi stand**, indicated by blue signs with "TAXI!" written in white: key central stands can be found at Termini, Piazza Venezia, Largo di Torre Argentina, Piazza San Silvestro, Piazza di Spagna, Piazza Navona and Piazza Sonnino (in Trastevere).
- When you pick up a cab, check that the **meter** is set at zero. As you set off it will jump to the current minimum fare (€6) for the first 200m (220 yards) and then rise quickly.
- **Supplements** are charged on Sundays, public holidays, for journeys between 10pm and 7am, for trips to and from Fiumicino, and for each individual item of luggage larger than 35 by 25 by 50cm (14 by 10 by 20 inches). All current supplements should be posted on a list inside the cab.
- Airport journeys fares are fixed at €35 to Ciampino and €48 to Fiumicino.
- If you suspect the driver has been dishonest, take the cab's name and number – making it clear to the driver that you are doing this is often enough to set matters right. Register any complaint with the drivers' co-operative – the number is displayed in cabs – or, in serious cases, with the police (➤ 189).
- The best way to be sure of a taxi is to call a **phone cab**. Give the address of where you wish to be picked up. The operator will give you a taxi-code (a geographical location followed by a number), plus the time you will have to wait: for example, "Londra dodici in cinque minuti" (London 12 in five minutes). Meters run from the moment a taxi sets off to pick you up.
- The following taxi companies are phone cabs that can be contacted by telephone, SMS or online, and are also available at taxi stands:
Taxi Roma tel: 06 3570, SMS 366 673 0000, www.3570.it
Cooperativa Samarcanda tel: 06 550 0036, SMS 3666 000 159, www.samarcanda.it
Societa la Capitale Radio Taxo tel: 06 49 94 (no website or SMS service)
Radio Taxi Cosmo tel: 06 881 77 (no website or SMS service).

Bikes and Scooters

Several outlets rent bicycles and scooters, but it is vital to realize that traffic is busy and potentially extremely dangerous. However, bicycles are good for exploring the quieter streets, and the open spaces of the Villa Borghese park.

- To rent a **moped** *(motorino)* you must be over 21. Rental requires a credit card, ID and/or a cash deposit. Helmets are compulsory.
- When you rent a **bicycle** it is usual to leave your passport or other ID such as driver's licence as a deposit.
- Rome has introduced a **bike-sharing scheme**, with 19 pick-up points across the centre; hop on and go, then leave the bike at the pick-up point nearest to your destination. Go to www.roma-n-bike.com for more information.

Admission Charges

The cost of admission for museums and places of interest mentioned in this guide is indicated by the following price categories:

Inexpensive under €5   **Moderate** €5–€10   **Expensive** over €10

Accommodation

Rome has hundreds of hotels in all price categories. Prices are often rather high for the facilities on offer, however, and good hotels in the mid-range bracket are in short supply. Rooms may be small, even in grand hotels, and noise is a problem just about everywhere. Central options are best, but you need to reserve early to be sure of securing a room.

Grading

Hotels are officially graded from one-star, the simplest accommodation, to five-star (luxury). Grading criteria are complex, but in a three-, four- or five-star hotel, all rooms should have an en-suite bathroom, a telephone and a TV. Most two-star establishments also have private bathrooms. Even in the smartest hotels, however, bathrooms may have only a shower *(una doccia)* and no bath *(una vasca)*. Always ask to see a selection of rooms – you may be shown the worst first. All-day room service and air conditioning are rare in all but four- or five-star hotels. Set prices for each room must by law be posted in individual rooms.

Location

In Rome it pays to be in the centre, despite the fact that traffic and other street noise may be worse here. The areas around Piazza Navona or Piazza di Spagna are best. Trastevere is pleasant, but has relatively few hotels. Via Vittorio Veneto (Via Veneto) is also a good, if slightly peripheral, place to stay but has mostly larger and grander hotels. The area around Stazione Termini has the biggest selection of inexpensive hotels, but this is not a pleasant area, especially at night, and is some distance from most of the key sights. Hotels north of St Peter's are also inconvenient, but this area is quieter and generally more pleasant than Termini. To reduce noise problems, try to choose a hotel away from main streets, or request a room at the rear or overlooking an internal courtyard.

Reservations

It is advisable to reserve all hotels in advance, especially in high season (Easter and May–September). Many hotels offer an online reservation system, often at better rates than a telephone booking. Whichever option you choose, make certain you request a written confirmation, either by email or fax. It's also a good idea to reconfirm reservations a couple of days before arrival. Hoteliers are obliged to register every guest, so on checking in you have to hand in your passport. Usually it is returned within a few hours, or on the day of departure. Check-out times range from 10am to noon, but you should be able to leave luggage at reception for collection later in the day.

Prices

All prices are officially set, and room rates must by law be displayed in the reception area and in each room. Prices for different rooms can vary within a hotel, but all taxes and services should be included in the rate. Hotels often levy additional charges for air conditioning and garage facilities, while laundry, drinks from mini-bars and phone calls made from rooms invariably carry surcharges.

Room rates usually include breakfast *(colazione)*, but where breakfast is optional (see rate cards in rooms), it always costs less to eat at the nearest bar. Breakfasts in better hotels are improving – buffets are now more common – but for the most part *colazione* just means a "continental" breakfast: coffee, roll and jam.

Reservation Agencies

If you haven't reserved a room, then *on no account* accept rooms from touts at the airport or railway station. Instead, contact **Enjoy Rome**, Via Marghera 8A (tel: 06 445 1843, www.enjoyrome.com), which operates a free room-finding service. Or try the free **Hotel Reservation Service** (tel: 06 699 1000, www.hotelreservation.it, 7am–10pm) at Fiumicino, Ciampino and Termini.

Budget Accommodation

Youth Hostel: Ostello del Foro Olimpico (Viale delle Olimpiadi 61, tel: 06 323 6267, www.ostellionline.org).

YWCA (Via Cesare Balbo 4, tel: 06 488 0460, www.ywca-ucdg.it). All welcome.

Sandy (Via Cavour 136, tel: 06 488 4585, www.sandyhostel.com). Dorm hostel-type accommodation.

Suore Pie Operaie (Via di Torre Argentina 76, tel: 06 686 1254). Centrally located, women only. Booking essential.

Accommodation Prices

Price categories below are for a double (**una matrimoniale**) or twin (**una camera doppia**) room for one night, and are given for guidance only. Seasonal variations may apply, with more reasonable rates in winter.

€ under €140   €€ €140–€250   €€€ over €250

Albergo Cesàri €€–€€€

Opened in 1787, the three-star Cesari has been in business long enough to get things right, and latterly has maintained its standards through the efficiency of its staff and regular renovation – the last major overhaul was in 1999. It also has the bonus of a quiet, central position in a hard-to-find little street between the Pantheon and Via del Corso. The 47 rooms are comfortable with modern decorative touches, as well as TVs and air conditioning. Prices are at the lower end of the expensive category.

🔢 194 B1 ✉ Via di Pietra 89/a ☎ 06 674 9701; www.albergocesari.it

Grande Hotel de la Minerva €€€

The Minerva does not yet have the cachet of Rome's other five-star hotels, but none of its upmarket rivals can claim such a central position – behind the Pantheon (► 90–94) and church of Santa Maria sopra Minerva. The hotel was first converted by Holiday Inn in the 1980s, but has since left the chain and enjoyed another makeover that

has improved still further the 135 rooms and suites and public areas. Service is excellent, the facilities are the equal of – and often superior to – similarly starred hotels, and little can beat the prospect as you step from the hotel's front door.

🔢 194 B1 ✉ Piazza della Minerva 69 ☎ 06 695 201; www.hotel-invest.com

Hotel Aberdeen €

Guests are made to feel very welcome at this friendly hotel, which is also excellent value for money. Set in a wonderfully quiet location just off the Via Nazionale, this is the perfect place to relax after a busy day sightseeing. The rooms are immaculately clean and relatively large for Rome. The transport links from here to all the main sights are excellent, though it's a little far from the *centro storico*. Breakfast buffet is served in a frescoed room.

🔢 195 E2 ✉ Via Firenze 48 ☎ 06 482 3920; www.hotelaberdeen.com

Hotel Accademia €€

If you're looking for a combination of modern design and historic surroundings, then the Accademia, near the Fontana di Trevi (► 124–125), is a good find. The building has retained its period exterior and has a patio. Inside, the rooms have the clean and minimalist lines of an up-to-the-minute boutique hotel. Owned by a small group, Travelroma, the other hotels on the website are also worth considering.

✚ 194 C2 ✉ Piazza Accademia di San Luca 74 ☎ 06 699 22607; www.accademiahotel.com

Hotel Bramante €€

The Mariani family have been welcoming pilgrims and tourists to their hotel since 1873, when they converted this old palazzo, once the home of the architect Domenico Fontana, into a hotel. Quietly set on a cobbled street, just a few minutes' walk from Basilica di San Pietro (► 156–161), the 16 rooms are all a good size, and furnished traditionally with restrained elegance. Breakfast is excellent and there's a small patio.

✚ 197 D4 ✉ Viccolo delle Pallini 24 ☎ 06 6880 6426; www.hotelbramante.com

Hotel Eden €€€

The five-star Eden ranks among Rome's three or so top hotels for its style, old-fashioned luxury, and a more relaxed atmosphere than many of its stuffier rivals on nearby Via Veneto. It's been an exclusive favourite among celebrities for more than a century, attracting European royalty and film stars. Renovation of the rooms and suites in 1994 ensured it reinforced its position as one of the world's great hotels. At the same time it retained its sumptuous decoration, enormous rooms, antique furniture and marble bathrooms. The Terrazza restaurant is also superb, with spectacular views from the terrace – perfect for a romantic dinner.

✚ 195 D3 ✉ Via Ludovisi 49 ☎ 06 478 121; www.edenroma.com

Hotel Fontanella Borghese €€

A hospitable welcome awaits you at this Roman-style, comfortable hotel, attractively situated on the upper floors of a 16th-century palazzo and close to Piazza di Spagna (► 126–127). Walk through the courtyard to discover a modern hotel with traditional style. Half of the rooms have bathrooms with tubs, and half have showers. The staff are exceptionally helpful and friendly, and the good public areas make a stay here a truly enjoyable and Roman experience.

✚ 194 B2 ✉ Largo Fontanella Borghese 84 ☎ 06 688 09504; www.fontanellaborghese.com

Hotel Navona €

Never mind that this hotel only has a one-star rating, it is part of Rome's history, as parts of the building were built over the ancient Baths of Agrippa, which date back to the first century AD, and the English Romantic poets Keats and Shelley once occupied the top floor. Plus, its position is unbeatable – one minute from Piazza Navona (► 82–85). Set in a quiet side street away from the hustle and bustle, the vast majority of its 21 rooms have been renovated to a standard that makes a nonsense of its lowly star rating. The owners are a friendly Italo-Australian couple who make light of any communication problems. The only drawbacks are breakfast (take it in a nearby bar instead), the air conditioning, which commands a hefty supplement, and credit cards are not accepted. If the hotel is full, the owners may suggest you stay in the smarter, co-owned and slightly more expensive Zanardelli hotel just north of Piazza Navona.

✚ 194 A1 ✉ Via dei Sediari 8 ☎ 06 683 01252; www.hotelnavona.com

Hotel Piazza di Spagna €€

The three-star Piazza di Spagna is not on the piazza, but in a side street nearby, a better location because it is considerably quieter. The attractive old building is covered in creeper. Its 20 rooms are not enormous, but the facilities are good: all rooms have air conditioning, a TV and telephone, and a bathroom. The location, especially if you intend to do a lot of shopping, could not be better.

🔒 194 B2 ✉ Via Mario de' Fiori 61
☎ 06 679 3061; www.hotelpiazzadispagna.it

Hotel Ripa €€€

Fans of sleek minimalism will be thrilled to find a hotel for the 21st century in the heart of the Trastevere district (► 95–98). Streamlined public areas give a taste of the bedrooms, where some might say style takes precedence over comfort. Classy and cool, this hotel will appeal to the discerning traveller.

🔒 198 C2 ✉ Via degli Orti di Trastevere 3
☎ 06 58611; www.ripahotel.com

Hotel San Francesco €€

The San Francesco in Trastevere is a good base from which to explore Rome. This comfortable hotel, which offers excellent value for money, has traditionally furnished rooms with white walls and rich textiles, and the public areas are delightful, with contemporary design. The breakfast buffet is generous, but the big bonus is the rooftop terrace, where you can enjoy a drink while looking over the rooftops to the trees on the Janiculum.

🔒 198 C3 ✉ Via Iacopa de' Settesoli 7
☎ 06 5830 0051; www.hotelsanfrancesco.net

Hotel Scalinata di Spagna €€€

What you pay for this three-star hotel might buy you a bigger room elsewhere, but it would take a considerable sum to purchase a setting quite as romantic – the hotel sits at the top of the Spanish Steps looking down over Keats' house and the Piazza di Spagna (► 126–127). Some of the 16 traditionally furnished rooms are small, but all are charming, as are the old twisting staircases and little roof garden.

🔒 194 C3 ✉ Piazza Trinità dei Monti 17
☎ 06 679 3006; www.hotelscalinata.com

Hotel Teatro di Pompeo €€–€€€

In Rome you walk through history, but in this three-star hotel you can sleep in it as well. On a quiet square east of Campo dei Fiori (► 80–81), the hotel occupies the site of the ancient Theatre of Pompey, which dates from the first century BC. Parts of the original building can still be seen in the remarkable rough-stone vaulted dining room and elsewhere. History aside, this is a pleasant hotel thanks to a welcoming owner, modest size – just 13 rooms – and the charm of many of the rooms: the attic rooms with their beamed ceilings and terracotta floors are among the best. Rooms have TVs and air conditioning.

🔒 197 F2 ✉ Largo del Pallaro 8
☎ 06 687 2812; www.hotelteatrodipompeo.it

Hotel Teatropace 33 €€–€€€

Location, location, location goes hand in hand with peace and quiet at this charming hotel, close to the iconic Piazza Navona (► 82–85), one of Rome's loveliest squares. The apricot-coloured washed building dates from 1585 and access to the upstairs rooms is by a beautiful, shallow-stepped, stone spiral staircase. As often in Rome, rooms are on the small side, but they're well designed to make the most of the space, and the marble-appointed bathrooms (mainly with showers) are state-of-the-art. Order breakfast the night before and it's brought to your room.

🔒 197 F3 ✉ Via del Teatro Pace 33
☎ 06 687 9075; www.hotelteatropace.com

Hotel Trastevere €€

The friendly two-star Trastevere is the best of a handful of hotels in the lively and atmospheric Trastevere district (► 95–98). Though the 20 rooms are small, they are well-appointed with modern bathrooms, terracotta floors and wood panelling. There are also four private apartments with kitchens available, which are good value if there are more than two of you or if you are staying more than a few nights. It can be noisy later in the evenings.

🔒 198 C3 ✉ Via Luciano Manara 24
☎ 06 581 4713; www.hoteltrastevere.net

Food and Drink

Eating out is one of Rome's great pleasures. The city has a huge range of restaurants, from humble trattorias and traditional dining rooms to sleek and expensive contemporary eateries, and there are plenty of places where you can get inexpensive snacks, pizzas and sandwiches. In summer – as an extra bonus – it's often possible to eat outside.

■ Don't be put off by Rome's specialities, many of which require a strong stomach (► 18), because most restaurants offer a broad range of **familiar Italian dishes**, which will delight most palates.

■ Differences between types of restaurants in Italy are becoming increasingly blurred. An *osteria* was once the humblest type of eating place, but now tends to describe new and unstuffy restaurants serving simple, often innovative, food in relaxed surroundings. Anywhere described as a **pizzeria** is likely to be even simpler; it will often serve a few pastas, salads and other dishes as well as pizzas. A **trattoria** is the general name for a traditional and unpretentious restaurant, while *un ristorante* is usually smarter and more expensive. A smart and expensive restaurant in Rome, more than most cities, does not guarantee good food; often you can eat well in the humblest places.

■ For most of the eating places listed in this guide it is well worth trying to **reserve**, the exception being pizzerias, which rarely take reservations. For more popular restaurants you may need to reserve a few days in advance.

■ Restaurant menus are usually broken down into a **number of courses**; these begin with *antipasti* (hors d'oeuvres), followed by *il primo* (pasta, gnocchi, risotto or soup) and *il secondo* (meat or fish). Vegetables *(il contorno)* or salad *(insalata)* are usually served separately from the *secondo*. For dessert you can choose between *il dolce* (sweet), *formaggio* (cheese) and *frutta* (fruit). Puddings are often disappointing; buying an ice cream from a *gelateria* can be a better choice (see panel, below).
　　You're not obliged to wade through all the courses on the menu, and none but the top-ranking restaurants should mind if you just have a salad and a plate of pasta, especially at lunch.

■ Romans take **lunch** *(il pranzo)* after about 12:30pm and **dinner** *(la cena)* from 8pm. The famous long Roman lunch followed by a lengthy siesta is largely a thing of the past, except on Sunday, which is still an excuse for a big traditional lunchtime meal.

■ **Service** *(servizio)* and *pane e coperto* (bread and cover charge) may bump prices up in all restaurants. Both should be itemized on the bill. If a service charge is not included, then you should **tip** at your discretion up to about ten per cent: in less expensive places it's enough to round up to the nearest €2.50 or €5.

Ice-cream Etiquette

Choose whether you want your ice cream in a cone *(un cono)* or a cardboard cup *(una coppa)*. Both come in different sizes, costing from about €1.50 for the smallest portion to €3 or more for the largest. You name your price and then choose flavours from the tubs laid out in front of you – usually you can choose a mixture of one, two or three flavours, even in the cheapest price band. You will usually be offered a topping of optional – and often free – whipped cream *(panna)*.

■ The **bill** (*il conto*) should be a properly printed receipt. If all you receive is prices scrawled on a scrap of paper then the restaurant is breaking the law and you are entitled to request a proper bill (*una ricevuta*).

Restaurant Prices

Expect to pay per person for a meal, excluding drinks and service:

€ under €30	**€€** €30–€50	**€€€** over €50

Eating Cheaply

■ Many restaurants, especially around Termini railway station, offer a set-price tourist menu (*un menù turistico*), but the food is often poor.

■ Keep costs down by drinking **house wine** (*vino della casa*), usually a good white Frascati or similar, available in a quarter-litre (around a half-pint) carafe (*un quartino*) or half-litre (around 1 pint) jug (*un mezzo litro*).

■ Most bars offer **sandwiches** (*tramezzini*), which are invariably made from the blandest white bread with crusts removed. Far better are *panini*, or filled rolls, which you can often have heated (*riscaldato*).

■ **Pizza** by the slice (*pizza al taglio*) is often sold from tiny hole-in-the-wall bakeries, but check the quality of the topping; in the worst places it amounts to no more than a smear of tomato.

■ A *pasticceria* specializes in cakes and pastries. A *torrefazione* is a bar that also roasts coffee for retail sale.

Best For

To sample the best that Rome has to offer, try the following places:

... **Tazza d'Oro** (➤ 94) for coffee
... **San Teodoro** (➤ 73) for fish
... **Il Gelato di San Crispino** (➤ 138) for ice cream
... **Leonina** (➤ 73) for pizza by the slice
... **Agata e Romeo** (➤ 136) or **Les Étoiles** (➤ 166) for a romantic meal
... **Bar della Pace** (➤ 108), **Ar Galletto** (➤ 107) or **Palatium** (➤ 137)
   for people-watching

What to Drink

■ The first drink of the day is generally **coffee** (➤ 40), usually a cappuccino accompanied by a sweet croissant (*un cornetto*). After lunch or dinner, Italians always drink an espresso, *never* cappuccino.

■ **Tea** (*un tè*) is common, but the Romans take it with lemon (*un tè al limone*) and without milk. If you want tea with milk, ask specifically for *un tè con latte* – sometimes you may have to insist on *latte freddo* (cold milk), otherwise it'll be the warm milk used for cappuccinos.

■ **Mineral water** (*acqua minerale*) is widely available, either fizzy (*acqua gassata*) or still (*acqua non gassata*). If you want a glass of water ask for *un bicchiere d'acqua*. If you prefer free tap water, ask for a *bicchiere d'acqua dal rubinetto* or *acqua normale*.

■ Bottled **fruit juice** (*un succo di frutta*) is often drunk at breakfast. Freshly squeezed juice is *una spremuta* of either orange (*una spremuta d'arancia*), grapefruit (*...di pompelmo*) or lemon (*...di limone*). Lemon Soda (the brand name), a bitter lemon drink, is another good soft drink.

■ **Beer** (*birra*) is lager, but darker-style beer (*birra scura*, *nera* or *rossa*) may be available. The cheapest way to buy beer is from the keg: ask for *un birra alla spina* and specify the size – *piccola* (small; 20–25cl/6.76–8.45

fluid ounces), *media* (medium; 40cl/13.5 fluid ounces) or *grande* (large; up to a litre/34 fluid ounces). Bottled beers are usually more expensive, except for Italian brands such as Peroni or Nastro Azzurro.

- **Aperitifs** include fortified wines such as Martini and Cinzano. Note that Campari Soda comes mixed in a bottle; for the real thing ask for *un bitter Campari*. You'll often see people drinking an orange-coloured aperitif – this is the non-alcoholic Crodino. Prosecco, a white sparkling wine from northeast Italy, is another popular *aperitivo*. Gin and tonic is *gin e tonica*.
- After-dinner **digestifs** include brandy (Vecchia Romagna is the best brand), *limoncello* (lemon-flavoured alcoholic drink), or *amaro*, literally "bitter". The last is the most Italian thing to drink, the best-known brand being the very bitter Fernet Branca; a good and less demanding brand is Averna. Romans may also have *grappa* after a meal, a strong clear *eau de vie*, or sweeter drinks such as the almond-flavoured Amaretto or aniseed-flavoured Sambuca (sometimes served with an added coffee bean).

Coffee Essentials

- **un espresso** (or, more colloquially, **un caffè**) – an espresso coffee (short and black)
- **una doppia** – double espresso
- **un lungo** – espresso with a little more water than usual
- **un macchiato** – espresso with a dash of milk
- **un caffè corretto** – espresso with a dash of whisky or other liqueur
- **un cappuccino** – espresso with added frothed milk
- **un caffè latte** – cappuccino with more milk and no froth
- **un americano** – espresso with hot water to make a long coffee drink
- **un caffè Hag** – decaffeinated coffee
- **un caffè freddo** – iced coffee. It is usually served with sugar already added. Ask for "*amaro*" if you want it without sugar.

Bar Etiquette

Waiter service at a table can cost twice or three times as much as ordering and standing at the bar. Prices for bar service and sitting *(tavola* or *terrazza)* should be listed by law somewhere in the bar. If you do sit down, remember you can occupy your table almost as long as you wish. Ordering at the bar means paying first, which you do by stating your order at the separate cash desk *(la cassa)*. After you've paid, the cashier will give you a receipt *(lo scontrino)*, which you then take to the bar and present to the bar person *(barista)*. If service seems slow, a coin placed on the bar as a tip with your *scontrino* often works wonders. Never try to pay at the bar, and never pay the standing rate and then try to sit down at a table.

Further Information

The following websites are useful for the latest information on restaurants:
www.gamberorosso.it – an easy-to-use site with an excellent selection of Roman restaurants
www.foodinrome.com – an informative, easy-to-use site with a good restaurant selection, updated weekly
www.060608.it – main tourism site with more than 2,200 restaurant listings and an essential source of information about Rome

Shopping

Rome might not be in the same shopping league as London, Paris or New York, and even in Italy takes second place to Milan, yet it has plenty of top designer stores and boutiques to choose from, as well as countless specialist shops and many interesting markets.

- The largest concentration of **designer, accessory and luxury goods** shops are concentrated in the grid of streets surrounding **Via Condotti,** or Via Frattina and Via del Belbuino.
- **Less expensive clothes and shoe shops** line several key streets, notably Via del Corso – which you'll find packed with shoppers on Saturdays – Via del Tritone and Via Nazionale. Shoes and clothes generally are good buys, as are food, wine, accessories such as gloves, leather goods, luxury items and fine antiques.
- Other smaller streets have their own specialities: **antiques and art galleries**, for example, on Via dei Coronari, Via Giulia, Via del Babuino, Via del Monserrato and Via Margutta; paper and wickerwork on Via Monterone; religious ephemera and clothing on Via dei Cestari. Via del Governo Vecchio or Via dei Banchi Nuovi, for example, are dotted with second-hand stores, jewellers and small artisans' workshops.
- Rome does not offer much in the way of one-stop shopping: there are only one or two **department stores** in the centre (the best is **La Rinascente**, ► 140) and no shopping malls.
- The city has several fine **markets**, notably the picturesque **Campo dei Fiori** (► 80–81), the **Nuovo Mercato Esquilino**, housed in a converted barracks on Via Lamarmora near **Piazza Vittorio Emanuele** (this is central Rome's main market, open Monday to Saturday 10am–6pm), and the famous Sunday flea market at **Porta Portese** southwest of the centre near Porta Sublicio in Trastevere. Porta Portese is reputedly the largest flea market in Europe, with around 4,000 stalls selling anything and everything, from antiques to organic food. It becomes extremely crowded by mid-morning, so try to arrive early (it finishes at 2pm). The market is particularly popular with pickpockets, so keep a close eye on your belongings at all times.
- Most food **shopping** is still done in tiny neighbourhood shops known as *alimentari*. These sell everything from olive oil and pasta to basic toiletries. They usually have a delicatessen counter, where you can have a fresh sandwich *(panino)* made up from the meats and cheeses that are on display.
- Rome shop assistants have a reputation for aloofness, especially in smarter boutiques. If they pretend you don't exist, ignore them or politely ask for help: the phrase is *mi può aiutare, per favore?*
- Don't be tempted to bargain – **prices are fixed**. Prices may drop in sales: look for the word "saldi".

Opening Times

- In the **city centre**, opening times are fast becoming closer to those of northern Europe, that is, Monday to Saturday 9–7 or 8pm. Even those shops that still close for lunch often close for only an hour or so from 1pm rather than observing the 1–4pm break of times past.
- The vast majority of shops are **closed on Monday morning**. Many food shops close on Thursday afternoon in winter and Saturday afternoon in summer.
- **In August many stores close** completely for weeks at a time (*chiuso per ferie* is the telltale sign – closed for holidays).

Entertainment

Rome's cultural scene was transformed in 2002 with the opening of the Auditorium-Parco della Musica, a world-class venue that offers a staggering range of music and the performing arts. The city is also noted for music festivals – often staged in beautiful churches and palazzi.

Information

- Information about most events and performing arts can be obtained from the main visitor centre and information kiosks around the city (➤ 30).
- The main **listings** magazine is *roma c'è* (www.romace.it), an invaluable weekly publication with details of classical and other musical events, theatre, dance, opera, nightclubs, current museum and gallery opening times, shopping, restaurants and much more. It also has a summary of key events and galleries in English at the back. It can be obtained from most newspaper stands and bookstores. The English-language *Wanted in Rome* (www.wantedinrome.com) is published every other Wednesday.
- If you read some Italian, listings can be found in *Time Out Roma* (issued on Thursday); *Trovaroma*, a "what's on" insert in the Thursday editon of *La Repubblica* newspaper; or daily editions of newspapers such as *Il Messaggero* (which has a detailed listings supplement, *Metro*, published on Thursdays).
- Alternatively, contact box offices listed in individual chapters – although sales staff may not speak much English.

Tickets

Rome does not yet have major one-stop ticket agencies, nor do all venues accept reservations and pre-payment with credit cards over the phone. Often you are obliged to visit individual box offices before a performance. The alternative is to visit a ticket agency such as **Orbis** (Piazza dell'Esquilino 37, tel: 06 474 4776, Mon–Sat 9:30–1, 4–7:30). They will give you information only over the phone; if you want tickets you must visit in person. Tickets for some classical, jazz and other concerts are also available from Ricordi music stores, of which there are five, and from Hellò Ticket (toll-free in Italy 800 907080, www.helloticket.it). Tickets for the Auditorium-Parco della Musica can be booked online.

Nightclubs

- Where nightclubs are concerned, be aware that a popular club one year can lose its following or re-emerge with a facelift and new name by the next.
- Long-established **gay bars and clubs** include L'Alibi (➤ 112). Other clubs such as Piper (➤ 142) often have gay nights.
- For most clubs **admission prices** are high, but entry often includes your first drink. For tax and other reasons, some clubs or bars define themselves as private clubs, which in practice means you have to fill out a (usually free) membership card. Remember, too, that many clubs close during summer or move to outdoor or seaside locations beyond the city.
- Dress codes for clubs are rare; remember clubs will be very hot.
- Most clubs open around 10pm with things hotting up after midnight and continuing through till 3am or later.

Classical Music

The key classical music and opera venues and companies remain fairly fixed but one area of classical music which is subject to change is the location of the city's outdoor summer concert cycles. These can be one of the city's best cultural attractions. Contact visitor centres for current information.

The Ancient City

Getting Your Bearings

What remains of ancient Rome is not confined to a single area of the modern city. Buildings and monuments from the era of the Roman Empire and earlier are scattered far and wide, yet the heart of the old city – around the Capitoline, Palatine and Esquiline hills – still boasts the largest present-day concentration of ancient monuments.

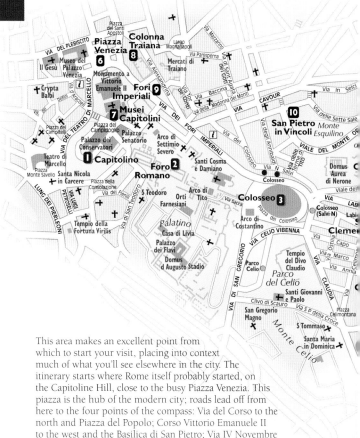

This area makes an excellent point from which to start your visit, placing into context much of what you'll see elsewhere in the city. The itinerary starts where Rome itself probably started, on the Capitoline Hill, close to the busy Piazza Venezia. This piazza is the hub of the modern city; roads lead off from here to the four points of the compass: Via del Corso to the north and Piazza del Popolo; Corso Vittorio Emanuele II to the west and the Basilica di San Pietro; Via IV Novembre to the east and Stazione Termini; and Via dei Fori Imperiali to the south and the Colosseo.

The Capitoline Hill, however, was the early focus of the ancient city. From its slopes you can look over and then explore the open spaces of the Foro Romano (Roman Forum), the social, political and mercantile heart of the old Roman

Page 43: A magnificent marble mosaic column in San Giovanni in Laterano

Climbing the steps to Piazza del Campidoglio and Palazzo Senatorio

0   250 m
0   250 yds

★ Don't Miss

At Your Leisure

Empire. From here it's only a few steps to the Colosseo, the greatest of all ancient Roman monuments, and then on to a quieter residential area and your first church, San Clemente, a fascinating historical hybrid which contains a beautiful medieval interior, the remains of an older fifth-century church, and the partially excavated ruins of a Roman temple.

Just a few minutes' walk away stands San Giovanni in Laterano, Rome's cathedral church, and among the most important churches in the city after St Peter's. In between times you can take time out in the park of the Colle Oppio, just a few moments from either the Colosseo or San Clemente. And if you still have some time, retrace your steps to the Capitoline Hill and explore the Capitoline Museums, which are filled with masterpieces from the Roman era.

In a Day

If you're not quite sure where to begin your travels, this itinerary recommends a practical and enjoyable day out in the Ancient City, taking in some of the best places to see using the Getting Your Bearings map on the previous page. For more information see the main entries.

9:00am

Begin the day by walking to busy **6 Piazza Venezia** (➤ 66), taking time to admire the colossal Monumento a Vittorio Emanuele II and **8 Colonna Traiana** (➤ 67). Then climb the shallow ramp of steps near the piazza's southwest corner to **7 Piazza del Campidoglio** (Capitolino, ➤ 48–49).

9:30am

Explore the church of **Santa Maria in Aracoeli** (➤ 49) and admire the view from the terraces of the Monumento a Vittorio Emanuele II. Then take the lane from the piazza's left-hand corner, admiring the Arco di Settimio Severo, a Roman triumphal arch.

10:00am

Go down the steps to one of five entrances to the **2 Foro Romano** (left, ➤ 50–55), one of the world's most historic ruins.

12:30pm

Emerge close to the **3 Colosseo** (top right, ➤ 56–60) and **Arco di Costantino** (➤ 58). You can visit them now or after lunch. You could have a snack lunch in **Cavour 313** wine bar (➤ 72), one of the cafés east of the Colosseo, a meal in **Il Bocconcino** (➤ 72), or buy provisions in Via Cavour and head for the Colle Oppio.

2:00pm

Spend time in the **11 Colle Oppio** (► 70), then either visit the Colosseo or walk through the park and spend time in the **13 Museo d'Arte Orientale** (► 71).

3:30pm

Walk a short distance on Via di San Giovanni in Laterano to **4 San Clemente** (► 61–63), in time for when it opens in the afternoon. The church not only has a lovely medieval interior – complete with superb frescoes and early mosaics – but also two fascinating subterranean places of Christian and pagan worship from earlier eras.

4:30pm

Make your way along Via dei Santi Coronati, a quiet side street, to visit the church **12 Santi Quattro Coronati** (► 70), before continuing toward the soaring **5 San Giovanni in Laterano** (► 64–65), the cathedral church of Rome and one of the most important places of worship in the city.

5:30pm

Explore **San Giovanni in Laterano**, not forgetting its ancient baptistery and cloister, the latter graced with countless superbly decorated columns. Then take a bus or the Metro if you don't want to retrace your steps to the Colosseo and Piazza Venezia.

∎ Capitolino

The Capitolino, or Capitoline Hill, is the smallest but most important of Rome's original Seven Hills. Home to Bronze Age tribes as early as the 14th century BC, it formed the city's birthplace, eventually becoming the hub of its military, religious and political life. Its history, position and many sights make it the perfect introduction to the ancient city.

Today, much of the Capitolino has been obscured by the Monumento a Vittorio Emanuele II, the huge white edifice that dominates Piazza Venezia (➤ 66). In the earliest times, however, the hill had two distinct crests: one to the north, which was known as the *Arx*, or Citadel, and is now the site of the church of **Santa Maria in Aracoeli**; and one to the south, known as the *Capitolium*, which is now largely given over to magnificent palaces such as the Palazzo dei Conservatori.

Between the two lay the *Asylum*, an area reputedly created by Romulus as a place of sanctuary, the aim being to attract refugees to the fledgling city. Today this area is occupied by **Piazza del Campidoglio**, a square largely laid out by Michelangelo and bounded by Rome's town hall, the Palazzo

View over the Piazza del Campidoglio toward the statue of Emperor Marcus Aurelius from Palazzo Senatorio

Senatorio (to the rear), and the **Musei Capitolini**, or Capitoline Museums, to either side (➤ 66–67).

Piazza d'Aracoeli

Ignore the steps to **Santa Maria in Aracoeli** – there's an easier entrance to the church in the piazza above – and climb the shallow stepped ramp (1536), or *cordonata*, in front of you. This was designed by Michelangelo for the triumphal entry of Emperor Charles V into Rome, and is crowned by two huge Roman statues of Castor and Pollux placed here in 1583. At the heart of the piazza stands a copy of a famous equestrian statue of Emperor Marcus Aurelius – the original is in the Palazzo Nuovo on your left, part of the Capitoline Museums (the rest of the museum is in the Palazzo dei Conservatori on your right).

Fresco of the *Life of San Bernardino* in the Chapel of St Bernardino of Siena, Santa Maria in Aracoeli

Head for the space between the Palazzo Nuovo and Palazzo Senatorio, where you'll find steps on the left into **Santa Maria in Aracoeli** (and the entrance to the Monumento a Vittorio Emanuele II, see below), a church already considered ancient when it was first recorded in AD574. The church is filled with chandeliers, ancient columns and a beautifully decorated ceiling. It also contains frescoes on the *Life of San Bernardino* (1486) by the Umbrian artist Pinturicchio (in the first chapel of the right, or south, aisle), and the *Tomb of Luca Savelli* (1287), attributed to the Florentine sculptor Arnolfo di Cambio (left side of the south transept).

TAKING A BREAK

The Capitoline Museums have a café (entrance on the lane to the right of Palazzo dei Conservatori; no ticket required), as does the terrace of the Monumento a Vittorio Emanuele II.

Santa Maria in Aracoeli

🔳 199 E5 🖂 Piazza d'Aracoeli 🕿 06 6976 3839 🕔 May–Sep daily 9–12:30, 3–6:30; Oct–Apr 9–12:30, 2:30–5:30 💲 Free 🍴 Cafés in Capitoline Museums and on terraces of Monumento a Vittorio Emanuele II 🚇 Colosseo 🚌 40, 44, 46, 60, 63, 64, 70, 75, 81, 85, 87, 175 and all other services to Piazza Venezia

---

CAPITOLINO: INSIDE INFO

Top tips Be sure to walk through the passages to the left and right of the Palazzo Senatorio for views over the Foro Romano (Roman Forum) (➤ 50–55).

■ It is worth visiting the Monumento a Vittorio Emanuele II (➤ 66, tel: 06 699 1718), the entrance to which is rather hidden at the top of the steps that also give access to Santa Maria in Aracoeli. Walk down the short corridor to emerge on the monument's colossal terraces, with superb views of the Fori Imperiali, and an excellent outdoor café. Café and monument open daily 9:30–5:30 (4:30 in winter); free.

②Foro Romano

The Foro Romano (Roman Forum) was the heart of the Roman Empire for almost 1,000 years. Today, its once mighty ensemble of majestic buildings has been reduced almost to nothing, yet the surviving ruins provide a romantic setting in which you can still catch a glimpse of the glory that was Rome.

Exploring the Forum

When exploring the Forum, it's essential to remember the site's 3,000-year history, and the degree to which monuments over this period were built, rebuilt, moved, destroyed, adapted, plundered or left to fall into wistful ruin. Only a handful of structures, therefore, such as the **Arco di Settimio Severo** or the **Basilica di Massenzio** hint at their original size or layout.

The remains of the Temple of Castor and Pollux at the Foro Romano

If monuments are all you seek, you'll probably leave disappointed, or at best bemused by the jumble of stones and columns. The trick here is to enjoy the beauty and romance of such ruins, and appreciate their historical associations: after all, you are literally walking in the footsteps of Julius Caesar, Nero, Caligula, Claudius, Hadrian and countless other resonant names from antiquity. With this in mind, allow anything up to two hours to amble around the site, more if you decide to see the Palatino.

Marsh to Majesty

The Forum was not Rome's original heart – that honour probably went to a fortress hamlet on the more easily defended Capitoline Hill to the northwest. The future hub of the empire actually began life as the *Velabrum*, a marshy inlet of the Tiber between the Capitoline and Palatine hills. This was the area that featured in the myth of Romulus and Remus (► 7), for it was here that the twins were found and suckled by the She-Wolf, and here that Romulus – according to legend – founded Rome in 753BC.

During the Iron Age, the area probably served as a local cemetery, and later as a meeting place, common land and rubbish tip for the shepherds and other inhabitants of these early settlements. It was at this point that the Forum may have acquired its name, for "*forum*" comes from a word that means "beyond" or "outside the walls" (*fuori* in modern Italian still means "outside").

HILL OF PALACES

The Palatino, or Palatine Hill (left), which rises above the Forum to the south, is one of Rome's Seven Hills. Sometimes called Rome's Beverly Hills, the area contains ruins of grand palaces built after the first century BC by the city's rich and powerful (the word "palace" comes from Palatino). You come here not so much for monuments – the ruins are even more confusing than those of the Forum – but to enjoy the area's gardens, shady walks, fountains, small museum, orange groves and pretty views over the Forum. It's a charming, atmospheric place, the perfect way to spend a couple of relaxing hours during the hottest part of the day.

As Rome prospered, so the area was drained by the first-century BC Cloaca Maxima, or Great Drain, and became the obvious place to build shops and houses, temples, courts, basilicas and the other great buildings of state. Successive emperors, consuls and other prominent power-brokers vied with one another to leave ever-grander memorials to their military and political achievements. This state of affairs continued until about the second century AD, when a growing shortage of space meant that political power followed the emperors to their new palaces on the Palatino, or Palatine Hill. Trade and commerce, meanwhile, moved to the Mercati di Traiano (➤ 68), while new building projects were diverted to the nearby Fori Imperiali, or Imperial Fora (➤ 68–69).

After the fall of Rome, the site declined swiftly; many of the monuments tumbled, and the stone was plundered to build Rome's medieval churches and palaces. By the 16th century the Forum was little more than an overgrown meadow. Excavations began around 1803, but remain far from complete. Major excavations to explore previously untouched ground around the Curia and Argiletum began in 1996, and are now proceeding apace, although much remains to be uncovered, not least under the Via dei Fori Imperiali.

Inside the Forum

You enter the Forum alongside the **Arco di Settimio Severo**, a huge arch raised in AD203 to mark the tenth year of the reign of Emperor Septimius Severus. It also commemorated the minor military victories of his sons, Geta and Caracalla, hence the battle scenes depicted in the large marble reliefs. To the left and a little in front of the arch, a line of stones indicates the remains of the **Rostra**, or orator's platform, where Mark Antony reputedly made his "Friends, Romans, countrymen" speech after the assassination of Julius Caesar. The platform took its name from the bronze prows (rostra), from ships that were captured by the Romans in battle, which decorated it. They have given their name to the speaker's "rostrum" ever since.

The eight-columned **Tempio di Saturno** (Temple of Saturn) to the south is one of the Forum's oldest temples – it dates from around 497BC – perhaps because Saturn, a god of agriculture, was one of Rome's most venerated gods from earliest times: the ancient Romans believed the city's initial prosperity and power were based on its agricultural prowess.

Walking away from the Capitoline Hill, you pass the **Basilica Giulia** on your right, begun by Julius Caesar in 54BC to complement the Basilica Aemelia opposite. The nearby **Tempio di Castore e Polluce**, or Temple of Castor and Pollux, was supervised by the city's *equites*, or knights, and was home to the Empire's weights and measures standards. To its south is the infrequently open **Santa Maria Antiqua**, the Forum's most important Christian building: it was converted from an earlier pagan monument in the sixth century.

Right: View from the Foro Romano toward the Palatino, which is remarkable for its tranquil gardens as much as its ruins

Below: Detail of a battle scene on the Arch of Septimius Severus in the Foro Romano

Along the Via Sacra

Cutting through the Forum is the **Via Sacra**, once the Forum's principal thoroughfare and the route taken by victorious generals and emperors parading the spoils of war. On your left as you walk along the surviving flagstones are the ruins of the Basilica Aemelia, built in 179BC as a business and moneylending centre. The large brick building ahead and to the right is the much-restored Curia, or Senate House, probably completed by Augustus in 28BC, when it was the meeting place of Rome's 300 or so senators.

The area to the Curia's right is the **Argiletum**, the site of a now-vanished temple that once held a statue of Janus, the two-faced god. Its twin doors were kept open in times of war and closed in times of peace: in 1,000 years, it is said, they were closed on only three occasions. In front of the Curia is the **Lapis Niger**, or Black Stone, a black marble slab which marks the site of a sanctuary to the god Vulcan. A staircase leads to a chamber beneath the shrine, where you'll see a headstone inscribed in Latin dating from the sixth century BC (the oldest example ever found). Modern scholars believe the inscription warns against profaning the sacred site.

Temples and the Vestal Virgins

The **Tempio di Antonino e Faustina**, built in AD141 by Emperor Antoninus to honour his wife, Faustina, is beyond the Curia. It makes a good introduction to the site, mainly because it is so well preserved, its survival due to its consecration as a church in the 11th century. Some of the oldest graves ever found in Rome were uncovered nearby.

Most visitors to Rome are drawn to the romantic remains of the Foro Romano

Beyond this point and the Temple of Castor and Pollux are the **Tempio di Vesta** and **Atrium Vestae**, respectively the Temple and House of the Vestal Virgins. It was in the temple that the Vestal Virgins tended Rome's sacred flame, a symbol of the city's continuity.

Part of the **Basilica di Massenzio** (begun AD306), beyond the Atrium on the left, is one of the Forum's most impressive monuments: in its day it would have been still more awe-inspiring, for what remains is only a single aisle of what was once a 100m (110-yard) nave. Remarkably, only one of what originally must have been dozens of columns from the basilica still survives, and now it stands in front of Santa Maria Maggiore (► 118–119).

Many of the ruins in the Foro Romano, such as the Temple of Antoninus and Faustina, are over 2,000 years old

The Arco di Tito

The Forum's last major monument before the Colosseo is the **Arco di Tito**, Rome's oldest triumphal arch, built in AD81 by Emperor Domitian to honour Titus (Tito), his brother and predecessor as emperor. Titus' most famous victory was over the Jews in AD70, and the arch's beautiful reliefs depict a series of scenes of the emperor's triumphal return to Rome with spoils from the campaign.

TAKING A BREAK

There are no places for refreshments inside the Forum: the nearest cafés are to be found off Piazza del Campidoglio (► 48), the grid of streets east of the Colosseo, or in Via Cavour. For a light snack in the last, try **Cavour 313** (► 72).

➕ 200 B3 ✉ Entrances by Arco di Settimio Severo, Largo Romolo e Remo, by Arco di Tito and off Via del Teodoro ☎ 060608; 06 399 67700; online booking at www.pierreci.it 🕐 Apr–Aug daily 8:30–7:15; Sep 8:30–7; Oct 8:30–6:30; Nov to mid-Feb 8:30–4:30; mid-Feb to mid-Mar 8:30–5; mid-Mar to last Sun in Mar 8:30–5:30 💷 Expensive. Combined ticket is also valid for the Palatino and Colosseo. Audioguides (70-minute tour) available in Italian, English, French, German, Spanish and Japanese: moderate Ⓜ Colosseo 🚌 75, 85, 117, 175, 810, 850 to Via dei Fori Imperiali

---

FORO ROMANO: INSIDE INFO

Top tips Before exploring the Foro Romano, **enjoy an overview of the site** from the steps and terraces on the rear eastern side of the Campidoglio, accessed from Piazza del Campidoglio (► 48). Steps from the balconies lead down to one of the Forum entrances alongside the Arco di Settimio Severo.

■ Avoid visiting the Forum in the heat of the afternoon – there is little shade on the site and sightseeing can be uncomfortable.

■ If you only have **limited time** to spend exploring the Forum, the most significant among the ruins (and sites definitely not to be missed) are the Curia, Arco di Settimio Severo, Tempio di Vesta and Basilica di Massenzio.

❸ Colosseo

Little else in Rome is likely to compare with your first sight of the Colosseo (Colosseum), once the scene of gladiatorial combat and other entertainment, and now the city's most majestic and awe-inspiring ancient monument.

First Impressions

To grasp the Colosseo's scale you need to admire it from afar. The best place for an overview is the **Colle Oppio** (➤ 70), a park to the northeast of the monument, or the belvedere (Largo Agnes) immediately above the Colosseo Metro station exit (best reached from Via Cavour via Via del Colosseo or up the steps just to the right of the Metro as you face the station exit). The more usual viewpoint – the open ground to the amphitheatre's west, alongside the flank of the **Foro Romano** (➤ 50–55) – is less satisfactory. The entrance to the monument's upper levels is nearby, and from here you can walk around a part of the exterior, well away from the roaring

Stripped of its marble facing, the underlying structure of the Colosseo still survives

traffic; you can also admire the **Arco di Costantino** from the same point (➤ 58, panel).

Early Days

The massive building project of the Colosseo was begun around AD70 by Emperor Vespasian. Its inspiration was the Teatro di Marcello and its site had previously been used for an artificial lake annexed to Nero's palatial Domus Aurea, or Golden House. The area's marshy conditions proved problematic, and required the laying of enormous drains – many of which still survive – and the creation of immense foundations. The costs of building the monument were met by the spoils of war, in this case the Romans' triumph over the Jews in AD70, which realized 50 tonnes of gold and silver from the temple of Jerusalem alone. Jewish slaves captured in the campaign provided the labour force.

By the time of Vespasian's death in AD79, the monument had been completed to its third tier. Additions were made by Vespasian's son, Titus, who inaugurated the Colosseo in AD80 with celebrations that saw the slaughter of 5,000 animals and 100 days of festivities.

The completed structure was an architectural triumph. Its simple design has provided a model for stadiums to this

day, with **tiered seating** and 80 exits, or *vomitoria*, that allowed huge crowds – estimates of the Colosseo's capacity range from 50,000 to 73,000 people – to leave the stadium in minutes. Above the seating, a vast sailcloth roof, or *velarium*, could be pulled into place by sailors of the Imperial fleets to shade spectators from the elements. It was supported by 240 wooden masts, the supports and sockets for which you can still see in a ring below the structure's uppermost cornice.

Inside the Colosseo

Inside, much of the original seating and flooring have disappeared. A major fire in AD217 devastated the upper levels and wooden arena (*arena* means sand, which covered the stage area). Other fires and earthquakes over the next 400 years further damaged the structure. By the sixth century the arena was being used as workshops and a cemetery; by 1320 the entire south side of the monument had collapsed.

Many of the sculptural reliefs on the Arco di Costantino were lifted from older monuments and then remodelled to fit their new home

ARCO DI COSTANTINO

In any other context, the Arch of Constantine (AD315) would be a major monument. Being overshadowed by the Colosseum, it is often ignored in favour of its neighbour. A triumphal arch like the Arco di Tito (► 55) and Arco di Settimio Severo in the Foro Romano (► 52), it was raised to commemorate the triumph of Emperor Constantine over Maxentius, his imperial rival, at the Battle of Milvian Bridge (AD312) just north of Rome. It is the city's largest and best-preserved arch, and one of the last major monuments built in ancient Rome.

Most of its materials were pilfered from other buildings. These included many of the sculptural reliefs, notably the eight reliefs framing the inscription, which portray scenes of an emperor at war or engaged in civic duties. They were probably removed from a monument raised to celebrate victories by Marcus Aurelius in AD176. Wherever the face of Aurelius appeared, masons simply recarved the reliefs to portray Constantine.

The same happened in the arch's central passage, where the two main reliefs show scenes carved during the reigns of Domitian or Trajan. With a little judicious recarving and relabelling (*Fundator quietis* – "founder of calm"), the panels were altered to show Constantine riding into battle against the barbarians (on the monument's west side) and being crowned by the figure of Victory.

Stone from the Colosseo was plundered to build many of Rome's churches and palaces, but the arena and arcades are still clearly visible

This and other parts of the building were then ransacked for building stone, most of which found its way into churches, roads, wharves and palaces such as the Palazzo Venezia and Palazzo Barberini. The desecration ceased in 1744, when Pope Benedict XIV consecrated the site in memory of the Christians who had supposedly been martyred there.

Contrary to popular myth, however, few if any Christians were killed in the Colosseo, whose primary function was to stage gladiatorial and other games. Today, you can look down on the **maze of tunnels and shafts** that lay under the stage, the means by which the games' animals, gladiators and other protagonists were brought to the stage from distant pens. Clever plumbing, it's said, also meant the stage area could be flooded to present mock sea battles.

The Spectators, the Emperor and the Sport

Spectators were rigidly segregated by status and sex, and they were expected to dress specially for the occasion. The emperor and Vestal Virgins faced each other at the lowest levels in special boxes. Alongside them, on wide platforms, sat the senators, all of whom were expected to dress in white togas and bring their own chairs (*bisellia*). Above them sat the knights and aristocrats, then came the ordinary Roman citizens (*plebeians*) and finally – some 40m (130 feet) up and 50m (165 feet) from the stage – the women, slaves and poor (though few women, by all accounts, ventured to the games). Some groups had separate sections, notably soldiers, scribes and heralds, and some were banned altogether, namely gravediggers, actors and retired gladiators. A special official, or *designator*, kept everyone in their rightful place.

Emperors and spectators often had control over a protagonist's destiny. A wounded man could appeal for mercy by raising a finger on his left hand; the wave of a handkerchief would then indicate a reprieve, while the sinister and still-familiar downturned thumb meant death. The wounded were often dispatched in any case, regardless of the crowd's verdict, and those who tried to escape by feigning death were poked with red-hot irons to discover if they were still alive.

TAKING A BREAK

Avoid the expensive cafés and bars in the monument's immediate vicinity. Instead, try Via Cavour or the streets off Via di San Giovanni in Laterano. Try **Café Café** (➤ 72) for a snack lunch or **Il Bocconcino** (➤ 72) for a meal.

🚹 200 C3 ⌧ Piazza del Colosseo, Via dei Fori Imperiali ☎ 060608; 06 3996 7700; online booking at www.pierreci.it ⏲ Interior: Apr–Aug daily 8:30–7:15; Sep 8:30–7; Oct 8:30–6:30; Nov to mid-Feb 8:30–4:30; mid-Feb to mid-Mar 8:30–5; mid-Mar to end Mar 8:30–5:30 💶 Expensive. Combined ticket with Palatino and Foro Romano. Audioguides (70-minute tour): moderate 🚇 Colosseo 🚌 30B, 75, 85, 87, 117, 175, 186

The floodlit Colosseo at night is one of Rome's unmissable sights

COLOSSEO: INSIDE INFO

Top tips Return to the Colosseo after **nightfall**, to see the monument floodlit.
■ The Colosseo's rather hidden entrance is on its southernmost side.
■ Climb to the monument's **upper tiers** for a proper idea of the structure's size and the complexity of the tunnels below the stage area.
■ If you're tired of all the bustle, walk to the nearby Colle Oppio park (➤ 70).
■ The Colosseo's "gladiators" often expect to be paid if you photograph them.

In more detail Once you've climbed up to the first tier, there's plenty of information on the Colosseo in the shape of a **permanent exhibition**, complete with excellent information in English, devoted to the Flavian dynasty, of which Vespasian was the founder. Fascinating insights are to be found in the displays of artefacts, which were found during excavations, such as gaming pieces used by members of the crowd to pass the time between contests, lost hairpins, combs and trinkets, and remnants of Roman lunch boxes and flasks that the spectators used to hold their picnics.

④San Clemente

Little in San Clemente's deceptively plain exterior suggests you are looking at one of Rome's most remarkable churches. Not only is the building home to the city's loveliest medieval interior – complete with some sublime frescoes and mosaics – but it also contains two earlier places of worship that span 2,000 years of religious observance.

The *Triumph of the Cross* above the high altar dates from the 12th century. The 12 sheep and 12 doves symbolize the Apostles

San Clemente divides into three sections, stacked one on top of the other: a 12th-century church above a fourth- or fifth-century church, which sits on a late second-century Mithraic temple. The church alone would be worth a special visit, but the two lower structures make the complex unmissable. Note that you enter the main church via a side door on Via di San Giovanni in Laterano, though the main entrance is occasionally open. You should allow around 40 minutes here, more if you are interested in the temple and excavations.

Medieval Interior

The main body of the church at ground level was built between 1108 and 1184 to replace the church that now lies beneath it, which was destroyed by Norman raiders in 1084. Inside, it retains Rome's finest medieval interior, most of the city's churches having been modified in the baroque age – only Santa Maria in Cosmedin (► 177) rivals San Clemente.

The highlights are many. Among the paintings, pride of place goes to a Renaissance **fresco cycle** of the *Life of St*

Catherine (1428), one of only a handful of works by the
influential Florentine artist Masolino da Panicale (it's in the
rear left aisle chapel, to your right as you enter).

Among the **mosaics**, the star turn is the 12th-century
Triumph of the Cross, which forms a majestic swathe of colour
across the apse. Scholars think its design was based on that
of a similar mosaic that was lost when the earlier church was
destroyed in the 11th century. The work is full of detail and
incident: note in particular the 12 doves on the cross and
the 12 sheep below, symbols of the Apostles, and the four
rivers of paradise which spring from the cross, their waters
quenching the thirst of the faithful, represented here by stags.
The imposing 14th-century tabernacle below and to the right
is by the Florentine sculptor Arnolfo di Cambio.

The marble-panelled walls of the **choir screen** (fifth–ninth
century) dominate the nave. Such screens were a typical
feature of early medieval churches but are now rare. Many
of the panels were salvaged from the earlier church, while
various of the columns originally hailed from the Foro Traiano
(Trajan's Forum) in the Fori Imperiali (➤ 68). Equally
beautiful and almost as venerable are the pulpit, candleholder
and altar canopy, or *baldacchino*.

The Temple and Excavations

Steps accessed from the rear right-hand (south) side of the
church lead down to what remains of the earlier church, the
existence of which was only discovered in 1857. The remains
here are relatively scant.

More is to be gained by dropping down yet another level,
where there are the remains of two Roman-era buildings, parts
of which are still only partially excavated. Almost the first
thing you encounter is the cast of a **Mithraic altar**. Mithraism
was a popular Roman cult that survived into the Christian
era. The bull was one of Mithraism's main symbols, hence the
beast portrayed on the altar being killed by the god Mithras,
along with the figures of torch-bearers and a snake, a symbol
of regeneration. The cult was finally suppressed in AD392.

The site of
San Clemente
has been used
as a place of
worship for
more than
2,000 years

Christ and Our Lady, one of the superb medieval frescoes that adorn the apse of San Clemente

A Roman House and Warehouse

This subterranean area of the church also includes part of a **Roman house** in which a *mithraem*, or place of worship, had been installed in the central room, probably toward the end of the second century. Such temples were meant to replicate Mithras' cave, so doors would have been blocked or narrowed to a slit to allow sunlight to strike the cult's icons and images. Benches were installed to enable the initiates to take meals and worship communally.

The house itself is much older, archaeologists having discovered date-stamps corresponding to the reign of Domitian (AD90–6) on the steps of the ancient staircase. In their day, these steps led into the basement of the house. Excavations suggest that the temple was walled up close to the year of Mithraism's fourth-century suppression, but that the basement continued to be used for a further six centuries.

The layout of the second structure here corresponds in part to that of a *horrea*, or warehouse, and may well have been a granary, although some early theories suggest it could have been the site of workshops belonging to the Imperial Mint, the *Moneta Caesaris*. Newer theories suggest the site contains two buildings, one being commercial premises, the other a house built over these premises which belonged to a wealthy Roman Christian. This Christian, so the theory goes, went by the name of Clemente, and founded a church on the site dedicated to his saintly namesake.

TAKING A BREAK

There are many small bars on Via di San Giovanni in Laterano and adjoining streets where you can stop for a coffee, a drink or a quick bite to eat. **Café Café** (➤ 72) is good for snacks.

✚ 201 D3 ✉ Via di San Giovanni in Laterano ☎ 06 774 0021; www. basilicasanclemente.com 🕐 Church and excavations: Mon–Sat 9–12:30, 3–6, Sun 12–6; closed during services 💶 Church: free. Excavations: moderate 🚇 Colosseo 🚌 75, 85, 87, 117, 175 to Piazza del Colosseo or 85, 117, 850 to Via di San Giovanni in Laterano

---

SAN CLEMENTE: INSIDE INFO

In more detail If the main door of the upper church is open, try to look outside at the *quadroporticus*, the distinctive square colonnaded courtyard that fronts the main facade. Such courtyards were once common features of early Roman basilica churches – rectangular churches with simple naves and no transepts – but are now rare.

5 San Giovanni in Laterano

San Giovanni in Laterano, not St Peter's, is the cathedral church of Rome; St Peter's lies in the Vatican, a separate sovereign state. Even without its exalted status, however, this great church would be worth visiting, both for its soaring facade and the beauty of its interior, cloister and baptistery.

San Giovanni in Laterano has venerable origins. It was in a Roman palace on the site, where Constantine, the first Christian emperor, met Pope Miltiades in 313, and here that Constantine raised the city's first officially sanctioned church (over what had been the barracks of his personal guard). From earliest times it housed the *cathedra*, or throne, of the Bishop of Rome. The church's importance continued for centuries – for example, popes were crowned here until the 19th century. During this time, the original church was destroyed by the Vandals, and subsequent churches were replaced or restored following fires and earthquakes.

In the portico at the foot of the immense facade (built in 1735) stands an **ancient statue of Constantine**, while to its

Baroque architect Francesco Borromini remodelled much of San Giovanni's sumptuous interior

right are the church's magnificent **main bronze doors**, which were brought from the Curia, or Senate House, in the Foro Romano (➤ 50–55).

The Interior and Baptistry

The church's restrained **interior** (1646–50) is largely the work of the baroque architect Borromini, who thoughtfully retained the nave's earlier gold-hued and beautifully **ornate ceiling**. The ceiling aside, you shouldn't miss the **papal altar and canopy** (begun in 1367) at the main crossing, where, until latterly, only a pope could officiate. It reputedly holds the skulls of saints Peter and Paul, and part of a table that is said to have been used by St Peter.

San Giovanni's real glory is its **cloister** (1215–32), entered from the south side of the church, a tranquil corner with dozens of variously shaped columns, many adorned with exquisite Cosmati work (an intricate inlay of beautiful coloured stones and marbles).

Outside the church to its rear – you need to exit the building and bear left – is Constantine's San Giovanni in Fonte, or **Baptistery of St John**, a building whose octagonal plan provided the blueprint for baptisteries across Italy for centuries to come. Some of the building has been altered over the years, but significant older parts survive, notably the fifth-century mosaic in the north apse and the Chapel of St John (461–68), which preserves its original doors.

Numerous statues adorn San Giovanni's facade, a prominent feature of Rome's skyline

➕ 201 E2 ✉ Piazza di San Giovanni in Laterano ☎ 06 6988 6433; www.vatican.va. Scala Santa: 06 772 6641 🕐 Church: daily 7–6.45. Cloister: daily 9–6. Baptistery: daily 7:30–12:30, 4–6:30. Scala Santa: daily 6:30–12, 3–6. Note that times can vary without notice 💷 Church, Scala Santa: free. Baptistery, Cloister: inexpensive 🚇 San Giovanni 🚌 3, 16, 81, 85, 87, 117, 218, 360, 590, 650, 714, 810, 850

SAN GIOVANNI IN LATERANO: INSIDE INFO

Top tips While visiting San Giovanni you might wish to visit the **flea market** (Mon–Fri 8:30–1:30, Sat 8:30–6) held along nearby Via Sannio, a right turn just through Porta San Giovanni.

■ If you baulk at the long walk back to the city centre from San Giovanni, consider taking the Metro from nearby Giovanni Metro station (just beyond Porta San Giovanni).

In more depth Stand with your back to San Giovanni's facade. The building ahead of you and a little to the left contains the **Scala Santa**, or Holy Staircase, 28 wood-covered marble steps reputedly removed from Pontius Pilate's palace in Jerusalem. Constantine's mother is said to have brought them to Rome, since when, as the steps that Christ ascended during his trial, they have been an object of veneration for the pilgrims who climb them on their knees.

At Your Leisure

6 Piazza Venezia

Piazza Venezia is the key to central Rome, a huge traffic-filled square from which some of the city's major streets strike off to the four points of the compass. But while you will probably pass through the piazza several times, it is not a place with many important things to see – save for the huge white edifice on its southern flank, the Monumento a Vittorio Emanuele II.

This magnificent marble monolith, built between 1885 and 1911, commemorates the unification of Italy and the country's first king, Vittorio Emanuele. It is also called the Altare della Patria, or Altar of the Nation – the tomb of Italy's Unknown Soldier is here – but Romans know it as the "typewriter" or "wedding cake" after its huge marble tiers. Its terraces (► 49) offer superb views of the surrounding area.

On the square's west side stands the Palazzo Venezia (1451), which for 200 years between 1594 and 1797 was the property of the Venetian Republic – hence its name and the name of the square. The palazzo is known for the balcony from which Mussolini once harangued crowds in the square below – the dictator kept an office in the building – and for the underrated Museo del Palazzo Venezia, used for temporary exhibitions and noted for its permanent collection of medieval paintings, textiles, ceramics, jewellery and other decorative arts. If it's open, you should also look into San Marco, a church best known for its beautiful gilt ceiling and magnificent ninth-century apse mosaic.

🔢 199 E5

Museo del Palazzo Venezia

🔢 199 E5 ✉ Via del Plebiscito 118
☎ 06 6999 4388; www.ticketeria.it
🕐 Tue–Sun 8:30–7:30 (hours vary for temporary exhibitions) 🎫 Museum: moderate
Ⓜ Cavour 🚌 All services to Piazza Venezia

7 Musei Capitolini

On the left (north) side of Piazza del Campidoglio stands the Palazzo Nuovo, whose inner courtyard

Fragments of a massive statue of the Emperor Constantine I in the courtyard of the Palazzo dei Conservatori

ontains the
olossal Roman
tatue of a river
od, Marforio,
particular
avourite with
hotographers.
As you
xplore the
wo floors of the
alace, you will
nd that it contains
nany beautiful
ntique sculptures, the
ighlights of which are the
)ying Gaul and the *Capitoline
/enus*, both Roman copies of
Greek originals.

Across the piazza, and linked to
he Palazzo Nuovo by an underpass,
s the Palazzo dei Conservatori,
which houses the rest of the
nuseum's impressive collections.
tar of the show, and housed in a
tunning modern space, the Esedra,
within the palazzo, is the celebrated
questrian statue of Marcus Aurelius
AD161–80). It originally stood in the
piazza outside but was brought inside
fter restoration for safekeeping (the
tatue outside is a copy). It is the
nly such statue to survive from this
period, and throughout the Middle
Ages was repeatedly referred to by
rtists and writers. It forms part of
he nucleus of the museum, founded
n 1471 by Pope Sixtus IV.

Other galleries here contain the
pinario (a first-century bronze of
boy removing a thorn from his
oot), the famous She-Wolf statue,
ymbol of Rome, an Etruscan bronze
lating from the fifth century BC and
paintings by Caravaggio, Veronese,
Tintoretto and Bellini.

Some 400 of the museum's
culptures have been relocated to
Centrale Montemartini, a converted
power station at Via Ostiense 106
south of the city).

🔟 199 E4 ⊠ Piazza del Campidoglio 1
☎ 060608 (daily 9–9 for bookings and info);
www.museicapitolini.org (bookings)
🕐 Tue–Sun 9–8 (last entry 7pm)
💶 Expensive 🍴 Museum Café 🚇 Colosseo
🚌 All services to Piazza Venezia

**Remains of the superb Temple of Minerva
at the Forum of Nerva, Fori Imperiali**

🔟 Colonna Traiana

Trajan's Column rises as a lonely,
majestic sentinel from the ruins of
Trajan's Forum. Built in AD113, it was
raised to mark two victorious military
campaigns over the Dacians, who
lived in what is now Romania. Like
triumphal arches, such columns were
typical of Roman victory monuments,
and likewise also invariably contained
friezes and reliefs recording details
of a campaign's battles and events.

Here, the reliefs run in a remarkable spiral – more than 200m (650 feet) of exquisitely carved marble, containing a continuous 155-scene sequence with more than 2,600 figures portrayed two-thirds of life size. The importance of the column is in the intense detail of these scenes, detail which has allowed scholars to learn much about the Roman military machine.

One reason for the column's survival is that it formed the bell tower of a Christian church, San Nicola de Columna. When this was demolished in the ninth century, the column became the first archaeological monument to be designated for protection by Rome's papal rulers. The structure comprises 29 vast drums of marble – eight for the base, nineteen for the column and two for the summit pedestal. Inside is a spiral staircase carved from the solid stone, a miracle of Roman engineering, but a miracle withheld from public view, for the column can only be admired from the outside. The figure crowning the summit is St Peter, added in 1588, replacing a bronze statue of Trajan, whose ashes once resided in a golden urn at the column's base.

➕ 199 F5 ✉ Via dei Fori Imperiali
🚇 Cavour 🚌 Services to Piazza Venezia

❾ Fori Imperiali

The Imperial Fora comprise five fora built when lack of space in the old Foro Romano forced emperors, from Julius Caesar onward, to look elsewhere for a site for their grandiose architectural schemes. Much of the area was lost when Mussolini forced the huge Via dei Fori Imperiali road through their heart in the 1930s. You can easily admire the Fora while walking down the Via dei Fori Imperiali, having

first made sense of it all by taking in the models and plans in the Visitor's Centre near the Colosseo end.

The best approach to the Fori Imperiali though, is to concentrate on the stunningly restored Foro Traiano, which houses the Museo dei Fori Imperiali and is home to the Colonna Traiana (➤ 67–68). Opened in 2007 after a massive clean-up job, the complex includes the forum itself and the towering remains of the Mercati (markets) behind. From the entrance on Via IV Novembre, you can walk through the Great Hall, past beautifully lit marbles, to the terrace above the Great Hemicycle, built in AD107. Stairs lead down through the different levels of this market, passing more than 150 Roman shops and offices, many with their doorjambs still showing the fitments for their night shutters. East of the Great Hall, you can access Via Biberatica, an ancient street lined with shops and bars.

Alongside Trajan's Forum to the right is the Foro di Augusto (begun in 42BC), part of an immense building project initiated by Augustus, whose most striking ruins are the remains of the Temple of Mars Ultor. Across the road lie the scant remains of the Foro de Cesare, or Caesar's Forum, the first of the Imperial Fora, built by Julius Caesar in 54–46BC. There

s even less to see of the remaining
'ora: the Foro di Nerva (AD96–98),
whose best surviving relic is a frieze
on the colonnade on the corner of Via
Cavour and Via dei Fori Imperiali, and
he Foro di Vespasiano (AD71–75),
also known as the Foro della Pace,
whose former library contains the
church of Santi Cosma e Damiano.

Mercati di Traiano

✚ 200 B4 ✉ Via IV Novembre 94 ☎ 060608;
www.mercatiditraiano.it 🕐 Daily 9–7
💶 Expensive Ⓜ Cavour 🚌 40, 64, 70

🔟 San Pietro in Vincoli

t takes only a couple of minutes
o walk to this church from the
Colosseum, and only a little
onger to see its main attraction
– an imposing statue of Moses
1503–13), one of Michelangelo's
sculptural masterpieces. The
statue was conceived as part of a
42-figure ensemble designed to
adorn the tomb of Pope Julius II,
one of Michelangelo's principal
patrons. In the event the project was
never realized, although it would
orment Michelangelo for much
of his life – he referred to it as this
"tragedy of a tomb". Instead he was
distracted by other works such as
he Sistine Chapel – another Julius
commission – and then after Julius'
leath deprived of funds by popes
who saw little glory in funding their
predecessor's obsession.

Michelangelo's masterpiece in San Pietro
in Vincoli depicts Moses receiving the
Ten Commandments

The statue of Moses hints at what
might have been, a monumental
figure captured at the moment
he receives the tablet of the Ten
Commandments (shown here under
his right arm). Michelangelo left
a famous signature in the statue's
beard – his profile – and gave Moses
a wonderfully equivocal expression
as he watches the Israelites dance
around the golden calf, his look of
divine illumination at receiving the
tablets mixed with fury at his people's
faithlessness and idolatry.

Note, too, the figure's horns, which
represent beams of light, features
ascribed to Moses in the iconography
of many medieval paintings and
sculptures. The main flanking
statues are also by Michelangelo, and
represent Rachel and Leah, symbols
of the active and contemplative life.
The other figures are the work of
Michelangelo's pupils.

✚ 200 C4 ✉ Piazza di San Pietro in Vincoli
4a ☎ 06 9784 4950 🕐 Apr–Sep daily
8–12:30, 3:30–7; Oct–Mar 8–12:30, 3–6
💶 Free Ⓜ Colosseo or Cavour 🚌 75 to Via
Cavour or 75, 85, 87, 117, 175 or 186 to Piazza
del Colosseo

ST PETER'S CHAINS

San Pietro in Vincoli was built in
432, reputedly on the site where
St Peter was condemned to death
during the persecutions of Nero. The
church takes its name from the highly
venerated chains (vincoli) that you
see in a casket under the main altar.
There are actually two sets of chains:
one is believed to have been used to
bind Peter in Jerusalem, the other
thought to have been used to shackle
him in Rome's Mamertine prison.
When the two were eventually united
they miraculously fused together.

⑪ Colle Oppio

The Colle Oppio is central Rome's most convenient park, a pretty area of grass, walkways, trees and archaeological remains spread over the slopes of the Esquiline Hill, one of the original Seven Hills. It is the perfect place to relax away from the hustle and bustle of the city, or for a picnic. It takes its name from one of the hill's two summits, the *Cispius* and *Oppius*. Although just across the street from the Colosseum, it is little used by visitors, but locals make full use of its café and quiet corners, particularly on Sundays. The park's loveliest area of grass, only faintly shaded by slender palms, is the section right by the entrance across from the Colosseum.

OFF THE BEATEN TRACK
The little-known park of **Villa Celimontana** south of the Colosseo (entered from Via della Navicella) is a good place to escape from the rigours of sightseeing. The area around the park is also relatively quiet and unexplored, with interesting churches, such as Santa Maria in Domnica and Santo Stefano Rotondo, and little lanes, such as Viale del Parco and Clivo di Scauro, which lead to Santi Giovanni e Paolo.

The superb interior of Santi Quattro Coronati, home to an enclosed order

The park makes a pleasant way to reach Santa Maria Maggiore (➤ 118–119) or Palazzo Massimo alle Terme (➤ 120–123), avoiding the busy Via Cavour and other roads. Avoid visiting the park at night.
➕ 201 D3 ✉ Via Labicana 136 🚇 Colosseo

⑫ Santi Quattro Coronati

The basilica of the Four Crowned Saints stands on the site of one of Rome's earliest churches and is now home to an enclosed order of Augustinian nuns – you'll have to ask them for the key to visit parts of the complex. It's dedicated to four Roman martyrs; take your pick as to whether they were Roman soldiers executed for refusing to pray before the statue of Esculapius, the god of healing, or stonemasons who refused to carve his statue – nobody knows for sure.

The first church was built in the fourth century and, like many others, was burned down during the 1084 Norman sack. It was rebuilt as a fortified monastery, incorporating the apse from the original church; you can still see traces of this basilica-form structure. Inside, the church has one of the loveliest of Rome's cosmatesque floors and retains its matrimonium – the upstairs gallery

where women sat during religious ceremonies. There's access to a secret cloister, complete with double columns and arches surrounding a flower-filled garden with a fountain. You can also take in the oratory outside the church (ring the bell and ask for the key), which contains a fresco cycle depicting the Donation of Constantine, an early Christian piece of propaganda, which claims that the Emperor Constantine gave the Pope authority over the West.

🚩 201 D3 ✉ Via Santi Coronati 20
☎ 06 7047 5427 🕐 Mon–Sat 9:30–12, 4–5:30, Sun 9:30–10:30, 4–5:30 🎫 Free
🚌 85, 87, 117, 850

⒔ Museo d'Arte Orientale

There is a spectacular wealth of artworks, pottery, jewellery and sculptures from the swathe of civilizations that runs from the Near to the Far East in this state museum,

housed in the 19th-century Palazzo Brancaccio.

The museum is also Italy's most important Oriental art research centre, but displays an eclectic collection of art from all over the East. Chinese and Korean ceramics shine, and there are some finds from Italian archaeological digs in the Swat region of Pakistan.

🚩 201 D4 ✉ Via Merulana 428 ☎ 06 4697 4832 🕐 Mon, Wed, Fri–Sat 9–2; Tue, Thu, Sun 9–7:30 🎫 Inexpensive 🚌 16, 360, 649, 714

FOR KIDS

The **Foro Romano** may be a little too ruined for young imaginations, but the scale of the **Colosseo** and its gladiatorial associations (► 56–60) should fire youngsters' minds. Kind parents will head for **Rewind Rome** (Via Capo d'Africa 5, tel: 06 770 76627, daily 9–7, expensive), an interactive, digital, 3D experience that takes you back to AD310. Children should also enjoy the dark and mysterious Mithraic bowels of **San Clemente** (► 61–63). The **Colle Oppio** park (left, ► 70) is a favourite among families – you can buy an ice cream or provisions for a picnic in streets to the south of the park. On Sundays, entertaining **street performers** can often be found on the nearby Via dei Fori Imperiali.

Where to...
Eat and Drink

Prices
Expect to pay per person for a meal, excluding drinks and service:
€ under €30   €€ €30–€50   €€€ over €50

The area of Rome that embraces the Capitoline Hill, Colosseo and Foro Romano is almost entirely given over to monuments, and the number of restaurants is correspondingly small. Though most are aimed at tourists, there are a handful of good places in the side streets close to the main sights.

Antica Birreria "Peroni" €
Don't be tempted into the overpriced cafés or snack bars on Piazza Venezia. Instead, walk just round the corner to this *birreria*, or beer hall. The term is slightly misleading for what is more a large, pleasant bar and simple restaurant. You could just have a beer: it's worth a visit simply to admire the original art nouveau interior. Romans pack the place at lunchtime to take advantage of the handful of inexpensive but well-prepared pasta and other dishes (though it is little known to visitors to the city). Service is canteen style; the seating is at simple wooden tables. The atmosphere is lively but not intimidating.

🚹 200 A5 🖾 Via di San Marcello 19 🕿 06 679 5310 🕒 Mon–Sat 12–12. Closed 2 weeks in Aug

Il Bocconcino €€
Simple surroundings and an accent on seasonal, regional produce are the hallmarks of this friendly trattoria, whose owners adhere to the principles of the Slow Food movement. The menu changes seasonally, but you can always expect high quality cured and fresh meat, excellent cheeses, home-made pasta, some vegetarian dishes and good puddings. Try the ravioli stuffed with spinach and ricotta followed by a grilled steak or rabbit casserole and vegetables fresh from the market. Service can be slow.

🚹 200 C3 🖾 Via Ostilia 23 🕿 06 7707 9175 🕒 Daily 11–11

Café Café €
A tiny, one-room café-restaurant just seconds from the Colosseo with a cosy, ochre-coloured interior, Café Café serves good cold snacks, with one or two hot dishes daily. It is perfect for lunch, tea, coffee or a glass of wine.

🚹 201 D3 🖾 Via dei Santi Quattro

(Coronati) 44 🕿 06 700 8743 🕒 Daily 11am–1am. Closed Aug

Cavour 313 €
This popular and long-established wine bar is surprisingly little patronized by tourists despite being less than a minute's walk from the main entrance to the Foro Romano. First impressions inside are of rather plain and uninspiring wood-dominated decor, but don't be put off: the atmosphere is informal and friendly, the many good hot and cold snacks are well priced, and there's a selection of more than 500 wines.

🚹 200 C4 🖾 Via Cavour 313 🕿 06 678 5496 🕒 Jun–Sep Mon–Sat 12:30–2:30, 7:30–12:30; Oct–May Mon–Sat 12:30–2:30, 7:30–12:30. Sun 7:30–12:30

Ciuri Ciuri €
Eight minutes' walk from the Colosseo and less than five from San Clemente, this splendid Sicilian *gelateria* and bar is a wonderful place for a quick, inexpensive

lunch. Here you'll find all the Sicilian specialities, *arancini* (deep-fried rice balls stuffed with meat and cheese), deep-fried vegetables in batter, *iris*, a pastry stuffed with ricotta cheese, and tiny pizzas. The big draws, though, are the *gelati* and *pasticceria* (pastries), all made to Sicilian, rather than Roman, recipes. Now's your chance to try *cannoli*, a pastry tube stuffed with sweetened ricotta and candied fruit, *cassata*, the quintessential Sicilian cake, and some of the creamiest, richest ices you've ever sampled – try the *amarena* (morello cherry) served, as in Sicily, in a sweet roll.

✚ 201 D3 ⊠ Via Labicana 126–128 ☎ 06 4542 4856 ⊕ Tue–Sun 8am–11pm

Leonina €

You can tell that you are in the presence of something special by the regular long lines of customers outside Leonina. They are waiting for some of Rome's best *pizza al taglia*, or pizza by the slice. Prices for what is usually the most inexpensive of snacks are higher here than elsewhere, but then so is the quality of the pizza.

✚ 200 C4 ⊠ Via Leonina 84 ☎ 06 482 7744 ⊕ Daily 8am–11pm

Luzzi €

For a real local and Roman trattoria experience, head for Luzzi, a good neighbourhood dive near San Clemente. It is packed inside and out (there are exterior tables all year round) with Romans enjoying basic favourites, such as good pizzas from the wood-fired oven, straightforward pasta dishes and simple *secondi*. It can be very busy, so come before 8pm to be sure of a table and get ready to enjoy the food and atmosphere.

✚ 201 D3 ⊠ Via Celimontana 1 (on corner of Via San Giovanni in Laterano) ☎ 06 709 6332 ⊕ Thu–Tue 12–3, 7–12. Closed 2 weeks in Aug

San Teodoro €€€

The time to eat at this decidedly upmarket restaurant is during the hot summer months, when tables spill out onto one of the neighbourhood's prettiest piazzas. The predominantly fish cooking covers a wide range of Italian cuisine, with some dishes, such as *minestra di broccoli* (broccoli ravioli served in fish broth) firmly rooted in *cucina Romana*, while other dishes are modern and imaginative fusions of seafood and crisp fresh vegetables. Leave room for some pudding because *pasticceria* and *gelati* are taken very seriously here.

✚ 199 E4 ⊠ Via dei Fienili 49–51 ☎ 06 678 0933 ⊕ Mon–Sat 1–3:15, 8–11:30. Closed 3 weeks in Dec–Jan

Trattoria Morgana €€

This quintessentially Roman restaurant has been going since 1935, when an older wine bar was transformed into a popular neighbourhood eating house. So it remains today; packed with locals enjoying Roman specialities such as snails, tripe and oxtail. But you'll also find a good range of more usual dishes, which include home-made pasta, drippingly fresh mozzarella from Campania, grilled meat and a selection of fresh fish. The wine list offers a good choice of regional wines.

✚ 201 D3 ⊠ Via Mecenate 19–21 ☎ 06 487 3122 ⊕ Tue–Sun 12:30–3, 7–11

Trattoria Sora Lella €€

Sora Lella lies on Isola Tiberina (Tiber Island) between the Capitoline area and Trastevere district. It is worth the detour, as the accomplished, authentic Roman cooking is a cut above what you would expect of somewhere that affects the informal atmosphere (but not the prices) of a simple trattoria. Sora Lella was a much-loved actress, and the restaurant was named in her honour by her son, Aldo Trabalza, after her death in 1993. Her portrait occupies pride of place alongside the bar.

✚ 199 D4 ⊠ Via di Ponte Quattro Capi 16, Isola Tiberina ☎ 06 686 1601 ⊕ Daily 12:30–2:30, 8–10.45. Closed Aug

Where to... Shop

This is a sightseeing area rather than an area of the city for shoppers to visit with any great expectations, though you may stumble across the odd artisan's workshop, gallery, antiques shop or specialist store in the side streets off Via Cavour (the best hunting grounds are Via dei Serpenti, Via del Boschetto and Via Madonna dei Monti). One such is **La Bottega del Cioccolato**, a vivid red chocolate shop at Via Leonina 82 (tel: 06 482 1473, Mon–Sat 9:30–7:30).

Otherwise most of the shops in the streets around Rome's ancient monuments are local food and general stores for those who live around Via Cavour (by the Forum) and in the residential enclave between the Colosseo and San Giovanni in Laterano.

Where to... Be Entertained

Ancient monuments and cultural life generally don't mix in Rome. Outdoor concerts were once regularly held in the Terme di Caracalla (Baths of Caracalla) south of the Colosseo, but for a variety of reasons, most significantly the preservation of the ruins, these now only take place very occasionally. Similar restrictions mean that there are no productions at the Colosseo, Foro Romano or other sites.

MUSIC AND THEATRE

The **Teatro di Marcello** provides a summer venue for classical concerts organized by the **Associazione Il Tempietto** (Via Rodolfo Morandi 3, tel: 06 8713 1590, www.tempietto.it). Between November and July the association's concerts move indoors to the church of **San Nicola in Carcere** (tel: 06 686 9972), south of the Teatro at Via del Teatro di Marcello 46. Tickets are available from both venues about two hours before each performance.

San Giovanni in Laterano is one of only a handful of churches to maintain a choir and present a sung Mass. The church is also a good place to hear organ music; the superb Luca Blasi organ is usually played during and after the 10am Sunday Mass. Contact visitor centres or the church itself for further details.

The tiny church of **San Teodoro** in Via San Teodoro on the western flank of the Palatine Hill is also used as a concert venue by the choral association "Agimus", short for the **Associazione Giovanile Musicale** (tel: 06 3211 1001, www.agimus.it). Theatre and dance productions are held at the **Teatro Colosseo**, east of the Colosseo at Via Capo d'Africa 5a (tel: 06 700 4932).

NIGHTLIFE

This is not an area rich in nightlife, but **Micca Club** (Via Pietro Micca 7a, tel: 06 8744 0079, www.miccaclub.com, Thu–Tue 7pm–3am, closes for summer break) has opened on its fringes and has a programme ranging from burlesque shows to jazz concerts.

A good place for a light meal or a late-night drink near Termini is the **Zest** bar in the sleek contemporary Radisson Blu es. Hotel (Via Filippo Turati 171, tel: 06 444 841, www.rome.radissonsas.com, daily 9am–1am). Alternatively, if you've been out late and need a drink or bite to eat, **La Base** at Via Cavour 274 (tel: 06 474 0659), which stays open until 4:30 every morning, is perfect for night owls and revellers.

The Heart of Rome

Getting Your Bearings

The heart of Rome – the area bounded by the curve of the Tiber in the west and Via del Corso in the east – is often described as "Renaissance Rome" or "Baroque Rome" or even "Medieval Rome". No description is quite right, for the area is a wonderful mixture of ancient monuments, churches, palaces, streets and squares that span 2,000 years of history.

The two-day itinerary in this chapter epitomizes this diversity perfectly, offering a superb amalgam of sights that cover Rome's rich history and artistic legacy. It will give you a real insight into the city's overlapping epochs. The area covered in the first day has an atmosphere and appearance all its own, thanks to its combination of tiny old cobbled streets, imposing Renaissance palaces, the occasional broad thoroughfare – Corso Vittorio Emanuele II is the axis around which the area hinges – and a sprinkling of larger or grander squares such as Campo dei Fiori and Piazza Navona. This is also an area where people live and work, and its artisans' workshops, neighbourhood shops and busy markets create the atmosphere of a village rather than a capital city.

It is also scattered with remnants of Imperial Rome, among them the Pantheon, which rivals the Foro Romano and the Colosseo, as well as a marvellous museum of antiquities, the Palazzo Altemps.

Two of Rome's most distinctive districts are also encompassed in this chapter. The medieval Jewish Ghetto, a web of streets just beyond Lungotevere di Cenci on the northern banks of the Tiber, is a mostly residential enclave of peaceful streets and small squares, with a handful of more traditional restaurants and shops. Across the river lies Trastevere, a self-contained corner of the city, filled with picturesque old streets and squares. It retains much of its old working-class character – despite the fact that its appearance has made it one of Rome's main restaurant districts. This is a good place to explore by day or in the evening, though it has relatively few churches, museums and monuments.

View of Rome through trees of the Botanical Garden located in Trastevere

Page 75: The magnificent Palazzo Spada, which is a just a couple of minutes' walk from Campo dei Fiori

★ **Don't Miss**

At Your Leisure

In Two Days

If you're not quite sure where to begin your travels, this itinerary recommends a practical and enjoyable two days exploring the Heart of Rome, taking in some of the best places to see using the Getting Your Bearings map on the previous page. For more information see the main entries.

Day 1

Morning
Breakfast in **1 Campo dei Fiori** (► 80–81), before exploring its wonderfully evocative morning food and flower market. Next, head off to **6 Piazza Farnese** (► 99), the Via Giulia – one of Rome's most elegant streets – and (perhaps) visit the small **7 Palazzo Spada** art gallery (► 99).

Walk back to **2 Piazza Navona** (left, ► 82–85), a baroque showpiece second only to St Peter's, meander the side streets off the square – notably Via della Pace – and stop for a coffee in one of its cafés.

Just north and east of Piazza Navona lie the churches of **9 Sant'Agostino** (► 100–101) home to a Raphael fresco and **10 San Luigi dei Francesi** (► 101), graced with three major paintings by Caravaggio.

Lunch
Try **Cul de Sac** or **Bar della Pace** (► 108) if you only want a snack lunch, **La Carbonara** (► 107) for an inexpensive meal al fresco, or indulge at **Ar Galletto** (► 107).

Afternoon
Visit **3 Palazzo Altemps** (► 86–89), one of Rome's most dazzling museums, where some of the greatest classical Roman sculpture is on display. Then make your way to the **4 Pantheon** (► 90–94), the most perfectly preserved of all Rome's ancient monuments.

Spend the rest of the afternoon exploring Via del Corso, one of the city's main shopping streets, and the streets to its west where you will find many interesting little specialist shops. Alternatively, visit the **12 Ara Pacis** (► 102), a Roman monument covered in intricate marble reliefs, and explore the art-filled church of **13 Santa Maria del Popolo** (► 103–104).

Day 2

Morning

Allow an hour or so to see the rich collection of paintings at the **14 Palazzo-Galleria Doria Pamphilj** (➤ 104–105); its state apartments typify the magnificent scale on which the aristocratic Roman families lived.

Walk to Trastevere by way of **Santa Maria in Cosmedin** and the **Ghetto** (➤ 176–179). Alternatively, take a bus to Trastevere from Via del Plebiscito just off Piazza Venezia.

Lunch

You can take lunch in any number of places on your walk to, or around, Trastevere: try **Alle Fratte di Trastevere** (➤ 107).

Afternoon

Spend time simply exploring **5 Trastevere's** pretty streets and squares (below, ➤ 95–98), before making your way to **Santa Maria in Trastevere** (➤ 96), which is usually open all day.

Trastevere has plenty of stylish places to eat, so you may wish to extend the day and stay in the area for dinner without returning to your hotel. Do this either by walking up to the **Gianicolo** (➤ 96) to enjoy good views over the city, or by visiting the church of **15 Santa Cecilia in Trastevere** (➤ 105–106).

◻Campo dei Fiori

Campo dei Fiori (Field of Flowers) is a place you will probably return to more than once during your stay. One of Rome's prettiest piazzas, it is the site of a wonderful outdoor market, with picturesque palaces and houses providing the backdrop for a colourful medley of stalls selling fruit, flowers and fish.

Take time to wander around these stalls and enjoy the street life: the old knife-sharpeners, the redoubtable Roman matriarchs trimming vegetables, the fishmonger bawling his wares, and the local housewives driving a hard bargain with knowing stallholders. When you have had your fill of sights, sounds and smells, pick one of the small cafés around the square and watch proceedings over a cappuccino.

In its earliest days the square really was a field of flowers: until the Middle Ages it formed a meadow that fringed the first-century BC Theatre of Pompey. Then it was built over and quickly became a bustling focus of city life. All manner of famous names were associated with the surrounding district: Lucrezia Borgia was born locally, her brother Cesare was assassinated nearby, and the artist Caravaggio murdered a rival after losing a tennis match in the square. Lucrezia's father, Alessandro, better known as Pope Alexander VI, would also have been familiar with the area, for one of his mistresses, Vanozza Cattenei, ran some of the inns and brothels for which the district became celebrated.

Today, there's relatively little to see here apart from the **market and the statue** at its heart (see Inside Info, opposite).

Stallholders at Campo dei Fiori, Rome's prettiest market

The Campo is a popular place to meet at night

However, be sure to explore some of the characterful surrounding streets, notably **Via dei Cappellari** (Street of the Hatters), a shadowy lane filled with furniture workshops and premises of other artisans. Also walk the short distance to Piazza Farnese to admire the square and its palace (➤ 99), and then continue to Via Giulia, one of Rome's most exclusive residential streets, to look at the church of Santa Maria dell'Orazione e Morte (➤ 100).

TAKING A BREAK

The Campo is full of small cafés and restaurants: one of the nicest is the **Caffè Farnese** (Via dei Baullari 106–7) just off the square on the corner with the grander Piazza Farnese. One of the best places for lunch or dinner is the old-fashioned **Ar Galletto** (➤ 107), a few steps off the square.

➕ 197 F2 ✉ Piazza Campo dei Fiori 🚌 40, 46, 62, 64 to Corso Vittorio Emanuele II or H, 8, 63, 271, 780 to Via Arenula

CAMPO DEI FIORI: INSIDE INFO

Top tips The Campo's cafés make a perfect place for breakfast; the market is also at its least crowded early on (it runs daily except Sunday from about 6am to 2pm).
- As in any busy part of the city, be sure to keep a tight grip on your valuables.
- The Campo is also popular at night: the **Vineria Reggio** wine bar (No 15) and the American-run **Sloppy Sam's** (No 10) in the piazza's eastern corner are among the liveliest bars.

In more detail At the heart of Campo dei Fiori stands a cowled and rather **ominous-looking statue**, easily missed amid the debris of the market. This depicts Giordano Bruno, a 16th-century humanist and scholar who was burned at the stake on this spot in 1600 for the crime of heresy. His secular outlook suits the square, which to this day remains unusual among Roman piazzas in having no church.

❷ Piazza Navona

None of Rome's many squares is as grand or theatrical as Piazza Navona. The magnificent piazza, one of the city's baroque showpieces, is dominated by three fountains, a ring of ochre-coloured buildings – many hung with flowers in the summer – and an almost constant throng of visitors, artists and stallholders.

You will probably be tempted back here many times during your visit, although whether your budget will stretch to too many drinks at the piazza's pretty but expensive cafés is another matter. You don't need to spend money, however, simply to enjoy the area, which is an **irresistibly atmospheric** place for meeting and people-watching at most times of the day and night.

Street traders and artists contribute to Piazza Navona's lively atmosphere

The piazza's distinctive elliptical shape betrays its origins, for the square corresponds almost exactly to the **outline of the racetrack** and stadium built on the site by Emperor Domitian in AD86. This was known as the *Circus Agonalis*, a name which by the Middle Ages had been modified to *in agone* and the dialect *n 'agone* before arriving at the present "Navona".

All manner of activities took place here over and above games and races, not least the martyrdom of Sant'Agnese (Saint Agatha), a 13-year-old girl killed in AD304 for her refusal to renounce her Christian beliefs and marry a pagan. She was thrown into a brothel close to the stadium, then paraded naked in the Circus, only for her nakedness to be covered by the miraculous growth of her hair.

The Church of Sant'Agnese in Agone

The simple oratory eventually built on the site of her death was superseded by the present church of **Sant'Agnese in Agone** (www.santagneseinagone.org, Mon–Sat 9:30–12:30, 3:30–7, Sun 10–1, 4–7) on the piazza's western edge in the mid-17th century. One of the architects involved in the

church was Borromini, the great but troubled rival of Rome's other baroque superstar, Gian Lorenzo Bernini, who designed the piazza's central fountain, the **Fontana dei Quattro Fiumi** (1648), or Fountain of the Four Rivers. The fountain's four major statues represent the four rivers of Paradise – the Nile, Ganges, Plate and Danube, and the four known corners of the world – Africa, Asia, Europe and America. Note the dove on the top of the obelisk, a symbol of Pope Innocent X Pamphilj, who commissioned the work.

Innocent was also responsible for other major changes to the square, notably the creation of the Palazzo Pamphilj (left of Sant'Agnese), now the Brazilian Embassy, changes which largely put an end to the horse racing, jousting and bullfights that had taken place in the square for much of the Middle Ages. At times the piazza was also flooded, allowing the city's aristocrats to be pulled around the resultant artificial lake in gilded carriages, an echo of the so-called *naumachia*, the mock seabattles staged by the ancient Romans under similar circumstances.

TAKING A BREAK

Most of the piazza's cafés are much of a muchness, though those on its eastern flanks enjoy a little more sun. Two of the best-known bars are **Caffè Bernini** (No 44) and **I Tre Scalini** (➤ 108), the latter celebrated for its sensational chocolate chip ice cream (*tartufo*). Don't forget the ever-popular **Bar della Pace** (➤ 108) nearby.

Bernini's Fontana dei Quattro Fiumi lies at the heart of the piazza

🔢 197 F3 ✉ Piazza Navona 🚇 Spagna 🚌 30, 70, 81, 87, 116, 492, 628 to Corso del Rinascimento or 40, 46, 62, 64 to Corso Vittorio Emanuele II

PIAZZA NAVONA: INSIDE INFO

Top tips Be warned that drinks at cafés around Piazza Navona are some of the most pricey in the city, but you can sit at your table as long as you wish.
■ Piazza Navona is busy with sightseers by day, but still busier by night, so **leave time for an after-dinner stroll** past the floodlit fountains and the many artists and caricaturists who set up shop here.

In more detail An often-told tale relates how Bernini deliberately designed one of the statues on his central fountain so that it appeared to be shielding its eyes or recoiling in horror at Sant'Agnese, the church of his great rival, Borromini. It's a nice story, but in truth the fountain was created before the church. In fact, the Nile hides its eyes, because its source was undiscovered when the statue was carved.

Hidden gems Most visitors overlook Piazza Navona's two lesser fountains. At the piazza's northern end stands the **Fontana del Nettuno**, or Fountain of Neptune, which shows the marine god grappling with a sea serpent. At the southern end is Giacomo della Porta's **Fontana del Moro** (1575), or Fountain of the Moor, whose central figure – despite the fountain's name – is actually another marine god: the erroneous name probably comes from the name of the sculptor, Antonio Mori, who added the dolphin from a design by Bernini.

❸ Palazzo Altemps

The Palazzo Altemps and its sister gallery, the Palazzo Massimo alle Terme (➤ 120–123), form the magnificent setting for the cream of Rome's state-owned antiquities. The Roman sculptures here are some of the city's finest, and are displayed in a beautifully restored Renaissance palace.

Above: The palazzo is built around a central courtyard

Left: Portraits and busts of the Caesars line the beautiful painted loggia of the Palazzo Altemps

The Palazzo Altemps was begun around 1477, but took its name from Cardinal Marco Sittico Altemps, its owner after 1568. Altemps was a collector of antiquities, and would have been pleased at what has become of his palace, for it now houses some of the most sublime sculptures of the classical age. These sculptures form part of the collection of the Museo Nazionale Romano, whose exhibits were split between several new homes at the end of the 1990s.

The Palace and its Exhibits

Spread over two floors, and unlike many similar museums, this one won't dull your senses with endless rows of busts and second-rate statues. Everything here is outstanding, with only a handful of exhibits in each room – some rooms have just one or two sculptures – with the result that each masterpiece has the space it needs to shine. As an added bonus, the palace itself has some beautifully decorated and frescoed rooms and chambers, not least the small church of Sant'Aniceto and the stunning painted loggia on the first floor.

After a small medley of rooms around the ticket hall you walk into the palace's airy central courtyard, flanked at its top and bottom (north and south ends) by two statue-filled arcades. Start your exploration by turning left, but note that although the rooms are numbered and named on the gallery plan, their open-plan arrangement encourages you to wander among the exhibits at random.

Room 7, the Room of the Herms, houses the first of the gallery's major works, two first-century figures of **Apollo the Lyrist**, both from the Ludovisi collection, a major group of sculptures amassed by Ludovico Ludovisi, a Bolognese nephew of Pope Gregory XV. The collection – purchased by the Italian government in 1901 – forms the core of the Altemps' displays. Another work from the collection, the **Ludovisi Athena**, dominates Room 9, a statue distinguished

Roman victory
portrayed in
the second-
century AD
*Grande
Ludovisi
Sarcophagus*

by the finely carved tunic and the snake twisting to stare at
the goddess. Room 14 contains a wonderful sculptural group
portraying Dionysus and satyr with a panther, full of beautiful
details such as Dionysus' ringleted hair and a bunch of grapes.

Gallery Highlights

The gallery's real stars are on the first floor. To reach them,
cross back over the courtyard and climb the monumental
staircase close to where you first entered. This will bring you
to the south loggia, where you should hunt out a second-
century **sarcophagus** embellished with scenes of Mars and
Venus, significant because it was drawn and much admired
by Renaissance artists such as Raphael and Mantegna. Room
19 at the far end of the loggia is known as the Painted Views
Room – for obvious reasons.

In the next room (Room 20, the Cupboard Room), you
come face to face with two sensational statues: the **Ludovisi
Orestes and Electra**, a first-century group by Menelaus (the
artist's signature can be seen on the supporting plinth), and
the **Ludovisi Ares**, a seated figure (possibly Achilles) with
sword and shield; the sculpture is probably a Roman copy
of a Greek original and was restored by Bernini in 1622.

The gallery's finest works occupy the next room (Room 21,
The Tale of Moses Room), which contains little more than two
monolithic heads and a deceptively humble-looking relief.
The heads are the **Ludovisi Acrolith** (left of the relief) and
the **Ludovisi Hera**. The latter was one of the most celebrated
and admired busts of antiquity, and has been identified as an
idealized portrait of Antonia Augusta, the mother of Emperor
Claudius, who was deified by Claudius after her death and
held up as an exemplar of domestic virtue and maternal duty.

Less striking, but more precious to scholars because of
its unusual nature and probable age, is the central relief, the
Ludovisi Throne, discovered in 1887 in the grounds of the
Villa Ludovis. Although some controversy surrounds the
piece, most critics believe it is a fifth-century BC work brought
to Rome from one of the Greek colonies in Calabria, southern
Italy, after the Romans conquered much of the region in the
third century BC. The scene portrayed on the front of the
"throne" probably shows the birth and welcome to land of

Aphrodite (literally "born of the foam"). Panels on the throne's sides show two young girls, both seated on folded cushions, one nude and playing a double-piped flute, the other clothed and sprinkling grains of incense from a box onto a brazier.

Magnificent Sculptures

Three further exceptional sculptures dominate the room (Room 29) at the end of the palace's west flank, a large salon with ornate fireplace once used for entertaining palace guests. At its heart stands the *Gallic Soldier and His Wife Committing Suicide*, one of the most dramatic and visceral sculptures in Western art. It was found with the *Dying Galatian* statue, now in the Musei Capitolini (➤ 66–67), and probably belonged to a group of linked statues based on three bronzes commissioned by Attalus I, king of Pergamum, to commemorate his victory over the Galatians. The marble copies here and on the Capitolino were commissioned by Julius Caesar to celebrate his victory over the Gauls. Like the *Ludovisi Throne*, the statue was found during construction of the Villa Ludovisi on land that once belonged to Julius Caesar. Finally, don't miss the room's superb helmeted head of Mars and the *Grande Ludovisi Sarcophagus*, a virtuoso sculpture portraying a battle scene divided into three: the victors at the top; the combatants at the centre; and the vanquished at the bottom.

One of the most dramatic sculptures in Western art is the *Gallic Soldier and His Wife Committing Suicide*

TAKING A BREAK

Stop for a coffee at the pretty and popular **Bar della Pace** (➤ 108), just off Piazza Navona.

➕ 197 F4 ✉ Piazza di Sant'Apollinare 46 ☎ 06 3996 7700; www.pierreci.it (bookings) 🕑 Tue–Sun 9–7:45 💲 Moderate 🚌 30, 70, 81, 87, 116, 492 and 628 to Corso del Rinascimento

---

PALAZZO ALTEMPS: INSIDE INFO

Top tips If you come to Rome outside the summer months, try to **visit the Palazzo Altemps after dark**: the superb lighting in the gallery adds immense drama to many of the exhibits.

■ Invest in the **gallery guide and plan** published by Electa-Soprintendenza Archeologica di Roma (available in English): it is beautifully illustrated and provides interesting background information about the main exhibits.

4 Pantheon

The Pantheon is the closest you'll come to a perfect Roman building. One of Europe's best-preserved ancient buildings, its majestic outlines have remained almost unchanged despite the passage of almost 2,000 years. No other monument presents such a vivid picture of how Rome would have looked in its ancient heyday.

The first sight of the Pantheon is one of many people's most memorable moments. The initial impact of the building is further reinforced when you move closer, for only then does the building's colossal scale become clear – few stone columns, in Rome or elsewhere, are quite as monolithic as the Pantheon's **massive pillars**. The building itself does not take long to admire, however – inside or out – for there's little specific to see, which means your best bet is to take in the former temple from the sanctuary of an outdoor café table in **Piazza della Rotonda**.

The impressive facade of the Pantheon, where Italy's kings and queens are buried

Imperial Design

The Pantheon you see today was built by Emperor Hadrian between AD118 and 125. It largely superseded two previous temples on the site, the first having been built some 150 years earlier between 27 and 25BC by Marcus Agrippa, the son-in-law of Emperor Augustus. This structure was damaged by a **momentous fire** that swept through Rome in AD80. A second temple, built by Emperor Domitian, suffered a similar fiery fate when it was **struck by lightning** in AD110.

Given this history, the large dedication picked out in bronze letters across the building's facade is puzzling, for it alludes to Marcus Agrippa: *m. agrippa l. f. cos tertium fecit* (Marcus Agrippa, son of Lucius, made this in his third consulship). This apparent anomaly is evidence of Hadrian's modesty, for he habitually retained the name of a building's original dedicatee on the monuments he rebuilt or restored.

Subsequent rulers were less modest, as you can see from the faint two-line inscription below in much smaller letters: *pantheum vetustate corruptum cum omni cultu restituerunt* ("with

UNKNOWN PURPOSE

For so great a building it is remarkable that no one really knows the Pantheon's purpose. Its name suggests it was a temple devoted to "all the gods", but there is no record of any such cult elsewhere in Rome. Some theories suggest it was devoted to the 12 Olympian gods of ancient Greece, others that it was not a temple at all in the accepted sense, but rather a place where rulers would glorify themselves by appearing in the company of statues of the gods.

every refinement they restored the Pantheon, worn by age").
This refers to renovations supposedly made by emperors
Severus and Caracalla in AD202. Not only were the pair
immodest in their claims, they were also dishonest, for it
appears the restorations never took place.

Hadrian's involvement was confirmed in 1892, when
archaeologists – who until then associated the building with
Agrippa – found that many of the Pantheon's bricks contained
the Emperor's personal seal. Hadrian's involvement probably
included the building's design, the squares and circles of
which created a structure of near-architectural perfection.

Temple to Church

Plenty of Roman buildings shared the Pantheon's mixed
fortunes, but few survived the passage of time in such pristine
form. The reason for its excellent condition is that it became
a Christian church in AD608, when Rome's then ruler, the
Byzantine emperor Phocas, presented the building to Pope
Boniface IV. This was the first time a temple constructed for
pagan rites had been **converted into a church** – worship in
such temples had previously been banned – and the change
brought with it the ruling that to remove even a single stone
from the site constituted a mortal sin.

Not all the building survived unscathed, however, as you'll
see from the **porch's exterior walls**, which were once largely

clad in white marble. The main body of the building to the rear was simply faced in stucco, a cheap way of imitating marble. Better preserved than the cladding are the **huge columns**, most of which are fashioned from Egyptian granite, together with their capitals and bases, which were carved from finest Greek Pentelic marble. Even here, though, certain contingencies had to be made: one column, for example, was brought from Emperor Domitian's villa in Castelgandolfo in the hills above Rome in 1626; two more – needed to replace damaged pillars – came from the Baths of Nero in 1666.

Damage was not always accidental, however. Sometimes it was inflicted, most notably when Emperor Constans II plundered the bronze gilding that covered many surfaces in 663–67: most of it found its way to Constantinople and was melted down and re-formed into coins. Something similar happened in 1626, when Pope Urban VIII was persuaded by Bernini, the celebrated architect and sculptor, to remove the ancient bronze gilding from the portico's wooden beams. Some 200 tonnes of metal were removed, most of which went to make Bernini's huge *baldacchino*, or altar canopy, in St Peter's (► 160). Enough metal was left over, it is said, to provide Urban with 80 new cannon for the Castel Sant'Angelo (► 164–165).

Dome and Interior

Walking into the interior usually produces a double take in visitors, for looking up at the great **coffered dome** reveals a 9m (30-foot) hole, or *oculus*, in the middle of the ceiling. This was a deliberate part of Hadrian's design, intended to allow those inside the building a direct contemplation of

MISSING STATUES
Among the treasures lost from the Pantheon over the centuries is a statue of Venus that once stood outside Agrippa's original version of the temple. The statue was celebrated for the earrings with which it was adorned, made by cutting in half a pearl that Cleopatra left uneaten after a famous bet she made with Mark Antony that she could spend 10 million *sesterces* on a single meal.

The 9m (30-foot) *oculus* in the middle of the dome dramatically illuminates the interior of the Pantheon

The Pantheon's dome is one of the marvels of Roman engineering. It becomes progressively thinner and uses lighter materials toward its top

the heavens. It is also a dramatic source of light, casting a powerful beam of sunlight into the marble-clad interior on sunny days and providing a glimpse of the beautiful starlit sky on clear evenings. On startling occasions, it also allows in birds and rain.

The dome is the Pantheon's greatest glory, measuring 43.3m (142 feet) in diameter – greater than the dome of St Peter's – exactly the same as the height of the building from floor to *oculus* (a perfect sphere would fit in the interior). This was the world's largest concrete dome until 1958, when it was superseded by the CNIT building in Paris.

The dome's distinctive **coffering**, or *lacunas*, was made by pouring material into moulds, just one of the cupola's many engineering subtleties. What you can't see is the way in which the dome's skin becomes thinner as it approaches its apex – from 7m (23 feet) to just 1m (3 feet) thick – so reducing its overall weight. Neither can you see the way in which progressively lighter materials were used: concrete and travertine at the base, volcanic tufa midway up, and featherlight pumice close to the *oculus*.

Lower down, little of the **marble veneer** you see on the walls is original, although it is thought to correspond closely to Hadrian's original decorative scheme. Much of the pavement, however, although extensively repaired, is believed to be original. Around the walls are seven alternating rectangular and semicircular niches, originally designed to hold statues, but now given over in part to the **tombs of the kings and queens** of Italy's monarchy (1870–1946). The third niche on the left contains the **tomb of the painter Raphael** (1483–1520), who was exhumed in 1833 and reburied here in an ancient Roman sarcophagus.

Horse-drawn carriage on the Piazza della Rotonda, outside the Pantheon

TAKING A BREAK

The **Tazza d'Oro** café (Via degli Orfani 84, tel: 06 678 9792, closed Sun) just off Piazza della Rotonda is considered by many to serve the best coffee in Rome, but unlike many of the cafés in the square, you can't sit down and there is no view of the Pantheon.

➕ 194 B1 ✉ Piazza della Rotonda ☎ 06 6830 0230 🕐 Mon–Sat 8:30–7:30, Sun 9–6, public holidays 9–1; Mass Sat 5pm, Sun 10:30am and 4:30pm 🎟 Free 🚇 Spagna 🚌 116 to Piazza della Rotonda, or 30, 40, 46, 62, 63, 64, 70, 81, 87 and all other services to Largo di Torre Argentina

---

PANTHEON: INSIDE INFO

Top tips The Pantheon is sometimes **closed on Sunday afternoon**.
- Don't look for the ticket office: the Pantheon is a church and **entrance is free**.
- **Come in the rain** to enjoy the remarkable spectacle of water pouring through the hole in the Pantheon's roof.
- The Pantheon can be seen quickly and easily in conjunction with two other smaller sights: the Caravaggio paintings in **San Luigi dei Francesi** (➤ 101) and the Gothic church of **Santa Maria sopra Minerva**, founded in the eighth century over a Roman temple to Minerva. Outside the church, look out for Bernini's elephant statue supporting an ancient Egyptian obelisk. Inside, be sure to see the frescoes of the *Annunciation* and *Assumption* by Filippino Lippi (in the Cappella Carafa in the right, or south, transept), the statue of *The Redeemer* by Michelangelo to the left of the high altar, and the tomb of Fra Angelico, patron saint of painters, who is buried in a passage at the end of the north (left) nave.

In more detail The date on which the Pantheon was consecrated as a church – 1 November, 608 – is interesting, for it marked the beginning of All Saints' Day, or the Day of the Dead. In another allusion to all the saints, as opposed to all the gods, the church was christened and dedicated to Santa Maria ad Martyres, the Virgin and the Christian Martyrs. Countless martyrs' bones and relics were brought here from catacombs around the city to mark the event.

⑤ Trastevere

Trastevere means "over the Tevere", and refers to a quaint enclave of the city on the southern bank of the Tiber (Tevere), an area that until recently was both the most traditional part of central Rome and the heart of its eating and nightlife district. Although no longer at the cutting edge, its cobbled streets and tiny squares are still picturesque places to explore and eat, either by day or night.

Trastevere is full of small bars and restaurants

Trastevere has an increasing number of hotels, but if you're staying elsewhere, it's not far to walk from the rest of the city. The routes you would take from places like the Capitolino or Campo dei Fiori run through interesting parts of the city such as the Ghetto, the Isola Tiberina and the cluster of churches and temples around Piazza Bocca della Verità (➤ 176). If you want to conserve your energy and catch a bus, there's plenty of choice, as Ponte Garibaldi, the main bridge linking the rest of Rome to Piazza Sonnino, one of Trastevere's main squares, is a major city thoroughfare.

As for what you should see, there are two main sights – the fine church of **Santa Maria in Trastevere** (➤ 96), the focus of the area's central square, and the **Villa Farnesina** (➤ 97), which contains rooms and ceilings adorned with frescoes by Raphael and others. Lesser attractions include the **Orto Botanico** (➤ 98, 101), but in the final resort, this is a place to explore and admire at random, particularly the web of streets sandwiched between Via Garibaldi and Viale di Trastevere.

The Heart of Rome

Santa Maria in Trastevere

There's nearly always something happening in Piazza Santa Maria in Trastevere: kids playing football, old men chatting, lovers canoodling, though late at night the atmosphere becomes seedier. Even when there are no people to watch, you can simply enjoy the facade of the church that dominates the square. Santa Maria in Trastevere was reputedly founded in 222, which – if true – would make it one of the city's oldest churches. It is first properly documented in 337, when a church was begun here by Pope Julius I, on the site where it was believed that a miraculous fountain of oil had flowed on the day of Christ's birth.

The mosaic in the upper apse of Santa Maria in Trastevere depicts Christ and the Virgin enthroned

The present church dates from the 12th century, and was begun by Pope Innocent II, a member of a prominent local family. Its most arresting features are its facade **mosaics** – many Roman churches would have once been similarly decorated – which portray, among other things, the Virgin flanked by ten figures. Like the identity of the figures themselves, the identity of the mosaics' creator is not known, although Pietro Cavallini is a possible candidate, if only because he was responsible for many of the even more spectacular mosaics inside the church. For instance, Cavallini's hand can be seen in the lively mosaics of the lower apse (1290), which portray scenes from the Life of the Virgin. The scenes in the upper apse are earlier (1140), and are executed in a more old-fashioned Byzantine style.

Don't miss the church's lovely inlaid medieval pavement and the nave's ancient columns, the latter brought here from the Terme di Caracalla, a sprawling Roman baths complex 15 minutes' walk beyond the Colosseo.

GIANICOLO

If you have the legs for a longer walk, then aim for the trees and greenery etched on the skyline above Trastevere. This is the Gianicolo, or Janiculum Hill, one of Rome's original "Seven Hills", and views over Rome from here make the climb worthwhile. Walk up Via Garibaldi and look at the **Fontana Paola** (1610–12), a monumental fountain created for Pope Paul V, and then see the late 15th-century church of **San Pietro in Montorio** at the top of Via Garibaldi, supposedly built over the spot on which St Peter was crucified (scholars believe he was actually martyred closer to the present-day site of the Vatican). In an adjoining courtyard stands the **Tempietto**, a tiny masterpiece of Renaissance architecture designed by Bramante, the architect partly responsible for the Basilica di San Pietro.

If you still have energy to burn, walk to the **Villa Doria Pamphilj**, Rome's largest park, a huge area of paths, pines, lakes and open spaces.

Villa Farnesina

From the church, walk northeast on Via della Scala and
continue on Via della Lungara, not an exciting walk, but
worth making for this beautiful Renaissance villa, built
in 1511 for Agostino Chigi, a wealthy Sienese banker. Its
highlight is the **Loggia of Cupid and Psyche** on the ground
floor, adorned with frescoes (1517) designed by Raphael but
largely painted by Giulio Romano. Upstairs is the **Sala delle
Prospettive**, a room entirely covered in frescoes containing
views of Rome and clever *trompe-l'oeil* tricks of perspective.
The adjoining room, formerly a bedchamber, contains vivid
16th-century frescoes by Sodoma.

The steep
walk up to
San Pietro
in Montorio,
Trastevere

A stone's throw from the villa you'll find the **Orto Botanico** (➤ 101), at the end of Via Corsini, a turn off Via della Lungara just south of the villa. Opened in 1883, its 12ha (30 acres) occupy the former gardens of the Palazzo Corsini, and spread up the slopes of the Gianicolo to the rear. It is famed for its palms and orchids, but is also a lovely place to take a shady time out from sightseeing.

TAKING A BREAK

The **Friends Art Café** (Piazza Trilussa 34, tel: 06 581 6111, daily 7:30am–2am) is a lively bar that serves everything from the morning cappuccino and *cornetto* (croissant) to after-dinner cocktails in surroundings of chrome and brightly coloured plastic.

Santa Maria in Trastevere	16th-century frescoes in the Renaissance Villa Farnesina
🞢 198 C4 ✉ Piazza Santa Maria in Trastevere ☎ 06 581 9443 🕙 Daily 7:30am–8pm, but may close 12:30–3:30 in winter 🎟 Free 🚌 23, 280, 780	

Villa Farnesina	Santa Maria in Trastevere lit up at night
🞢 197 E2 ✉ Via della Lungara 230 ☎ 06 6802 7397; www.villafarnesina. it; www.lincei.it 🕙 Mon–Sat 9–1 🎟 Moderate 🚌 23, 780 and 280 to Lungotevere della Farnesina or H, 8, 630 and 780 to Viale di Trastevere	

TRASTEVERE: INSIDE INFO

Top tips Try to see Santa Maria in Trastevere at night, when its facade and mosaics are usually **floodlit** to memorable effect.

■ Trastevere is generally safe, but you should take care late at night in the darker and more outlying streets.

At Your Leisure

🔢 Piazza Farnese

Piazza Farnese lies just a few steps from Campo dei Fiori, yet it's hard to think of two more contrasting Roman squares. While Campo dei Fiori is shabby and cramped, Piazza Farnese is broad and august, graced with elegant fountains, and unlike the Campo, which has no buildings of note, is dominated by the magnificent Palazzo Farnese. The palace, which has housed the French Embassy since 1871, is normally closed to the general public. The exterior was commissioned in 1515 by Cardinal Alessandro Farnese, later Pope Paul III. There are guided tours of the interior (book well in advance), giving you the chance to admire the magnificent ceiling frescoes by Annibale Caracci (1597–1603).

Much of the stone for the palace was pilfered from the Colosseo, and utilized here by the Tuscan architect Antonio da Sangallo the Younger. When Sangallo died in 1546 he was replaced on the project by Michelangelo, who designed much of the palace's cornice, many of the upper windows and the loggia. For one of Rome's grandest buildings, the French government pays the lowest rent in the city: set, before the advent of the euro, at one lira every 99 years. The Italians pay a similarly nominal sum for their embassy in Paris.

The fountains in the square were originally massive baths of Egyptian granite from the Terme di Caracalla. They were brought to the piazza in the 16th century by the Farnese family, who used them initially as a *dais* from which to admire the square's entertainments (look out for the carved lilies, the Farnese family symbol). They were turned into fountains in 1626.

➕ 197 F2 ✉ Piazza Farnese 🏛 Palazzo Farnese: Mon, Thu 3, 4, 5pm (pre-booked tours only). Email visitefarnese@franceitalia.it
🚌 40, 46, 62, 64, 916 to Corso Vittorio Emanuele II or H, 8, 63, 630, 780 to Via Arenula

🔢 Palazzo Spada

There are three modest reasons to visit the magnificent Palazzo Spada.

The first is the palace itself, which was built for Cardinal Girolamo Capo di Ferro in 1548. Much of the building's charm derives from the facade, added between 1556 and 1560, which is covered in beautifully patterned stucco work.

The second is an architectural *trompe-l'oeil* created in 1652 by the craftsman Francesco Borromini. It involves what appears to be a long columned corridor between two courtyards, which is in fact a passage a little under 9m (30 feet) long. The illusion is achieved by the deliberate narrowing of the corridor and foreshortening of the columns.

The third reason is to see its small, but very fine collection of paintings, among them works by Titian, Albrecht Dürer, Jan Brueghel the Elder and Guido Reni's portrait of his patron, Cardinal Bernardino Spada, who bought the palace in 1632.

➕ 197 F2 ✉ Piazza Capio di Ferro 13 ☎ 06 683 2409; www.galleriaborghese.it/spada; www.ticketeria.it 🕐 Tue–Sun 8:30–7:30 💶 Moderate 🚌 H, 8, 40, 46, 64, and other services to Via Arenula or Corso Vittorio Emanuele II

8 Santa Maria dell'Orazione e Morte

After looking at Piazza Farnese, walk along Via dei Farnesi. This soon brings you to Via Giulia, laid out by Pope Julius II between about 1503 and 1513, and still one of the city's most elegant and coveted residential thoroughfares. It's worth admiring, though perhaps not along its full length, for it runs for virtually 1km (0.6 miles) towards St Peter's.

Even if your itinerary doesn't take you down the street, devote a couple of minutes to the church on the junction of Via Giulia and Via dei Farnesi. Look for the unmistakable facade, decorated with stone skulls and, on the right side of the facade, looking down Via Giulia, the figure of a beaked bird – Osiris, the Egyptian god of death. A cheering inscription reads, in translation: "Me today, thee tomorrow". Santa Maria dell'Orazione e Morte (Our Lady of Oration and Death) was once the headquarters of a religious body known as the Compagnia della Buona Morte, or the "Company of the Good Death". Its charitable duties included collecting the unclaimed bodies of the poor and giving them a Christian burial. The corpses were stored in three tunnels running down to the Tiber, all but one of which were sealed up during construction of the river's modern embankment.

➕ 197 E2 ✉ Via Giulia 🕙 Sun 4–7pm
🚌 23, 63, 280

9 Sant'Agostino

The church of Sant'Agostino, built between 1479 and 1783, lies tucked away in the streets just north of Piazza Navona. The exterior is plain and unprepossessing, although the facade was one of the earliest Renaissance frontages in the city. The interior, which was extravagantly

The elaborately painted ceiling of the church of Sant'Agostino

efurbished in 1750, is that bit more
promising, and holds some unlikely
treasures for so modest a church. The
first is a Michelangelo-influenced
fresco of the Prophet Isaiah (1512)
by Raphael, commissioned by a
humanist scholar, Giovanni Goritz,
as an adornment to his tomb (the
painting is on the third pillar of the
left, or north side, of the church).

The first chapel on the same side
of the church features Caravaggio's
Madonna di Loreto (1605). Turn
around, and against the west wall
– the wall with the entrance door –
stands a statue by Jacopo Sansovino
known as the *Madonna del Parto*, or
Madonna of Childbirth (1521), much
venerated by pregnant women or
couples wanting a child.

➕ 194 A1 ✉ Piazza Sant'Agostino
☎ 06 6880 1962 🕐 Daily 7:30–12:30,
4–6:30 🎫 Free 🚌 30, 70, 81, 87, 116, 492
and 628 to Corso del Rinascimento

Detail of *The Martyrdom of St Matthew*
by Caravaggio, in San Luigi dei Francesi

⑩ San Luigi dei Francesi

The French national church in Rome,
built between 1518 and 1589, is
easily seen on the short walk between
Piazza Navona and the Pantheon, and
it is well worth stopping for the five
minutes it takes to see its principal
attractions: three superlative paintings
by Caravaggio.

The paintings were Caravaggio's
(► 24–25) first major Roman
commission (1600–02), and all
demonstrate the dramatic handling
of light and shade, or *chiaroscuro*
(literally "clear and dark") for which

Caravaggio was famed. They all
deal with the same theme – the life
of St Matthew – and portray *The
Calling of St Matthew* (the saint hears
God's summons while collecting
taxes); *St Matthew and the Angel*
(the altarpiece); and *The Martyrdom
of St Matthew*.

➕ 194 A1 ✉ Piazza di San Luigi dei
Francesi at the corner of Via Giustiniani
and Via della Scrofa ☎ 06 6882 8271
🕐 Fri–Wed 10–12:30, 4–7, Thu 10–12:30
🎫 Free 🚌 30, 70, 81, 87, 116, 492 and 628
to Corso del Rinascimento

FOR KIDS
Children will probably enjoy looking around the **Campo dei Fiori** market (► 80–81)
and watching the artists and occasional street performers in **Piazza Navona**
(► 82–85). They'll also relish the ice cream at **I Tre Scalini** (► 108) or a trip to
Bertè (Piazza Navona 108, tel: 06 687 5011, Tue–Sun 9–1, 3:30–7:30, Mon
3:30–7:30), one of Rome's oldest toy shops. **Legno e Fantasia** (Via del Governo
Vecchio 102, tel: 06 6813 9000, Tue–Sat 10–8, Sun 11–7) near Piazza Navona
has wonderful wooden toys and puppets, as well as necklaces and bracelets that
little girls will love. The **Orto Botanico** (Largo Cristina di Svezia 24, tel: 06 4991
2436, Tue–Sat 9:30–6:30 or dusk, closed Aug, inexpensive) provides plenty of
outdoor playing space for children who need to work off some energy (popular with
local mothers with children), but no playing equipment. The **Villa Sciarra**, however –
to the southwest of Trastevere – has a playground and mini roller-coaster.

⓫ Sant'Ivo alla Sapienza

The fact that Sant'Ivo is rarely open matters little, for the church's main attraction is its extraordinary spiralling dome and lantern, the work of Borromini, a leading baroque architect and rival of Gian Lorenzo Bernini. Borromini received his commission from Pope Urban VIII, a member of the powerful Barberini family, and it is said the architect based his spiky and eccentric dome on the family's symbol, the bee, taking the bee's sting as his inspiration. You'll catch a glimpse of the dome if you walk from the Pantheon to Piazza Navona via Piazza

Sant'Ivo alla Sapienza's spiral cupola was inspired by the sting of a bee

Sant'Eustachio. For a closer look you need to enter the Palazzo alla Sapienza, part of the papal university first founded in 1303.

➕ 194 A1 ✉ Corso del Rinascimento 40 ☎ 06 686 4987 🕐 Sun 9–12 💲 Free 🚍 30, 70, 81, 87, 116, 492 and 628 to Corso del Rinascimento

⓬ Ara Pacis

There's no easy way to see this Roman monument, which lies in an isolated position near the Tiber and to the northeast of the Castel Sant'Angelo. It's well worth making a detour, however, for the "Altar of Peace" (13–9BC), now within architect Richard Meier's controversial modern pavilion (2006), contains some of the city's best-preserved Roman bas-reliefs.

The altar was commissioned by the Senate to commemorate Emperor Augustus' military victories in France and Spain. The most striking and detailed of several sculpted friezes shows the procession that accompanied the altar's consecration, and includes the figures of Augustus, a number of high-ranking Roman officials and members of Augustus' family.

➕ 194 A2 ✉ Via di Ripetta ☎ 060608; www.arapacis.it 🕐 Tue–Sun 9–7 💲 Moderate 🚍 224, 628, 926 to Passeggiata di Ripetta

The Ara Pacis, the "Altar of Peace" is a memorial to Augustus' military victories

⓭ Santa Maria del Popolo

This church receives fewer visitors than it deserves, mainly because it lies on the northern fringe of the old city. Founded in the 11th century – allegedly over the tomb of Emperor Nero – it was much restored in later centuries by leading architects such as Bramante and Bernini. Inside the church, there are four outstanding artistic treasures worth seeing. The first is a series of frescoes (1485–89) behind the altar of the first chapel on the right (south) side by the Umbrian Renaissance painter Pinturicchio; the second is a pair of tombs (1505–07) in the choir by Andrea Sansovino; the third a pair of paintings by Caravaggio, *The Conversion of St Paul* and *Crucifixion of St Peter* (1601–02) in the first chapel of the left transept; and the fourth is the Cappella Chigi (1513), a chapel (second on the left, or north, side) commissioned by the wealthy Sienese banker Agostino

One of the ornate corridors within the Palazzo-Galleria Doria Pamphilj, which contains more than 1,000 rooms

Chigi. The last is noteworthy because virtually all of its component parts were designed by Raphael.

➕ 194 A4 ✉ Piazza del Popolo 12 ☎ 06 361 0836 🕐 Mon–Sat 7–12, 4–7, Sun 7:30–1:30, 4:30–7:30 💶 Free Ⓜ Flaminio 🚌 117, 119 to Piazza del Popolo

🄸 Palazzo-Galleria Doria Pamphilj

You'd never imagine looking at the Palazzo Doria Pamphilj's blackened exterior that it contained a multitude of beautifully decorated rooms and galleries, the succession of which provides a sumptuous setting for one of Italy's most important private art collections. There's no shortage of great pictures in Rome, but what makes the Palazzo so appealing is its sheer beauty and the opportunity to see behind the scenes of a truly grand, private palace.

The Doria Pamphilj palace is one of Rome's largest, with more than 1,000 rooms, five courtyards and four colossal staircases. Its size – in an age when the upkeep of such buildings is astronomical – is all the more remarkable given that it's still owned, and in part occupied, by the Doria Pamphilj family, headed today by two half-British siblings. This venerable papal dynasty was created when two families were united by marriage: the Doria, a Genoese merchant dynasty, and the Pamphili (or Pamphilj), a pillar of the Roman aristocracy.

From the entrance, climb the monumental stairway to the *piano nobile* and pick up one of the excellent multilingual audio guides (included in the ticket price), which will guide you round the palazzo, picking out highlights along the way; you should allow about 90 minutes for your visit. Five superbly decorated chambers, the state apartments, each more sumptuous than the last, open out one from the other. The ballroom, with its white and gold stucco decoration, mirrors and chandeliers is hung with figured silk. From here, you reach the private chapel, designed by Carlo Fontana in 1690, and the entrance to the picture galleries. These run round all four sides of the largest of the inner courtyards, and perfectly reflect 18th-century taste, with Flemish and Italian works hung alongside each other – the arrangement preferred by Prince Andrea Doria IV in 1760.

The collection's most famous work is Velazquez's *Portrait of Innocent X* (1650). A pope of notoriously weak character, Innocent is said to have remarked of the likeness that it was "too true, too true"; beside it stands Bernini's bust of Innocent, so that you can compare two different

likenesses. Most of the greatest names of Italian art are also represented in the galleries, including Caravaggio's *Rest on the Flight into Egypt* and the very beautiful *Magdalen*, Raphael's *Double Portrait* and Titian's dreamily seductive *Salome with Head of John the Baptist*. Other unmissable highlights include Filippo Lippi's *Annunciation* and Hans Memling's supremely pathetic *Pietà*.

🔢 199 E5 ✉ Via del Corso 305 ☎ 06 679 7373; www.dopart.it 🕐 Daily 10–5 💶 Expensive 🚇 Barberini 🚌 60, 62 and all other services to Piazza Venezia

⓯ Santa Cecilia in Trastevere

This church sits slightly west of Viale di Trastevere and the rest of Trastevere and can be included as part of a Trastevere stroll or a walk from the other side of the Tiber by way of the Isola Tiberina. Much of its appeal is wrapped up in the story of its dedicatee, St Cecilia, who is said to have lived here with her husband Valerio, a Roman patrician figure, in the fourth century. Valerio joined his chaste wife as a Christian, only to be rewarded with martyrdom. Cecilia's own martyrdom was protracted: attempts to scald and suffocate her failed, and she finally succumbed to three blows to her neck, but only after singing throughout her ordeal – one of the reasons why she is the patron saint of music.

The present church is a fascinating mixture of styles, ranging from the 12th-century portico to the grand 18th-century facade and chill baroque interior. Several fine

OFF THE BEATEN TRACK

To escape the hordes, visit the Trastevere's botanical gardens, Orto Botanico (▶ 101), off Via Corsini or the Villa Doria Pamphilj, a huge park on the western flanks of the Gianicolo. It is a long walk to the latter, however, so take either a cab or bus 870 from the western end of Corso Vittorio Emanuele II, or 115 or 125 from the southern end of Viale di Trastevere.

works of art survived the years, notably a statue of St Cecilia by Stefano Maderno. The sculptor was apparently present when the saint's tomb was opened in 1599, her body having previously been moved from the catacombs outside the city on the orders of Pope Paschal I in the ninth century. Maderno made a drawing of her reputedly uncorrupt body, and in his statue clearly depicted the three cuts left by the Roman executioner's unsuccessful attempts to cut off Cecilia's head. Today, the saint's tomb is in the church's crypt which can be visited, along with excavations which reveal the remains of a Roman house.

Above the church's altar is a lovely Gothic *baldacchino*, or altar canopy (1293), the work of Arnolfo di Cambio. The apse is adorned with a beautiful and almost glowing ninth-century mosaic which shows Pope Paschal I presenting Cecilia and her husband Valerio to Christ. The cloister features celebrated frescoes of the *Last Judgement* (1293) by the Roman painter and mosaicist Pietro

Cavallini, a contemporary of Giotto.
🚩 199 D3 ⊠ Piazza di Santa Cecilia in Trastevere ☎ 06 589 9289 🕐 Church: Mon–Sat 9:30–1, 4–6:30; Sun 11:30–12:30, 4–6:30. Cavallini frescoes: Mon–Sat 10:15–12:15, Sun 11:30–12:30. Excavations: daily 9:30–12:30, 4–6:30 💷 Inexpensive 🚌 56, 60, 75, 710, 780

Stefano Maderno's poignant sculpture of St Cecilia portrays the saint as she was found when her tomb was opened in 1599

Where to...
Eat and Drink

Prices
Expect to pay per person for a meal, excluding drinks and service:
€ under €30   €€ €30–€50   €€€ over €50

Alle Fratte di Trastevere €€

This wonderfully traditional Trastevere restaurant typifies everything that's best about a Roman family-run trattoria. It serves generous portions of freshly prepared seasonal and regional food. Dishes include *penne all'arrabiata* and *spaghetti alla carbonara*, baked fish and veal escalopes with different sauces. Desserts are home-made, there are tables outside, service is brisk and friendly, the staff speak English and prices are very reasonable.

➕ 198 C3 ✉ Via delle Fratte di Trastevere 49 ☎ 06 583 5775 🕓 Mon–Tue, Thu–Sat 12:30–3, 6:30–11:30, Sun 12:30–3. Closed 2 weeks in Aug

Ar Galletto €€

Overlooking one of Rome's loveliest squares, this cheerful and straightforward but stylish restaurant offers by far the best value for money of the restaurants on Piazza Farnese. Professionally and efficiently run, staples include a wonderful selection of vegetable antipasti such as *fiori di zucchi* (stuffed courgette flowers) and *puntarelle* (wild chicory shoots). Main courses range from Roman pasta specialities to grills and fish.

The house white comes from the Alban hills, but it's worth perusing the wine list. Sit at one of the pretty tables outside in summer, right across from Palazzo Farnese.

➕ 197 F2 ✉ Vicolo del Gallo 1 ☎ 06 686 1714 🕓 Mon–Sat 12:15–3, 7:15–11. Closed 10 days in Aug

La Carbonara €–€€

This popular Campo dei Fiori fixture is the best restaurant on the square, and serves perfectly acceptable food at decent prices. The large number of outdoor tables means you shouldn't have to wait too long to be seated.

➕ 197 F2 ✉ Campo dei Fiori 23 ☎ 06 686 4783 🕓 Wed–Mon 12:15–3, 7–11.30. Closed 3 weeks in Aug

Da Francesco €

This is the best of the pizzerias near Piazza Navona, a cramped, quintessentially Roman eating house that serves some of the best paper-thin pizzas in the city. There is also an antipasto buffet to start

with and the menu offers good, basic Roman *primi* and *secondi*. Factor in a jolly atmosphere, tables outside in summer and great value for money and you'll see why you may have to wait for a table.

➕ 197 F3 ✉ Piazza del Fico 29 ☎ 06 686 4009 🕓 Mon, Wed–Sun 12–3, 7–12:30: Tue 7–12:30

'Gusto €–€€

'Gusto's atmosphere and decor are chic and sophisticated but also informal. Downstairs in the busy split-level eatery you can sample pizzas, generous salads and other light meals (be prepared for lunchtime crowds), while upstairs in the restaurant there is a more ambitious and eclectic menu, combining Italian traditions and Eastern stir-fry cooking. Quality is good (rarely more), but you're here for the atmosphere as much as the food.

➕ 194 A3 ✉ Piazza Augusto Imperatore 9 ☎ 06 322 6273; www.gusto.it 🕓 Daily 1–3, 7:30–1

Il Leoncino €

Other pizzerias in the city may be better known, but Il Leoncino, located just a couple of blocks west of Via del Corso, offers the authentic Roman pizzeria experience – and is likely to be busy with locals. Pizzas are made traditionally behind an old marble-topped bar and cooked in wood-fired ovens.

🔢 194 B2 ⊠ Via del Leoncino 28, off Piazza San Lorenzo in Lucina 🕿 06 686 7757 🕐 Lunch: Mon–Tue, Thu–Fri 1–2.30. Dinner: Thu–Tue 6:30–12

Myosotis €€

The vivid modern dining rooms and light, innovative cooking at Myosotis are something of a departure from Rome's often rather traditional and decoratively uninspired restaurants. Service is amiable, the atmosphere relaxed and the prices reasonable. Menus change with the season, but almost always include Roman classics such as spaghetti alla carbonara and a selection of fish.

🔢 194 A1 ⊠ Vicolo della Vaccarella 3–5 🕿 06 686 5554 🕐 Mon–Sat 7:30pm–11pm. Closed 3 weeks in Aug

L'Osteria €€

Run by the same team as 'Gusto (▶ 107), this bustling restaurant on two levels applies the Spanish tapas approach to traditional trattoria cooking, so you can sample a wide range of dishes in the shape of tasters. Follow a few mouthfuls of fritti (deep-fried seafood or vegetables) with a couple of tastes of different pasta dishes, and then move on to traditional Roman meat dishes featuring offal. There's a great wine list that includes a good choice of wines by the glass.

🔢 194 A3 ⊠ Via della Frezza 16 🕿 06 322 6273 🕐 Daily 12:30–3:30, 7–1

Sora Margherita €

It's worth getting your head around the somewhat bizarre opening times to come here for a unique Roman experience. This hole-in-the-wall restaurant (find it by its

number not some fancy sign) offers superlative Roman-Jewish cooking at bargain prices. The friendly welcome matches the quality of the food, such as pasta e fagioli (pasta and beans) and a mouth-watering ossobuco (veal shank). The wine is local, the napkins paper – no frills, just genuine Roman cooking.

🔢 199 D4 ⊠ Piazza delle Cinque Scole 30 🕿 06 687 4216 🕐 Oct–Mar Tue–Thu, Sun 12:30–3, Fri–Sat 12:30–3, 8–11:30 (2 sittings at 8, 9.30, booking required); Apr–Sep Mon–Thu 12:30–3, Fri 12:30– 3, 8–11:30 (2 sittings at 8, 9.30, booking required)

BARS AND CAFÉS

Bar della Pace €

Frequent visitors to Rome may be cynical about this place just off Piazza Navona, but they still come back. By day, the bar is a pretty place for a coffee; by night it is one of the city's buzziest spots. The pizzeria-trattoria alongside is good.

🔢 197 F3 ⊠ Via della Pace 3–7 🕿 06 686 1216 🕐 Daily 9am–2am

Cul de Sac €

This wine bar, founded in 1968, close to Piazza Navona, has plenty of ambience and serves a large selection of wines, as well as snacks and appetizers.

🔢 197 F3 ⊠ Piazza Pasquino 73 🕿 06 6880 1094 🕐 Daily 12–4, 6–12:30

Il Goccetto €

An intimate and cosy wine bar close to Cul de Sac (see above). Il Goccetto takes its wine seriously. The setting, part of a grand medieval house, is lovely, with original frescoed ceilings.

🔢 197 E3 ⊠ Via dei Banchi Vecchi 14 🕿 06 686 4268 🕐 Mon–Sat 11:30–2, 7–11. Closed 3 weeks in Aug and Sat lunch Jul and Aug

I Tre Scalini €

I Tre Scalini would be just one more Piazza Navona bar were it not for its rightly celebrated tartufo ice cream. It's perfect for a hot afternoon.

🔢 197 F3 ⊠ Piazza Navona 28–32 🕿 06 6880 1996 🕐 Daily 9am–1am

Where to...
Shop

The heart of Rome is a large and varied area and the shopping opportunities here are correspondingly mixed and extensive. Small side streets often prove a happy hunting ground for specialities, notably Via dei Coronari (antiques), Via dei Giubbonari (inexpensive clothes and shoes), Via Giulia (art and antiques), Via dei Cappellari (furniture), Via dei Sediari (religious ephemera), and Via del Governo Vecchio, Via dei Banchi Nuovi and Via del Governo Vecchio (gift shops, clothes and antiques). Although Trastevere also has its share of small craft, antiques and speciality shops, it is not a major shopping area; it does, however, have a large general market in Piazza San Cosimato. The other main market

in the area is at Campo dei Fiori (▶ 80–81).

BOOKS

Feltrinelli

Part of a large, modern nationwide chain, Feltrinelli stocks a good range of English-language titles. It also sells a wide selection of attractive cards, magazines and posters, as well as children's toys and games.

Largo di Torre Argentina 11 ☎ 06 6866 3001 ◷ Mon–Fri 9–9, Sat 9am–10pm, Sun 10–9

Libreria del Viaggiatore

This book shop specializes in travel literature, maps and guides, and stocks some English-language titles.

Via del Pellegrino 78 ☎ 06 6880 1048 ◷ Tue–Sat 10–2, 4–8, Mon 4–8

CLOTHES

Arlette

Among the clothes shops that line this street near Piazza Navona, Arlette stands out for its relaxed, elegant and easy-to-wear women's clothes. Classic natural fabrics combine with good cuts to produce eminently desirable styles that have that Italian touch. They also sell accessories, such as scarves, bags and a few men's accessories.

Via del Governo Vecchio 49 ☎ 06 688 06837 ◷ Mon–Sat 10–8, Sun 12–7

Arsenale

Patrizia Pieroni shows her easy-to-wear and stylish collection in an airy white space; expect fashion with a distinctly boho twist, with great lines and a spread of colour and detail, as well as accessories.

Via del Pellegrino 172 ☎ 06 6880 2424 ◷ Tue–Sat 10–7, Mon 3–7

The Place for Kids

Quirky and colourful Italian children's clothes are on offer at this great little shop opposite the Pantheon, with frequently changing stock and a wide selection for boys and girls. Styles reflect what's what in the grown-up world with modern fabric and designs, and accessories, which will keep most children and their parents happy.

Salita dei Crescenzi 32 (Pantheon) ☎ 06 689 3183 ◷ Mon–Sat 10–8

COSMETICS AND TOILETRIES

Officina Profumo-Farmaceutico di Santa Maria di Novella

This Roman outlet for a Florence-based shop sells a wide range of good quality cosmetics, perfumes, and herbal and other natural beauty products, the majority of which are made to traditional methods originally devised by Dominican monks.

Corso del Rinascimento 47 ☎ 06 687 2446 ◷ Mon–Sat 9:30–7:30

Bassetti

Rows of fabrics fill this store, along with clothes and home furnishings.

☒ Corso Vittorio Emanuele II 73 ☎ 06 689 2326 ☻ Jul–Aug Tue–Sat 9–7:30, Mon 3:30–7; Sep–Jun Tue–Sat 9–1, 4–6, Mon 4–6

Ai Monasteri

This intriguing shop is across from Officina Profumo-Farmaceutico (▲109) at the northern end of Piazza Navona. It sells honey, oils, jam, liqueurs and other products from Italian monasteries.

☒ Corso del Rinascimento 72 ☎ 06 6880 2783 ☻ Mon–Wed, Fri–Sat 9–1, 4:30–7:30, Thu 9–1

Moriondo e Gariglio

This family-run concern makes and sells outstanding chocolate in all shapes, sizes and varieties.

☒ Via del Pie' di Marmo 21–22 ☎ 06 699 0856 ☻ Daily 9–7:30

Valzani

A long-established Trastevere institution celebrated for its cakes, chocolate, pastries and other sweet-toothed treats.

☒ Via del Moro 37b ☎ 06 580 3792 ☻ Mon, Tue 2–8, Wed–Sun 9:30–8

House & Kitchen

Unlike Spazio Sette, this traditional shop sells a full range of kitchen utensils – basic and exotic – and other household goods.

☒ Via del Plebiscito 103 ☎ 06 6992 0167 ☻ Mon–Sat 9:30–8, Sun 10:30–2:30. Closed Sun in Jul and Aug

Ornamentum

Rome has several shops offering a beautiful range of furnishing and other fabrics, but none perhaps quite as sumptuous as Ornamentum on Via dei Coronari. This is the ultimate emporium for silks, damasks and other fabrics, as well as an enormous range of tassels, brocades and assorted furnishing accessories.

☒ Via dei Coronari 227 ☎ 06 687 6849 ☻ Tue–Fri 9–1, 4–7:30, Sat 9–1, Mon 4–7:30. Closed Aug

Spazio Sette

Old mixes with new at Spazio Sette, the city's best furniture, household and design store, where a huge range of consumer desirables are spread over three floors of a Renaissance palace complete with frescoed ceilings and a pretty courtyard garden. This is a truly Italian shopping experience.

☒ Via dei Barbieri 7 ☎ 06 686 9747 ☻ Tue–Sat 9:30–1, 3:30–7:30, Mon 3:30–7:30

La Fiorentina

Located right on the busy Corso, this tiny shop is a treasure trove with a vast selection of beautiful semi-precious stones and coral, made up into tempting necklaces, earrings, bracelets and rings. Pieces are mounted on gold or silver, and there's such a range there's something to suit every pocket. They'll also make up pieces from their stock of loose stones in a couple of days.

☒ Corso Vittorio Emanuele II 95A–97 ☎ 06 686 5043 ☻ Tue–Sat 10–1, 4–7, Mon 4–7

Il Papiro

Italian paper products make wonderful gifts to take home and add a little Italian elegance to any desk. This lovely shop sells desirable notebooks, photo albums, desk accessories and frames all made from superb Florentine figured and marbled paper in beautiful designs. This is also an excellent shop if you want to purchase pencils, stylish pens and multicoloured inks.

☒ Via del Pantheon 50 ☎ 06 679 5597 ☻ Mon–Sat 10–8, Sun 11–8

Where to…
Be Entertained

CLASSICAL MUSIC

One or two classical music organizations have their headquarters in the centre of Rome (even if they stage their concerts elsewhere). One is the **Associazione Musicale Romana** (AMR) on Via Gregorio VII 216 (tel: 06 3936 6322, 06 686 8441, www.assmusrom.it), which usually puts on **chamber concerts** in spring and early summer; tickets are obtainable from individual venues. Another organization is the important **Oratorio del Gonfalone** (tel: 06 687 5952), which has its own orchestra and choir who usually perform at the Oratorio del Gonfalone in Via del Gonfalone, a tiny street between Via Giulia and Lungotevere Sangallo. It specializes in hosting small chamber recitals, but also presents concerts by visiting Italian ensembles.

Many of the city's major church **music** concerts – usually performed by visiting choirs – are staged in the central **Sant'Ignazio**, a large church in Piazza di Sant'Ignazio almost midway between the Pantheon and Via del Corso. Unfortunately, the building has poor acoustics – the best place to sit is as close to the front as possible, so you need to arrive early. Contact visitor centres (▶ 30) for details of forthcoming concerts, or look for posters outside the church. Recitals are usually free.

Several churches in the area offer **organ recitals**, but you will need to keep your eyes peeled for posters in the local area advertising concerts. A good bet is **San Giovanni de' Fiorentini** in Via Giulia where, at afternoon Mass on Sunday, you may be treated to the sound of the church's wonderful late 17th-century instrument being played. The AMR (see left) generally organizes an organ festival in the church during September.

NIGHTLIFE

Campo dei Fiori

Campo dei Fiori has become something of a focus for bars that come into their own at nightfall. The place that started the trend is the piazza's gritty **La Vineria** (Campo dei Fiori 15, tel: 06 6880 3268, Mon–Sat 8:30am–2am, Sun 5pm–1am), also known as Da Giorgio, as authentic a Roman wine bar as you could hope for. It makes few concessions to interior decoration – there is just one plain bar – and the characters who collect here can be colourful, to say the least. The outside tables are a favourite rendezvous on summer evenings. Almost immediately alongside La Vineria is the **Drunken Ship** (Campo dei Fiori 20–21, tel: 06 6830 0535, daily 4pm–2am), a boisterous and brash place much favoured by young Romans and foreign visitors alike. It serves mostly beer rather than wine and is further distinguished from its adjacent rival by its bold design and the fact that it has DJs and music most evenings: happy hour usually runs from about 5pm to 8pm.

Piazza Navona

For a somewhat calmer alternative to the trendy and busy bars on Campo dei Fiori, try **Cul de Sac** (▶ 108), **Il Goccetto** (▶ 108) and the perennially hip **Bar della Pace** (▶ 108), the latter perhaps the most popular place to hang out in this part of Rome. For something almost equally trendy but a little less busy, wander round the corner to **Bar del Fico** (Piazza del Fico 26–28, tel: 06 686 5205, Mon–Sat 9am–2am, Sun 6pm–2am). It is a touch less expensive and in winter has outdoor heating so you can still sit outside.

Jonathan's Angels (Via della Fossa 14, tel: 06 689 3426, Mon–Fri 8pm–3am, Sat–Sun 6:30pm–3am), just off Piazza Navona, is an eccentric but delightfully decorated bar, decked out with candles and plenty of kitsch and overpowering paintings on the walls.

Also close to Piazza Navona is **Anima** (Via Santa Maria dell'Anima 57, tel: 06 6889 2806, daily noon–4am), a small and welcoming bar and club with an eclectic music policy. A few minutes from the Pantheon is **Salotto 42** (Piazza di Pietra 42, tel: 06 678 5804, Tue–Sun 10am–2am), a cosy place for lunch or, later, cocktails in a stylish setting.

Piazza Venezia

Irish bars are big in many Italian cities, and Rome is no exception. One of the biggest and best in the city is **Trinity College**, housed near the Palazzo Doria Pamphilj over two floors of a beautiful Renaissance palace at Via del Collegio Romano 6 (tel: 06 678 6472, www.trinity-rome.com, daily noon–3am). Good and inexpensive Irish food is served along with the inevitable bottles of beer and stout.

Trastevere

In Trastevere, the best of the night-time bars and pubs is **Caffè della Scala** (Via della Scala 4, tel: 06 580 3610, www.caffedellascala. com, daily 5pm–2am), a big and bustling place for beer, wine by the glass, cocktails and light meals and snacks. It is definitely not the place for a quiet drink. For something quieter, try **Sacchetti** (Piazza San Cosimato 61–2, tel: 06 581 5374, Tue–Sun 6am–midnight), a family-run bar with tables outside. It serves delicious ice cream and home-made cakes and pastries.

Best of the live jazz and blues joints is long-established **Big Mama** (Vicolo San Francesco a Ripa 18, tel: 06 581 2551, www.bigmama. it, Oct–Jun Tue–Sat 9pm–1.30am). It describes itself, with some justification, as the "Home of Blues in Rome", staging around 200 concerts a year. Stars of today and yesteryear perform alongside up-and-coming Italian musicians.

Testaccio

Though Trastevere is still lively at night and has many good bars and clubs, it is no longer as trendy as it was a few years ago. The axis of night-time action has now shifted to **Testaccio** and **Ostiense**, traditional working-class districts farther south. In summer the district buzzes with clubs, bars and outdoor venues, but it's peripheral to the city centre, so you'll need to take a bus or taxi to get there.

Venues of the moment change with some regularity, but you can always be sure to find something to suit your tastes. Two of the more permanent fixtures for live music and dancing are **Akab** (Via di Monte Testaccio 69, tel: 06 5725 0585, www.akabcave.com, Tue–Sat 11pm–4am) and **Alpheus** (Via del Commercio 36, tel: 06 574 7826, Fri–Sun 10:30pm–4am). **l'Alibi** (Via di Monte Testaccio 40–7, tel: 06 574 3448, Wed–Sun 11pm–4:30am), a primarily (though not exclusively) gay club, is one of the most established and popular venues in the city.

CINEMA

If you're desperate to catch a film in its original language (*versione originale* or VO), then head over to the **Nuovo Olimpia** (Via in Lucina 16G, tel: 06 686 1068). This a comfortable, two-screen cinema just off Via del Corso. It's an art-house-oriented venue run by the Circuito Cinema (www.circuitocinema. com). Alternatively, VO films are occasionally shown at **Filmstudio** (Via degli Orti di Alibert 1C, tel: 334 178 0632) in Trastevere.

Northern Rome

Getting Your Bearings

This chapter encompasses two contrasting areas of Rome. The first is around Termini, the city's main railway station, which you'd avoid were it not for a superb museum and major church; the second is around Piazza di Spagna, renowned for the Spanish Steps, full of wonderful streets, fantastic shops, memorable views, and compelling museums and galleries.

The mid 20th-century architecture of Termini railway station has its admirers, but in truth there is little in the area around the station – which is all traffic and cheap hotels – to tempt you into staying longer than it takes to see the distinguished church of Santa Maria Maggiore and the magnificent collection of Roman statues, mosaics and wall paintings at Palazzo Massimo alle Terme.

Once your sightseeing in this part of the city is finished, you could catch the Metro from Repubblica to Spagna station to visit Piazza di Spagna, a means of avoiding a mostly uninteresting and far from pretty 19th-century part of the city. Alternatively, you could walk from the Palazzo Massimo alle Terme towards Via Vittorio Veneto (often known simply as Via Veneto), famous in the 1950s and 1960s as the focus of Rome's *dolce vita* days of hedonism and high living: today, sadly, it lives largely on its past reputation. You could also take in the works of art at Palazzo Barberini, as well as the interior of Santa Maria della Vittoria, home to a notorious Bernini sculpture.

By the time you reach the Fontana di Trevi, the most spectacular of the city's many fountains, you have re-entered Rome's old historic core and are close to its most exclusive shopping district, the grid of streets centred on Via Condotti. You could easily spend a couple of hours here window-shopping, perhaps followed by a lazy half-hour people-watching in Piazza di Spagna. Literary pilgrims may want to visit the small museum on the piazza devoted to the poets John Keats and Percy Bysshe Shelley.

Climb the Spanish Steps for views over Rome, and, if the weather's fine, walk northwest from Piazza di Spagna along Viale della Trinità dei Monti. This street offers fine views and leads into a more open part of the city, allowing you to strike into the Pincian Hill, and from there into the park and gardens of the Villa Borghese. A 1km (half-mile) walk through the park brings you to the Borghese gallery and museum, home to superb sculptures by Bernini and paintings by Caravaggio, Raphael and other major painters. If you don't want to walk, take a cab or bus 116 from Piazza di Spagna.

Page 113: Fontana della Barcaccia and the magnificent view to Trinità and the Spanish Steps
Right: One of the treasures in the Palazzo Barberini is the erotic *La Fornarina* by Raphael, completed in 1633, a painting which many believed to be a portrait of his lover

In a Day

If you're not quite sure where to begin your travels, this itinerary recommends a practical and enjoyable day exploring Northern Rome, taking in some of the best places to see using the Getting Your Bearings map on the previous page. For more information see the main entries.

8:30am

Make your way to Piazza dei Cinquecento on foot, or by bus, Metro or taxi, and then walk the short distance to **1 Santa Maria Maggiore** (➤ 118–119). Explore the magnificently decorated church, especially its mosaics, then visit the small nearby church of **6 Santa Prassede** (➤ 132).

9:15am

Walk to the **2 Palazzo Massimo alle Terme** (➤ 120–123) and allow a couple of hours to explore the museum's superb collection of classical sculpture and rare Roman mosaics and wall paintings.

11:00am

Walk west toward Piazza di Spagna, perhaps stopping off en route to visit Santa Maria della Vittoria, home to Bernini's erotic sculpture of St Teresa, **Santa Maria della Concezione** (➤ 10) and the **8 Palazzo Barberini** (below, ➤ 133), to see works by Raphael, Caravaggio (➤ 24–25) and Titian.

12:30pm
Make your way to the **3 Fontana di Trevi** (➤ 124–125) and then continue north toward Via Condotti (left) and Piazza di Spagna. If you have time, visit the **7 Museo Nazionale delle Paste Alimentari** (➤ 132–133).

1:00pm
Stop for a snack or a leisurely lunch in the streets around the Fontana di Trevi and Piazza di Spagna.

2:00pm
After lunch you might stop for a coffee in the historic **Antico Caffè Greco** (➤ 138). Serious shoppers will want to spend plenty of time in the area around **Via Condotti** (➤ 139); others can visit the **9 Museo Keats-Shelley** (➤ 134). Everyone should walk to the top of the **4 Spanish Steps** (➤ 126–127) to admire the marvellous views of the city.

3:00pm
Meander through the parkland of the Villa Borghese to the **5 Museo e Galleria Borghese** (right, ➤ 128–131), one of Rome's greatest museums. Remember pre-booking by phone or online is mandatory (➤ 131). If the walk is too far, take a 116 bus or taxi from Piazza di Spagna.

5:30pm
After seeing the Galleria you'll be far from the city centre. You could walk west through the park to **12 Villa Giulia** (➤ 135) or **11 Museo Carlo Bilotti** (➤ 134–135) or catch the 52, 53, 910 or 116 bus (Piazzale Brasile) back to the city centre.

❶ Santa Maria Maggiore

Santa Maria Maggiore is the most important – and possibly the oldest – of some 80 churches in Rome dedicated to the Virgin Mary. Its surroundings are not the prettiest in the city, but the ancient basilica's richly decorated interior is one of the most sumptuous in Italy.

According to legend, the church was built after the Virgin appeared to Pope Liberius in a vision on 4 August 356 and told him to build a church on the spot where snow would fall the following day. Snow duly fell, despite the fact that it was the middle of summer, leading not only to the foundation of a church, but also to the instigation of a feast day – Our Lady of the Snow – on 5 August. In truth, the church was probably founded in the middle of the fifth century, on the ruins of a Roman building dating back to the first century, or earlier.

A sublimely rich mosaic, depicting the Coronation of the Virgin, decorates the apse

This building was probably a temple to Juno Lucina, a mother goddess, much revered by Roman women, and it is probably no accident that a pagan cult was replaced by its Christian equivalent: the new church was dedicated to the mother of Christ as *Santa Maria ad Praesepe* (St Mary of the Crib). The church's maternal link was further reinforced by relics of Christ's Holy Crib, fragments of which were enshrined beneath the high altar.

Obelisks and pillars stand sentinel outside the church's (usually closed) north and south entrances, one a Roman copy of an Egyptian obelisk (in Piazza dell'Esquilino) removed from the Mausoleo di Augusto, the other a column removed from the Basilica di Massenzio in the Foro Romano (▶ 55). The main south entrance is the usual entry point for visitors.

Glorious Additions

Much has been added to the church since the fifth century, not least its immense weight of decoration, but the original basilica-shaped plan survives, a design probably adapted directly from the site's earlier structure. Almost the first thing to strike you inside is the magnificent coffered **ceiling**, reputedly gilded with the first gold to be shipped from the New World, a gift from Ferdinand and Isabella of Spain to Pope Alexander VI. A small museum details the basilica's history.

The colossal columns supporting the ceiling lead the eye upward to a superb 36-panel sequence of **mosaics**, fifth-century works portraying episodes from the lives of Moses, Isaac, Jacob and Abraham. A later, but equally magnificent mosaic (1295) depicting the

Confessio with a kneeling statue of Pope Pius IX. Mass has been celebrated in Santa Maria Maggiore for more than 1,500 years

Coronation of the Virgin swathes the apse, the area behind the high altar, the work of Jacopo Torriti. Complementary swirls of colour adorn parts of the church floor, examples of Cosmati inlaid marble work dating from the middle of the 12th century. More 13th-century mosaics can be seen on guided tours to the basilica's loggia.

Among the interior's most impressive additions are a pair of large facing chapels: the **Cappella Sistina** (on the right as you face the altar) and the **Cappella Paolina** (on the left), completed for popes Sixtus V and Paul V in 1587 and 1611 respectively. Little in either is individually outstanding, but the overall decorative effect is overwhelming.

TAKING A BREAK

If you want a leisurely drink, the best advice is to continue on towards Piazza di Spagna.

⊞ 201 D5 ☒ Piazza di Santa Maria Maggiore and Piazza dell'Esquilino
☎ 06 6988 6800 🕓 Daily 7–7; times may vary 💷 Free 🚇 Termini or Cavour 🚌 5, 14, 16, 70, 71, 75, 84, 105

SANTA MARIA MAGGIORE: INSIDE INFO

Top tip Santa Maria Maggiore is in a relatively unappealing part of the city close to the Termini railway station, but can be easily combined with a visit to the nearby Palazzo Massimo alle Terme (➤ 120–123). Unlike many churches in the city, it remains open all day.

Hidden gem Look out for the **tomb of Cardinal Consalvo Rodriguez** in the chapel to the rear right (south) of the high altar as you face it. The cardinal died in 1299, and the tomb was completed soon after. Its sculptor is not known, but the beautiful inlaid marble is the work of Giovanni di Cosma, one of the family first responsible for this distinctive "Cosmati" decorative style.

② Palazzo Massimo alle Terme

The Palazzo Massimo alle Terme houses part of the Museo Nazionale Romano, one of the world's greatest collections of ancient art. Among the city's newer museum spaces, it provides a magnificent showcase for some of the most beautiful sculptures, paintings and mosaics of the Roman age.

The Palazzo lies close to Rome's unlovely Termini station, but don't be put off, for once inside the superbly restored 19th-century building you're confronted by beauty at every turn. The gallery spreads over three floors: the first two levels (ground and first floor) are devoted largely to sculpture, the top (second floor) mostly to mosaics and a series of frescoed Roman rooms moved from sites around the city. Such painted rooms are extremely rare, most frescoes of this age having long been lost to the elements. They are also surprisingly beautiful, so leave enough time to do them justice.

The Collections

These mosaics and paintings distinguish the Palazzo Massimo from its sister museum, the Palazzo Altemps (➤ 86–89), which is smaller and devoted to sculpture, and in particular, to the superb sculptures of the Ludovisi collection.

Beyond the ticket hall and vestibule, bear to your right for the first of the ground floor's eight rooms, which are arranged around the palace's interior central courtyard. Ahead of you, along the courtyard's right-hand side, runs a gallery – one of three – filled with portrait busts and statues that served as funerary or honorary monuments in the last years of the Republican era (the end of the second and beginning of the first century BC). Room I opens to the right, where the highlight among several busts and statues of upper-class Roman figures is the *General of Tivoli*. It was probably the work of a Greek sculptor and is thought to have been executed between 90 and 70BC, at a time when the Romans were conducting numerous military campaigns in Asia.

The exquisitely detailed statue of Emperor Augustus

A collection of superb mosaics is housed on the second floor

Room III contains a collection of Roman coins, while the highlight of Room V is a virtuoso statue of **Emperor Augustus** – note the exquisite detail of the emperor's toga. Different in style, but no less compelling, is Room VII's statue of **Niobede**, one of the mythical daughters of Niobe murdered by Apollo and Artemis: the statue shows Niobede trying to remove an arrow shot by Artemis. Other rooms and galleries on this floor contain many more similarly outstanding sculptures, as well as small areas of wall painting that whet the appetite for the exhibits on the museum's top floor.

Sculptures on the first floor move chronologically through the Roman era, continuing the theme from the floor below in Room I with work from the era of the Flavian emperors (after AD69) – Vespasian, Titus and Domitian. The following rooms contain exhibits spanning 400 years.

Themed Rooms

Interspersed with these are rooms arranged by theme, notably Room VI, which is devoted to the idealized sports and other statues that once adorned ancient Rome's gymnasiums and sporting arenas. Here you'll find the gallery's most famous statue, the *Discobolo Lancellotti*, or **Lancellotti Discus-Thrower** (mid-second century AD), the finest of several Roman copies of a celebrated fifth-century BC Greek bronze original. This original was widely celebrated by classical writers as a perfect study of the human body in motion.

A very different, but equally beguiling statue resides in Room VII, devoted to gods and divinities, and shows *L'Ermafrodito Addormentato*, or **Sleeping Hermaphrodite** (second century AD). Like the Discus-Thrower, the sculpture is the best of several known copies made from a popular Greek original created some 400 years earlier. The statue's sensuous appearance made it a popular adornment for gardens and open spaces in the grand houses of private individuals. A far cruder statue, depicting a **masked actor in the guise of Papposileno**, is the most striking figure in Room IX, which is given over to the theatre and performing arts.

Much of your time in the gallery should be spent on the top (second) floor. Its first highlight is Room II, which contains **exquisite wall paintings** removed from the **Villa di Livia**, owned by Livia Drusilla, mother of Emperor Augustus (who reigned 27BC–AD14). The murals portray a garden scene, filled with finely painted birds, flowers and trees, suggesting the original room was part of a summer house.

Wall Paintings

From here, walk back through Room I and along the floor's right-hand (north) gallery to Rooms III to V. These contain **wall paintings** removed from the Villa Farnesina (► 97), uncovered in 1879. Probably from a villa originally built for the wedding of Augustus' daughter, Julia, these are the most important Roman paintings of their kind, and embrace several distinct styles, from traditional Greek-influenced landscapes and mythological scenes to Egyptian-style friezes and architectural motifs. You rarely see such paintings, making their delicacy, skill and sublime colouring all the more

The wall paintings from the Villa di Livia are part of the rare collection of frescoes and mosaics

The Palazzo Massimo contains a wealth of fine Roman sculpture, such as this altar to Mars and Venus

surprising and memorable. Much the same can be said of the many **mosaics** exhibited on this floor, whose beauty and detail are in marked contrast to later – and supposedly more sophisticated – medieval mosaics across the city.

TAKING A BREAK

Places to stop for a drink or snack on the Piazza della Repubblica are somewhat uninspiring, but walk a little farther to Via Vittorio Emanuele Orlando 75 and you'll find **Dagnino** (Galleria Esedra, tel: 06 481 8660, daily 7am–10pm), a lovely old-fashioned pastry shop selling Sicilian specialities.

195 F1 Largo i Villa Peretti 1 06 3996 7700; www.archeoroma. beneculturali.it; online booking at www.pierreci.it Tue–Sun 9–7:45 Expensive. Combined pass available (➤ 190) Termini 64 and all other services to Piazza dei Cinquecento, Repubblica

PALAZZO MASSIMO ALLE TERME: INSIDE INFO

Top tips The gallery is not difficult to navigate, but the **gallery guide** (see below) contains a good plan of each floor.
■ The gallery shop has many beautiful gifts and books, so bring money and credit cards in case you're tempted.

In more detail The beauty of the Palazzo Massimo – unlike many galleries of antiquities – is that it's not crammed with endless rows of dull statues: quality rather than quantity has been its guiding principle. There are relatively few works, and each is well labelled and well presented. Should you want to know more, it's worth investing in the excellent guides to the gallery published by Electa-Soprintendenza Archeologico di Roma. Copies in English are generally available from the gallery shop.

❸ Fontana di Trevi

The Fontana di Trevi (Trevi Fountain) is the most beautiful of Italy's many fountains. It is perhaps most famous for its tradition – throw a coin in the waters and you will return to Rome – and for actress Anita Ekberg's nocturnal visit in Federico Fellini's classic film, *La Dolce Vita*.

One of the Fontana di Trevi's main attractions is that you stumble across it almost by accident. There it is as you turn from one of the three streets that lend the fountain its name (*tre vie* means "three streets") into the small piazza, a sight Charles Dickens described as "silvery to the eye and ear".

The fountain's waters were originally provided by the *Acqua Vergine*, or *Aqua Virgo*, an aqueduct begun by Agrippa in 19BC to bring water to the city from the hills outside Rome. It took its name from the legend that it was a young girl *(vergine)* who showed the original spring to a group of Roman soldiers. Today, the fountain disgorges a colossal 80,000cu m (2.8 million cubic feet) of water daily; in its Roman heyday the aqueduct could carry over 100,000cu m (3.5 million cubic feet) an hour.

Romantic and atmospheric, the Fontana di Trevi attracts crowds of admirers in the evening

Water Bounty

The first major fountain to take advantage of this watery bounty was built in 1453 by **Pope Niccolò V**, who financed the project with a tax on wine. This led irate Romans of the time to sneer that the pontiff had "taken our wine to give us water". The present fountain was begun by another pope, **Clement XII**, in 1732 – an inscription above the fountain's main arch records the fact – and inaugurated 30 years later by **Clement XIII**.

The *fontana's* designer – probably **Nicola Salvi** – came up with the novel idea of draping the fountain over the entire wall of the Palazzo Poli, thus adding to its

The triton blowing into the conch represents calm seas

monumental scale and dramatic impact. The fountain's central figure represents **Neptune**, or Oceanus. In front stand two tritons (1759–62) by sculptor Pietro Bracci: the one on the left as you face the fountain represents the stormy sea (symbolized by the agitated horse), while the figure on the right blowing into a conch shell represents the sea in repose.

Few visitors can resist the temptation to **cast a coin into the waters**. The tradition echoes the practice of both the ancient Romans, who often threw coins into certain fountains to appease the gods, and early Christians, who would scatter coins onto the tomb of St Peter and other saints and martyrs.

TAKING A BREAK

For superlative ice cream head to **Il Gelato di San Crispino** (➤ 138). Alternatively, stop for a coffee at **Antico Caffè Greco** (➤ 138) – you'll pay a price to drink here as it is one of Rome's most historic cafés.

➕ 194 C1   ✉ Piazza di Trevi   💲 Free   🚇 Barberini   🚌 52, 53, 61, 62, 63, 71, 80, 95, 116, 119, 175, 492 and 630 to Via del Tritone

---

FONTANA DI TREVI: INSIDE INFO

Top tips Come to admire the fountain **late in the evening**, when the crowds are thinner and the fountain is usually floodlit.
■ Alternatively, your best option may be to get up early and come before the tour groups arrive, though typically, the area is jam-packed from morning until night throughout the year.

In more detail The **figures in the rectangular niches** either side of Neptune are allegorical figures symbolizing "Health" (with a relief above it of the young girl showing soldiers the source of the Acqua Vergine's spring) and "Abundance" (with a relief depicting Agrippa approving the aqueduct's design).

❹Piazza di Spagna

The Piazza di Spagna is one of Rome's great outdoor salons, a beautiful square that dominates the city's most elegant shopping district and whose famous Spanish Steps provide a magnet for visitors at all hours of the day and night.

The **Spanish Steps** are the piazza's most celebrated sight. More properly known as the Scalinata della Trinità dei Monti, they comprise a majestic double staircase that cascades down the slopes of the Pincian Hill from the church of **Trinità dei Monti**. Built between 1723 and 1726, they provide not only one of Rome's most celebrated scenic set pieces – especially in spring, when huge pots of azaleas adorn the steps – but also a forum that has proved a favoured meeting place for Romans and visitors alike for several centuries.

Both the square and the steps take their name from the Palazzo di Spagna, built in the 17th century as the Spanish Embassy to the Holy See. Before that, part of the piazza was known as the Platea Trinitatis, after the Trinità church.

The Fontana della Baraccia with the Spanish Steps and the church of Trinità dei Monti in the background

The English Ghetto

Many foreign visitors made the area their home during the 18th-century heyday of the Grand Tour. The English, in particular, were passionate admirers, so much so that the district became known as the "English ghetto" and boasted a famous café, the Caffè degli Inglesi, a favourite drinking den for expatriates. That particular establishment is no more, but there are two other historic cafés on or near the square: **Babington's Tea Rooms** (to the left of the steps as you face them), founded in the late 19th century by two English spinsters, and the **Antico Caffè Greco** in Via Condotti, founded in 1760 and patronized by the likes of Goethe, Casanova, Shelley, Byron, Baudelaire, Wagner and Liszt.

Another visitor to the area's cafés would probably have been John Keats, who lodged – and died – in a house to the right of the Spanish Steps. Today, the building is given over to a **museum** (➤ 134) devoted to the poet and other literary exiles, including Shelley.

At the foot of the Spanish Steps is the tiny **Fontana della Barcaccia**, literally the "Fountain of the Rotten (or Worthless) Boat". Its name derives from the centrepiece, a half-sunken boat with water spilling lazily from its sides; the fountain's low level and less than spectacular display are the result of the low pressure of the Acqua Vergine aqueduct (➤ 124) which feeds it. The baroque design – possibly based on an earlier Roman model – was probably a joint effort on the part of Pietro Bernini and his more famous son, Gian Lorenzo Bernini. It was commissioned in 1629 by Pope Urban VIII, a member of the Barberini family, whose sun and bee emblems adorn the stonework.

TAKING A BREAK

Both **Babington's** (➤ 138) and the **Antico Caffè Greco** (➤ 138) are pretty but expensive, and only worthwhile if you want to savour their historic ambience. Better choices of cafés and bars can be found close by: try **Ciampini al Café du Jardin** (➤ 138), the pretty **Antica Enoteca** (➤ 138) or GiNa (➤ 137), off the west end of the piazza.

➕ 194 C3 ✉ Piazza di Spagna 🚇 119

PIAZZA DI SPAGNA: INSIDE INFO

Top tips Climb to the top of the Spanish Steps from Piazza di Spagna for **good views**. Watch for pickpockets if the square is crowded.

■ The Trinità church, begun in 1502, has immense scenic appeal, but nothing inside that really merits a visit.

⑤ Museo e Galleria Borghese

The Borghese gallery and museum may be relatively small, but the quality of its paintings and sculptures – notably works by Bernini, Canova, Raphael and Caravaggio – make it one of the jewels of Rome's rich artistic crown.

Wealthy Roman prelates and aristocrats over the centuries often amassed **huge private art collections**, many of which were later sold, broken up or passed to the city or Italian state. The finest of all such collections was accumulated by Cardinal Scipione Borghese (1579–1633), a nephew of Camillo Borghese, later Pope Paul V. Many works were sold to the Louvre in Paris in 1807, mostly under pressure from Napoleon, whose sister, the infamous Paolina, was married to Prince Camillo Borghese. Nevertheless, the surviving exhibits – which were bequeathed to the state in 1902 – make this the finest gallery of its kind in Rome, its appeal enhanced by a lovely setting, the beautifully restored **Casino** (1613–15), or summer house, of the Villa Borghese.

The lavish interior of the Galleria, once the Casino, or summer house, of the Villa Borghese, has been beautifully restored

The Collection

The collection is simply arranged over two floors and around some 20 **gloriously decorated rooms**, the lower floor being devoted mainly to sculpture, the upper floor to paintings. One of the gallery's most famous works greets you in the first room, Antonio Canova's erotic statue of **Paolina Borghese**, in

the guise of **Venus**. This is one of the most sensual sculptures of the Borghese or any other gallery; so sensual, in fact, that Paolina's husband, Camillo Borghese, forbade anyone to see it after its completion – even Canova. Paolina was a willing and knowing model, who when asked how she could possibly have posed naked for the work is said to have replied "the studio was heated". The next room introduces the work of Gian Lorenzo Bernini, the presiding genius – with chief rival Borromini – of the baroque in Rome. The room's principal sculpture is a statue of **David** (1623–24) in the process of hurling his slingshot stone at Goliath, the face of which is said to be a self-portrait of the sculptor. It was commissioned by Scipione – the cardinal became one of Bernini's main patrons – who is said to have held a mirror for Bernini while he worked on the self-portrait.

Room III contains what many consider Bernini's masterpiece, *Apollo and Daphne* (1622–25), which portrays the flight of Daphne from Apollo, capturing the moment Daphne turns herself into a laurel tree to escape the god. An

Bernini's statue of David, one of the gallery's principal works

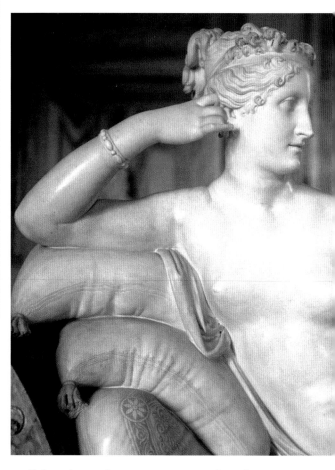

equally bewitching work awaits you in Room IV, *Pluto and Proserpina* (1622), renowned for the detail of Pluto's hand grasping Proserphine's thigh – rarely has the softness of flesh been so convincingly portrayed in stone. The following room contains a statue of a hermaphrodite, a Roman copy of a Greek original – you may already have seen a similar work in the Palazzo Massimo alle Terme (▶ 120–123). Room VI has more works by Bernini: *Aeneas and Anchises* (1613), probably carved by Bernini in collaboration with his father when he was just 15, and the much later allegorical work *Truth* (1652), which remains unfinished.

In Room VIII you find another Roman original, a celebrated second-century statue, a ***Dancing Satyr***. The room is better known, however, for **several major works by Caravaggio**, many of which were snapped up by Scipione when they were turned down by others as too shocking. Caravaggio is said to have painted self-portraits in at least two of the pictures – as

Antonio Canova's erotic reclining statue of Paolina Borghese scandalized her husband

the *Sick Bacchus* (*c*.1593) and as Goliath in *David with the Head of Goliath* (1609–10). His best works here, though, are the **Madonna dei Palafrenieri** (1605–06) and the **Boy with a Basket of Fruit** (1593–95), both notable for their realism. The former picture shows the Virgin crushing a serpent, a symbol of evil and heresy, an allusion to the confrontation at the time between the Catholic and Protestant churches.

Exceptional Art

There are many other paintings on the gallery's upper floor. Among the finest is **Raphael's Deposition** (1507). Other paintings include works by Perugino, Andrea del Sarto, Correggio – the outstanding *Danaë* (1530–31) – Lorenzo Lotto, Bronzino, and Giovanni Bellini. One of the best pictures is **Antonello da Messina's Portrait of a Man** (*c*.1475), the prototype of this genre of portrait painting.

🚩 195 D4 ✉ Piazzale del Museo Borghese 5 ☎ 06 3996 7800; 06 32810; www.galleriaborghese.it 🕐 Tue–Sun 8:30–7:30 💶 Expensive 🍴 Gallery café 🚇 Spagna or Flaminio 🚌 52, 53 and 910 to Via Pinciana or 116 to Viale del Museo Borghese

MUSEO E GALLERIA BORGHESE: INSIDE INFO

Top tip Numbers of visitors to the Galleria Borghese are limited, so it's obligatory to reserve your entry ticket. Call 06 3996 7800, 06 32810 or visit www.ticketeria.it to make reservations. The reservation service is open Monday to Friday 9–7, Saturday 9–1. Call well in advance, especially in high season (Easter–Sep).

In more detail One of the Galleria Borghese's most mysterious and out-standing paintings is Titian's beautiful and little-understood *Sacred and Profane Love* (1514). Some claim its subject is actually Venus and Medea or Heavenly and Earthly Love; most critics, though, think it is an allegory of spring, and was inspired by the same strange dream romance, *Hypnerotomachia di Polifilo*, which provided Bernini with the idea for his eccentric elephant statue outside Santa Maria sopra Minerva (► 94).

At Your Leisure

⑥ Santa Prassede

This tiny church, in a side street immediately south of Santa Maria Maggiore, is celebrated for its mosaics, in particular those of the Cappella di San Zeno, situated on the left near the church's entrance. The gold-encrusted chapel was commissioned in 822 by Pope Paschal I as his mother's mausoleum. The square halo of Theodora, Paschal's mother, in the mosaic left of the altar, indicates that she was still alive when the work was commissioned. Other mosaics on the church's triumphal arch portray Christ flanked by angels in a heavenly Jerusalem, while those in the apse depict saints Prassede and Pudenziana. Prassede is said to have witnessed the martyrdom of 24 Christians who were then hurled into a well (marked by a marble slab on the church's floor): the saint then miraculously soaked up their blood with a single sponge.

➕ 201 D4   ✉ Via Santa Prassede 9a
☎ 06 488 2456   🕐 Mon–Sat 7:30–12, 4–6:30
(but hours may vary), Sun 8–12, 4–6   💵 Free
🚇 Termini   🚌 5, 14, 16, 70, 71, 75 and other
services to Piazza dell'Esquilino

⑦ Museo Nazionale delle Paste Alimentari

If you love pasta, then you'll enjoy this modest but well-organized museum, which is due to re-open after restoration at the end of 2011. Close to the Fontana di Trevi it is one of Rome's more unusual (but over-priced) museums, thanks to its unique theme – pasta. The displays in its 11 rooms cover every aspect of the delicious food, from its history, cooking techniques and place in art to a collection of pasta-making equipment, models, dietary tips and photographs of famous people

Pope Paschal I commissioned mosaics to cover the shrine in the Cappella di San Zeno and the church of Santa Prassede

enjoying Italy's
national dish.

Visitors are
given an audio guide
with an informative
multilingual commentary
to guide them around the
various exhibits.

🔠 194 C1 ✉ Piazza Scanderberg 117
☎ 06 699 1120; www.museodellapasta.
it ⏰ Daily 9:30–5:30. Check website for
re-opening 🎫 Expensive 🚇 Barberini
🚌 52, 53, 56, 60, 61, 62, 71, 80, 81, 95, 116
and 119 to Via del Tritone or Via del Corso

🅘 Palazzo Barberini

The Palazzo Barberini was begun
in 1625 for Cardinal Francesco
Barberini, a member of one of
Rome's leading patrician families. A
magnificent baroque building in its
own right, it is also a major museum,
housing the lion's share of the
collection of the Galleria Nazionale
d'Arte Antica (the rest resides across
the Tiber in the Palazzo Corsini).

Recent restorations have seriously
given back the Palazzo's wow factor,
seen at its best in the palace's superb
centrepiece, the Gran Salone, a vast
and fantastically decorated room
dominated by Pietro da Cortona's
allegorical ceiling frescoes depicting
The Triumph of Divine Providence
(1633–39).

Other paintings are displayed
chronologically in a series of
beautiful rooms, and include major
works by Caravaggio, El Greco,
Tintoretto, Titian and many more.

The most famous picture is *La
Fornarina*, attributed to Raphael,
a work considered to portray the
artist's mistress, the daughter of a
baker (*fornaio* in Italian). Gossips
of the time suggested that Raphael's
premature death (in 1520) was
brought on by his lover's voracious
sexual appetite.

🔠 195 D2 ✉ Via Quattro Fontane 13
☎ 06 32810; www.galleriaborghese.it/
barberini ⏰ Tue–Sun 8:30–7:30 🎫 Moderate
🚇 Barberini 🚌 52, 63, 116, 119, 175 and 630

FOR KIDS

Most children will enjoy the **Time
Elevator** (Via dei Santi Apostoli 20,
06 6992 1823, www.time-elevator.
it, daily 10:30–7:30, expensive) an
hour-long, 3-screen show that uses
state-of-the-art sound and graphics
to re-create Rome's history and its
most famous monuments. You could
also take in the **Museo Nazionale
delle Paste** (▶ 132), or head for
the **Villa Borghese** (▶ 128), which
has swings, paddleboats, pony rides
and a toy train near the Viale delle
Belle Arti entrance. North of Piazza
del Popolo is **Explora** (Via Flaminia
82, 06 361 3776, www.mdbr.it,
Tue–Sun 10–6:30, expensive), a
hands-on science museum aimed at
the under-12s, while farther out, near
the Villa Torlonia, is **Rome's Technotown**
(Via Lazzaro Spallanzi 1A, 060608,
www.technotown.it, Tue–Sun 9–7,
expensive). Seven rooms concentrate
on modern technology for the 11–15
age group, with interactive exhibits,
time machines, 3D adventures and the
chance to compose electronic music.

9 Museo Keats-Shelley

Literary pilgrims will enjoy this lovely old house to the right of the Spanish Steps, where the 25-year-old English poet John Keats died in 1821 having come to Rome to seek a cure for consumption.

Since 1909, the house has been lovingly restored and preserved as a small literary museum and working library for scholars of Keats and his fellow English poet, Percy Bysshe Shelley, who also died in Italy, drowned off the Tuscan coast.

The fusty rooms are filled with old books, pamphlets and manuscripts, as well as literary mementos such as Keats' death mask, a lock of the poet's hair, part of Shelley's cheekbone, and a reliquary containing strands of John Milton's and Elizabeth Barrett Browning's hair.

🚩 194 C2 ✉ Piazza di Spagna 26 ☎ 06 678 4235; www.keats-shelley-house.org ⏰ Mon–Fri 10–1, 2–6; Sat 11–2, 3–6 💶 Inexpensive 🚇 Spagna 🚌 117 and 119 to Piazza di Spagna

10 MACRO

Contemporary art fans should head for Rome's newest space, the Museo d'Arte Contemporaneo di Roma (MACRO), housed in a wonderfully imaginative conversion of an old brewery. This huge 10,000sq m (107,639sq ft) extension, designed by superstar architect Odile Decq, finally

The elaborate columns and railings of the boundary of the Palazzo Barberini

gives Rome a space that attracts big international names in the modern art world, as well as providing room for large-scale multimedia installations and young artists. It works with MACRO Future, another stunning space in an old slaughterhouse, the Mattatoio, in Testaccio, Rome's most vibrant late-night area.

🚩 195 F4 ✉ Via Nizza 131 (corner of Via Cagliari) ☎ 06 6710 70400; www.macro.roma. museum ⏰ Tue–Sun 11–11 💶 Expensive 🚌 90

MACRO Future

🚩 199 D1 ✉ Piazza Orazio Giustiniani 4 ☎ 06 6710 70400; www.macro.roma.museum ⏰ Tue–Sun 4pm–midnight 💶 Moderate 🚇 Laurentina 🚌 719

11 Museo Carlo Bilotti

The billionaire Carlo Bilotti, an Italian-American perfume tycoon, converted this 17th-century *aranceria* (orangery), built for the Borghese, in 2006 as a showcase for his superlative collection of modern art. His passion was de Chirico, and 22 works by this artist and other late 20th-century luminaries are displayed in the permanent collection, along with a Larry Rivers portrait of Mr Bilotti and a 1981 Warhol of his wife and daughter. The ground floor holds changing exhibitions featuring the work of all the big names on the contemporary scene.

⊞ 194 C4 ⊠ Viale Fiorello La Guardia ☎ 060608; www.museocarlobilotti.it ⏰ Tue–Sun 9–7 💰 Moderate 🚌 52, 53, 95, 910

⑫ Museo Nazionale Etrusco di Villa Giulia

The Villa Giulia, tucked away in the northern reaches of the Villa Borghese, is worth the journey if you have a passion for the Etruscans, for a large part of the huge building is given over to the art and artefacts of that mysterious civilization. The collection is the greatest of its type in the world, but for too long has been neglected and left to gather dust. Many of the rooms contain unexciting rows of urns and other funerary sculpture. Rather more inspiring are

Villa Giulia contains an important collection of Etruscan art and artefacts

the museum's many exquisite pieces of gold and other jewellery, some of the larger sculptures, and the reconstructed Etruscan temple in the villa's extensive gardens.

⊞ 194 B5 ⊠ Piazzale di Villa Giulia 9 ☎ 06 322 6571; reservations 06 824 620 or www.ticketeria.com ⏰ Tue–Sun 8:30–7:30 💰 Moderate 🚇 Flaminio 🚌 3, 19, 231, 926

[Map showing Museo Nazionale Etrusco di Villa Giulia, Galleria Nazionale d'Arte Moderna, Bioparco, Museo Carlo Bilotti, Museo e Galleria Borghese, Villa Borghese, SALARIO, MACRO and surrounding streets]

OFF THE BEATEN TRACK

Much of the area surrounding Stazione Termini is given over to government ministries or the buildings of the main city university, and holds little visitor appeal. **San Lorenzo**, a traditional residential and student district with a sprinkling of inexpensive restaurants and pizzerias, east of Termini, is an exception (though probably not worth a separate trip unless you are on an extended visit). More worthwhile is the trip along Via Nomentana to the northeast to visit the **catacombs and churches of Santa Costanza** and **Sant'Agnese fuori le Mura**.

Around Piazza di Spagna, you can escape the crowds on **Via Margutta**, a pretty street filled with commercial art galleries, or in the web of **old streets between Piazza del Parlamento and the ruins of the Mausoleo di Augusto**, the circular mausoleum of the Emperor Augustus.

Where to...
Eat and Drink

Prices

Expect to pay per person for a meal, excluding drinks and service:

€ under €30 €€ €30–€50 €€€ over €50

Neither of the two main areas in and around Termini and Piazza di Spagna are known for their restaurants: Termini is too downbeat, Piazza di Spagna too full of shops and sights. Yet both areas have good places to eat in all price brackets, and offer an excellent selection of bars for coffee and snacks, including some of Rome's most historic cafés. Both areas also have small establishments from another age – the discreet Fiaschetteria Beltramme (▶ 137), for example – and more modern establishments such as Palatium (▶ 137), whose sleek minimalism wouldn't be out of place in London, Sydney or New York.

Agata e Romeo €€€

The environs of Termini railway station are an unlikely location for this excellent restaurant. The cooking is modern Roman mixed with pan-Italian and international dishes, and gives the lie to the notion that creative cuisine, especially in Italy, is invariably pretentious or unsuccessful. Thus you might eat a traditional dish such as baccalà (salt cod), but salt cod that has been smoked and cooked with an orange sauce;

or be tempted by a flan of pecorino (sheep's cheese) with honey. The setting is simple but comfortable – brick arches and plain walls with the occasional painting. The wine list contains an interesting selection of regional Italian and other wines. Reservations are essential.

➕ 201 E4 ☒ Via Carlo Alberto 45
☎ 06 446 6115; www.agataromeo.it
⏰ Mon–Fri 12:30–2:30, 7:30–10. Closed 2 weeks in Aug and 1–2 weeks in Jan

Al Presidente €€€

You are guaranteed a memorable – albeit expensive – evening at Al Presidente. With its cool, elegant design, this restaurant near the Quirinale and the Fontana di Trevi is a good bet for a leisurely meal, which you can eat outside in warm weather. The cooking is Italian but distinctly modern, so expect a twist on traditional favourites, which include soups, pasta and risottos, and some wonderful fish dishes – the coda di rospe (monkfish) served with lentils is recommended.

➕ 194 C2 ☒ Piazza Mignanelli 18
☎ 06 678 2621 ⏰ Mon–Sat 12–3, 7:30–10:30

The wine list has more than 500 varieties, including wines by the glass. In the evenings you can try one of the taster menus to sample the full range of the kitchen's capabilities.

➕ 194 C2 ☒ Via in Arcione 94–95 ☎ 06 679 7342 ⏰ Tue–Sun 1–3:30, 8–11:30. Closed 3 weeks in Jan and 3 weeks in Aug

Alla Rampa €–€€

It may be packed with tourists but this cheery restaurant, with its lovely outside terrace, is a great place for an excellent-value meal. Take advantage of the delicious spread of antipasti on the buffet before moving on to a simple pasta or grill. Credit cards are not accepted.

➕ 194 C2 ☒ Piazza Mignanelli 18
☎ 06 678 2621 ⏰ Mon–Sat 12 –3, 7:30–10:30

Antica Birreria Peroni €–€€

This wonderful old beer hall, wood-panelled and frescoed, has been serving Peroni on draught since

1906. They pride themselves on the beer and the straightforward, hearty cooking, which specializes in well-sourced grilled meat and *Würstel* (frankfurters). It's ideal for both a quick lunch or a good-value dinner, served with true Roman spirit.

🚼 194 C1 ⊠ Via San Marcello 19 ☎ 06 679 5310 🕙 Mon–Sat 12–12. Closed Aug

Cantina Cantarini €€

The tiny tables may be cramped, but the food makes up for it at this well-priced trattoria. Menus are meat-based for the first half of the week, then feature fish and shellfish from Thursday to Saturday; the locals ensure a great atmosphere. There are tables outside in summer.

🚼 195 E3 ⊠ Piazza Sallustio 12 ☎ 06 485 528 🕙 Mon–Sat 12:30–2:15, 7:30–10:15. Closed 3 weeks in Aug, 2 weeks in Dec–Jan

Fiaschetteria Beltramme €–€€

You could easily miss this historic but humble-looking trattoria,

which is incongruously located on one of the smart streets near Via Condotti. That may be the idea, for this is a deliberately understated place frequented by locals, artists, shopkeepers, society ladies and – on one famous occasion – by the pop legend Madonna. The interior is little more than a long single room whose walls are topped with wicker-covered wine bottles and almost completely covered in paintings left, bought or donated by locals over the years. Food is simple, well cooked and thoroughly Roman. Everything is recommended. You can't reserve a table here, so just turn up and hope that you'll be lucky. Credit cards are not accepted.

🚼 194 B3 ⊠ Via della Croce 39 🕾 No phone 🕙 Mon–Sat 12–3, 7:30–10:30

GiNa €

The cool, clean lines as much as the food and ambience draw all-day grazers to this relaxed and good-value bar-cum-café-restaurant off

the west end of Piazza di Spagna. People drop in for everything from a late breakfast through lunch to a light dinner, or just to enjoy a well-made aperitif. The menu is eclectic, with Italian staples on offer beside home-made soups, imaginative salads and delicious ice-cream sundaes. They also prepare picnic hampers, complete with glasses and cutlery; order ahead for a romantic outing to the Borghese gardens.

🚼 194 B3 ⊠ Via San Sebastianello 7A ☎ 06 678 0251; www.ginaroma.com 🕙 Daily 11–8. Closed 2 weeks in Aug

Il Margutta €–€€

Il Margutta has been in business for many years, which is no small achievement given that it is a vegetarian restaurant, something that until recently was barely known in Italy. The stylish dining area is airy and filled with modern art, a nod to the restaurant's position on Via Margutta, home to many of the city's leading

commercial art galleries. The food is always imaginative, never worthy and dull, and the wines, beers and ciders served are all organically produced. At lunch there's a good set-price all-you-can-eat buffet menu. You can also drop by most of the day for a tea or snack in the bar area.

🚼 194 B3 ⊠ Via Margutta 118 ☎ 06 3265 0577; www.ilmargutta.it 🕙 Daily 12:30– 3:30, 7:30–11

Palatium €–€€

The decor of this wine bar and eatery reflects its position right on one of Rome's trendiest streets, but the selection of wines from the Lazio region is long while the menu too, features dishes typical of Rome's surroundings. Choose from anything from a plate of cheese and a glass of wine to several courses with a fine vintage, and sit back for some serious people-watching.

🚼 194 B2 ⊠ Via Frattina 94 ☎ 06 692 02132 🕙 Mon–Sat 11–11

Piccolo Abruzzo €€

This restaurant, tucked away from the tourist crowds east of Via Veneto, specializes in dishes from the mountainous Abruzzo region. The menu often goes unregarded, so just expect a string of delicious, straightforward regional and seasonal plates of food to arrive on your table throughout the evening.

🚇 195 E3 ☒ Via Sicilia 237 ☎ 06 428 0176 🕐 Daily 12–4, 7–1:30

BARS AND CAFÉS

Antica Enoteca €

This wine bar opened in 1842 and has been restored in order to retain its pretty old-world appearance. You can order wine by the glass or bottle – or buy fine wines to take away – and choose nibbles from a cold buffet or eat in the restaurant to the rear.

🚇 194 B3 ☒ Via della Croce 76b ☎ 06 679 0896 🕐 Wine bar: daily 11:30am–midnight. Restaurant: daily 12:30–3, 7–10:30

Antico Caffè Greco €

The long-established Caffè Greco is Rome's most famous café, and since it was founded in 1740 has played host to the likes of Casanova, Wagner, Lord Byron, Shelley, Stendhal and Baudelaire. Though it has had its ups and downs in recent years (and may no longer be the city's best café), it is still worth the price of a cappuccino to enjoy the venerable interior and savour its historic atmosphere. Locals stand; tourists tend to crowd the sofas. Expect to pay slightly over the odds.

🚇 194 B2 ☒ Via Condotti 86 ☎ 06 679 1700 🕐 Tue–Sat 9–7:30, Sun–Mon 10:30–7:30

Babington's €–€€

Babington's was founded by two British women at the end of the 19th century and has affected the look and feel of a British tea room ever since. You can sip fine teas (reputedly the best in the city) and nibble dainty cakes here, but the high prices for such simple offerings reflect its smart Piazza di Spagna location.

🚇 194 C3 ☒ Piazza di Spagna 23 ☎ 06 678 6027 🕐 Daily 9–8:15

Ciampini al Café du Jardin €

You will escape the crowds in Piazza di Spagna at this lovely café near the Villa Medici, but you won't escape the area's relatively high prices. However, it's worth paying a little extra for the setting – a calm outdoor area with pond and creeper-covered walls – and the superlative views. The café serves sandwiches, light pasta meals, snack lunches, breakfast, ice cream and cocktails.

🚇 194 C3 ☒ Piazza Trinità dei Monti ☎ 06 678 5678 🕐 Thu–Tue 8am–1am (closes earlier in spring and autumn). Closed Nov–Mar

Dolci e Doni €

The perfect place to take a cake break just a few steps from Piazza di Spagna is in this chic pastry shop and tea room. Alternatively, indulge in a late breakfast, brunch or light lunch.

🚇 194 B2 ☒ Via delle Carrozze 85b ☎ 06 6992 5001 🕐 Daily 11–9 or 10. Closed 2 weeks in Aug

Il Gelato di San Crispino €

Walk just a few paces from the Fontana di Trevi and you arrive at this temple to the gelato. Most Romans consider it sells the city's best ice cream and sorbets: some say they are the best in Italy, which is close to saying the best in the world. There are no cones here, just cups: San Crispino's perfectionist owners, brothers Giuseppe and Pasquale Alongi, claim that cones, with their artificial additives, interfere with the purity and flavour of their fresh fruit and myriad other iced delights. Flavours change with what is seasonally available.

🚇 194 C2 ☒ Via della Panetteria 42 ☎ 06 679 3924 🕐 Wed–Mon 12–12 or later. Closed mid-Jan to mid-Feb

Where to... Shop

The streets at the foot of the Spanish Steps are the epicentre of Roman chic and the only area for shoppers in search of designer labels and luxury goods. Although **Via Condotti** is the best-known street, the parallel streets of Via Frattina and Via Borgognona are almost equally full of designer names. Smaller side streets in the vicinity increasingly have smart boutiques selling shoes, lingerie, leather goods and accessories. Some streets specialize in particular items: Via della Croce, for example, has a scattering of good food shops, while Via Margutta is home to commercial galleries and antiques shops. Via del Corso and Via del Tritone are lined with mid-market clothes, shoes and accessory shops, providing a good

alternative to the designer stores.

The area around Piazza Vittorio Emanuele south of Termini is a different world. It is home to many of Rome's most recent immigrants, and as a result is full of specialist food and other stores selling Chinese, Korean, Somalian and other Asian and African goods. The piazza is also the site of central Rome's main food and general market (Mon–Sat 6–2). Both the square and the surrounding streets are filled with colourful stalls selling fruit, vegetables, cheap shoes, clothing and household goods.

DESIGNER STORES

The outlets of principal Italian and international designers are listed below by street. Note, however,

that new outlets open regularly in these streets, and stores often change their locations. Opening hours for the designer stores are generally Tuesday to Saturday 10–7:30 or 8; some may close Monday morning.

Walk along Via Condotti to find designer shops, including **Dolce e Gabbana**, **Giorgio Armani**, **Gucci**, **La Perla**, **Max Mara**, **Prada**, **Salvatore Ferragamo**, **Trussardi** and **Valentino**.

Designer shops on Via Borgognona include names such as **Ermenegildo Zegna**, **Fratelli Rossetti** and **Roberto Cavalli**.

Other designer shops in and around Via Condotti and Piazza di Spagna include **Missoni** (Piazza di Spagna 78, tel: 06 679 2555); **Krizia** (Piazza di Spagna 87, tel: 06 679 3772); **Valentino Donna** (women; Via del Babuino 61, tel: 06 3600 1906); **Emporio Armani** (Via del Babuino 140, tel: 06 3600 2197); and **Armani Jeans** (Via del Babuino 70a, tel: 06 3600 1848).

ANTIQUES

Antichità

Serious antiques hunters wanting to furnish their homes with traditional Italian style and prepared to pay for quality goods will have a field day in Via del Babuino and Via Margutta northwest of Piazza di Spagna. Antichità is one of several tempting shops on these streets, specializing in old fabrics and furnishings.

Via del Babuino 83 06 320 7585
Tue–Sat 9–1, 3:30–7:30

Bottega del Marmorato

Here you'll find all manner of grand ornaments in marble, including copies of ancient busts and other antiquities.

Via Margutta 53b 06 320 7660
Mon–Sat 9–1, 3:30–7:30

BOOKS

The Lion Bookshop

A great range of English-language books is stocked here, and there is

a pleasant reading room where you can read a book over a coffee.
🖂 Via dei Greci 36 ☎ 06 3265 4007
🕙 Tue–Sun 10–7:30, Mon 3:30–7:30. Mid-Jun to mid-Sep closed Sun

CHILDREN'S CLOTHES

La Cicogna

This chain of shops sells an excellent range of sweet and practical clothes for babies and toddlers. There are several outlets in Rome.
🖂 Via Frattina 138 ☎ 06 679 1921
🕙 Mon–Sat 10:30–7:30, Sun 11–7

COSMETICS

Materozzoli

If you want to purchase quality beauty products, then you will enjoy shopping in Materozzoli. This refined shop dates from 1870 and sells a variety of top-of-the-range toiletries, perfumes, cosmetics and bathroom items.
🖂 Piazza San Lorenzo in Lucina 5

☎ 06 6889 2686 🕙 Tue–Sat 10–1:30, 3–7:30, Mon 3:30–7:30

DEPARTMENT STORES

Energie

This is not a department store in the accepted sense, but if you're looking for unique style, then this large shop has a selection of distinctive clothes, denim, shoes, bags and other accessories. The emphasis is on innovation rather than following the latest trends.
🖂 Via del Corso 179 ☎ 06 678 1045
🕙 Mon–Sat 9:30–8, Sun 10:30–8

La Rinascente

This is the only traditional department store in central Rome that is worth a mention – but it's an excellent one. It is a great place to spend a couple of hours and sells high-quality clothes, accessories, lingerie and household items.
🖂 Galleria Alberto Sordi 53, Piazza Colonna
☎ 06 784 209 🕙 Mon–Sat 9am–9:30pm, Sun 10–9

TAD

There are plenty of goodies under one roof at trendy TAD, where you can buy clothes, shoes, perfumes and cosmetics, browse the CDs and magazines, have your hair done or grab something to eat or drink. Expensive labels and expensive people make for a truly high-end Roman shopping experience.
🖂 Via del Babuino 155A ☎ 06 3269 5131 🕙 Tue–Fri 10:30–7:30. Sat, Mon 12–7:30

FOOD AND WINE

Buccone

This is one of the biggest and best places in Rome to buy good quality wine – thousands of bottles line the shelves – and a range of other alcoholic drinks such as *grappa* and *amaro*. Wine is available by the glass, and a small but excellent selection of snacks and fine foods.
🖂 Via di Ripetta 19 ☎ 06 361 2154
🕙 Mon–Thu 12:30–2:30, 9–10:30, Fri–Sat 8–midnight

Pasta all'Uova

Via della Croce does not have as many delicatessens as it once did, but there are still a few like this little place that sells a variety of fresh and dried pasta. The pastas in unusual colours and designs make inexpensive gifts.
🖂 Via della Croce 8 ☎ 06 679 3102
🕙 Mon–Wed, Fri–Sat 7:30–7:30, Thu 8–3:30 (8–7:30 in summer)

Salumeria Focacci

Like Pasta all'Uova, this is one of Rome's landmark food stores. You will find a truly excellent selection of cheeses, meats and other gastronomic treats and the service is attentive and helpful. It's the perfect place to buy picnic provisions.
🖂 Via della Croce 43 ☎ 06 679 1228
🕙 Mon–Sat 8–8

HATS AND GLOVES

Borsalino

Hats, hats and more hats: this is the only place in Rome you need to visit if you are looking for something to wear up top.

⊠ Via di Campo Marzio 72A ☎ 06 678 3945
🕑 Mon–Sat 10–7:30, Sun 10:30–7:30

Sermoneta

Giorgio Sermoneta's intimate shop has been selling just about every size, colour and style of Italian glove for over 35 years.

⊠ Piazza di Spagna 61 ☎ 06 679 1960
🕑 Mon–Sat 9:30–7:30, Sun 10:30–7

JEWELLERY AND WATCHES

Bulgari

Whether or not you are going to buy anything – and you'll need a huge credit card limit – it is worth browsing in Bulgari, easily Rome's most exclusive jewellers.

⊠ Via Condotti 10 ☎ 06 696 261
🕑 Mon–Sat 10:30–7:30, Sun 11–7

Swatch Store

This store is about as far removed as is possible from Bulgari, and sells a wide range of the familiar Swatch

brand watches and straps in a variety of colours and designs.

⊠ Via Condotti 33a ☎ 06 679 1253
🕑 Daily 10–7:30

LINENS

Frette

Hotels or Italian households who have any pretensions to style would not use anything but Frette bed or table linens. Goods are expensive, but you can expect outstanding quality and excellent service too.

⊠ Piazza di Spagna 11 ☎ 06 679 0673
🕑 Mon–Sat 10–7:30

LINGERIE

Demoiselle

If you adore gorgeous lingerie, the truly exquisite and sensual whisps of silk and lace nightwear and lingerie will send you diving for the plastic in this pretty store, which also sells swimsuits and beachwear by luxury designers such as Missoni and Pucci.

⊠ Via Frattina 93 ☎ 06 679 3752
🕑 Mon–Sat 10–8

Rossati

The window displays may be a little dated, but step inside this traditional lingerie shop to find the best of Italian products. They stock everything from soft silk and wool vests, pyjamas and nightgowns, to gossamer fine silk peignoirs trimmed with lace. Shops such as this are an essential destination for Italian women, and this is reflected in the service and quality goods.

⊠ Piazza di Spagna 52 ☎ 06 679 0016
🕑 Mon 3–8, Tue–Sun 10–8

SHOES AND BAGS

Fausto Santini

For something a little different, visit the city's foremost shoe designer. Some of the designs may seem far-fetched, but none can be called boring, and the quality is excellent.

⊠ Via Frattina 120 ☎ 06 678 4114
🕑 Mon–Sat 10–7:30, Sun 12–7:30

Tod's

For years, no one took much notice of Tod's in Italy. But since they became coveted by the rest of the world – and customers in the US in particular – the locals are as keen as everyone else to purchase the distinctive footwear.

⊠ Via Fontanella Borghese 56a ☎ 06 6821 0066; www.tods.com 🕑 Daily 10–7:30

STATIONERY

Pineider

The pens and stationery here are the finest and most exclusive in the city.

⊠ Via dei Due Macelli 68 ☎ 06 678 9013
🕑 Mon–Sat 10–7, Sun 10–2, 3–7

Vertecchi

This pretty shop crammed with pens, paints, stationery and all manner of items covered in marbled paper is a good place for gifts to take home.

⊠ Via della Croce 70 ☎ 06 332 282
🕑 Mon–Sat 9:30–7:30

Where to...
Be Entertained

CLASSICAL MUSIC

The opera season in Rome runs from November to May at the 19th-century auditorium, the **Teatro dell'Opera**, which lies just a few steps from Piazza dei Cinquecento at Via Firenze 72-Piazza Beniamo Gigli 8 (tel: 06 481 601, 06 481 7003, www.operaroma.it). The reputation of Rome's opera house is not exceptional, however, it is often easier to obtain tickets here than in Milan or elsewhere. The box office is generally open Tuesday to Saturday 9–5, Sunday 9–1:30 on days when there is no performance or 10:45am to hall an hour before the start of any performance. Free phone in Italy for information (tel: 800 016 665) between 10am and 1:30pm. Making a booking by

phone is almost impossible, so visit the box office in person or book online. Contact the visitor centre or the opera house for information on summer outdoor performances.

North from here is Rome's best performing arts centre, the **Auditorium-Parco della Musica** (Viale Pietro de Coubertin 15, 060608, 892982, 06 370 0106, www.auditorium.com). This is a superb complex of concert and exhibition spaces, designed by Renzo Piano (2006) and now offers a programme of extraordinary scope that includes everything from symphony to jazz. The box office is open Monday to Friday. Browse the website and book ahead online; alternatively, just go for a look at this exciting venue – worth it for the architecture alone.

NIGHTLIFE

If you are looking for places to drink in the evening, close to Santa Maria Maggiore lie two of Rome's oldest and best Irish pubs: the **Druid's Den** (Via San Martino ai Monti 28, tel: 06 4890 4781, daily 5pm–2am), and the **Fiddler's Elbow** (Via dell'Olmata 43, tel: 06 487 2110, daily 5pm–1:30am or later). They lie about a minute or so apart if you want to compare and contrast. If the thought of an Irish establishment doesn't appeal, try the more Italian **Monti DOC** (Via Giovanni Lanza 93, tel: 06 487 2696, Tue–Sun 7pm–1am, also Mon–Fri 1pm–3:30pm), just to the south of Santa Prassede and Santa Maria Maggiore. This easy-going wine bar has a good selection of wines and a range of snacks.

In a similar vein is **Trimani** wine bar (Via Cernaia 37b, tel: 06 446 9630, Mon–Sat 11:30–3, 6–12:30am), close to Piazza della Repubblica.

At the other end of the city, near Piazza del Popolo, you can drink and nibble snacks at **Lowenhaus** (Via della Fontanella 16d, tel: 06 323 0410, Fri–Mon 11am–2am, Tue–Thu 4pm–2am). If pubs or pub-like bars are not for you, don't forget the various alternatives offered by wine bars in the area covered by this chapter, notably the Antica Enoteca (▶ 138) or Ciampini (▶ 138).

If you want to dance or listen to live music you've something of a problem. The only club is the busy **Gregory's** (Via Gregoriana 54a, tel: 06 679 6386, Tue–Sun 7pm–2am), a live jazz venue with drinks and snack food near Piazza di Spagna. As for dancing, one of the main venues locally is **Piper**, one of the longest-running clubs in Rome – frequent revamps have allowed it to ride out changes of fashion. It lies some way from the centre to the northwest of Termini at Via Tagliamento 9 (tel: 06 855 5398, Thu–Sat 11pm–4am).

Vatican City

Getting Your Bearings

The Vatican is the world's smallest independent state – yet it contains two of the highlights of any visit to Rome: the immense Basilica di San Pietro (St Peter's), and the Musei Vaticani (Vatican Museums), home to one of the world's richest and largest collections of paintings, sculptures and other works of art accumulated by the papacy over the centuries.

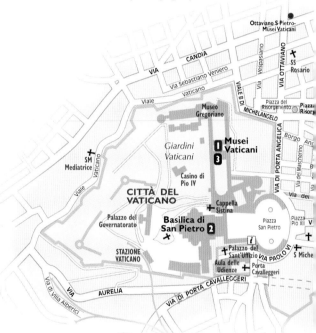

The Vatican has a long history. Once, the hilly area of Rome west of the Tiber was a place of execution, and later the site of imperial gardens and a circus, or race track, built for the emperors Caligula and Nero in the first century AD. In the fourth century, part of the area became the site for a huge basilica – the first St Peter's – built over or close to the tomb of St Peter, who was crucified in the area sometime between AD64 and 67.

By the 10th century, attacks by Lombards and Saracens had led to the building of a defensive wall around part of the district, and later to the use of the Castel Sant'Angelo – previously the mausoleum of Emperor Hadrian – as a papal fortress. After the sack of Rome in 1527, the area lost its strategic importance, and the popes moved their residential palace and offices to the safety of Lateran (San Giovanni in Laterano) and then the Quirinale, which now house government buildings.

By the 19th century, the papacy had controlled vast areas of central Italy, including Rome, for more than 1,000 years. Much of its domain, known as the

★ Don't Miss

At Your Leisure

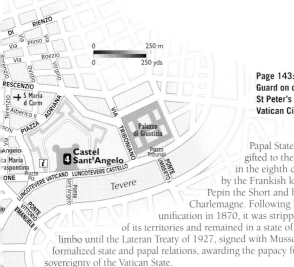

Page 143: Swiss Guard on duty in St Peter's Square, Vatican City

Papal States, was gifted to the popes in the eighth century by the Frankish king Pepin the Short and his son Charlemagne. Following Italian unification in 1870, it was stripped of its territories and remained in a state of limbo until the Lateran Treaty of 1927, signed with Mussolini, formalized state and papal relations, awarding the papacy full sovereignty of the Vatican State.

Today, the area has its own shops, banks, newspaper, helicopter pad and radio station. Most is out of bounds to the general public, with the important exceptions of San Pietro, the Musei Vaticani and – if you reserve a visit in advance – parts of the Vatican Gardens. No documents are needed to enter these areas, and no barriers exist between them and the city at large.

It should take just a couple of hours to see St Peter's, though you may be tempted to linger in the dome, which offers the best views in Rome. Just before (or after) seeing Basilica di San Pietro you might spend an hour in the Castel Sant'Angelo – these days outside the Vatican – a fascinating Roman building overlaid with later fortifications and papal apartments.

Though you could see the highlights of the Musei Vaticani – notably the Cappella Sistina and Raphael Rooms – in half a day, if the museums appeal, or you have particular interests, you could just as easily spend several days in the complex, whose 12 museums contain Egyptian, Etruscan, Greek, Roman, medieval and Renaissance treasures. There are also countless beautifully decorated salons and corridors, plus a Pinacoteca, or art gallery, crammed with masterpieces by Raphael, Leonardo da Vinci and others.

In a Day

If you're not quite sure where to begin your travels, this itinerary recommends a practical and enjoyable day exploring Vatican City, taking in some of the best places to see using the Getting Your Bearings map on the previous page. For more information see the main entries.

9:00am

The Musei Vaticani are always crowded, so get there early. Check the screens at the entrance to see what's open, then spend a few minutes planning your visit. You could follow one of the official itineraries, or start with the **1 Museo Pio-Clementino** (below, ➤ 148–149), which contains the best of the Vatican's sculpture collection.

10:00am

Have a quick look at the Etruscan highlights in the **3 Museo Gregoriano Etrusco** (➤ 162) before moving from its upper floors through the **Sala della Biga** (➤ 162) to the Gallerie. These corridors link the main museum buildings to the rooms that form part of the Vatican palace: the Galleria dei Candelabri, the Galleria degli Arazzi, and the Galleria della Carte Geografiche (➤ 149) – respectively adorned with statues, tapestries and frescoed maps.

11:00am

The Gallerie funnel visitors through to the **Stanze di Raffaello** (➤ 151), rooms covered in frescoes by Raphael, and the Cappella di Niccolò V (➤ 151), before steps take you down to the tiny **Appartamento Borgia** (➤ 162–163) and on to the glories of the **Cappella Sistina** (➤ 152–154).

12:30pm

Follow the signs through the **Biblioteca Vaticana** (➤ 163) to the Cortile and the **Pinacoteca** (➤ 164), well worth a quick glance.

1:00pm

The Musei Vaticani have a cafeteria, or you could try **Taverna Angelica** (► 167), which would leave you in the proximity of Castel Sant'Angelo for the afternoon.

2:00pm

Explore 🖪 **Castel Sant'Angelo** (above, ► 164–165) and Ponte Sant'Angelo.

3:00pm

Walk down Via della Conciliazione to Piazza San Pietro. Stroll around the piazza to admire its columns and the facade of 🖸 **Basilica di San Pietro** (right, ► 156–161), then explore the interior. Security queues into Basilica di San Pietro may take as long as an hour to get through at the busiest times of day.

5:00pm

Catch a 40 or 64 bus back to the heart of Rome, or walk back via the Ponte Vittorio Emanuele II.

ⓞ Musei Vaticani

Start a visit to the Musei Vaticani (Vatican Museums) by concentrating on the main highlights – the Museo Pio-Clementino, which contains the best of the Vatican's many classical sculptures; the frescoes in the Stanze di Raffaello (Raphael Rooms); and the Cappella Sistina (Sistine Chapel), celebrated for Michelangelo's famous ceiling paintings.

Since the inauguration of the new entrance complex in 2000, and extended opening hours, visiting the museums has become slightly less daunting. The scale is vast, and you'll have to be prepared for lengthy queues, random route changes and sudden gallery closures, but judicious planning will help. Check the screens near the ticket desk to see which galleries are open, and then take the elevator up to the gallery entrance to pick up an audio guide. You can get background information on the most popular sights – the **Cappella Sistina** and the **Stanze di Raffaello** – via the information boards in the **Cortile della Pigna**.

Museo Pio-Clementino and Galleries

Founded by Pope Clement XIV in 1771 and augmented by his successor, Pius VI, this museum made use of the papacy's already immense collection of Greek and Roman antiquities. Here, as elsewhere, the order in which you move through the museum may vary: the highlights, however, are easily seen.

These start with the Vestibolo Rotundo, which leads to the Gabinetto dell'Apoxyomenos, dominated by the **Apoxyomenos**, the only known Roman copy of a fourth-century BC Greek masterpiece. It shows an athlete scraping the sweat and dust from his body in the wake of victory. Returning to the Vestibolo, you move left to the Cortile Ottagono, which contains some of the greatest classical statues. The most famous is the **Laocoön**, an intricately carved sculptural group dating from around 50BC. Created by sculptors from Rhodes, it was found near the Domus Aurea in 1506 and had a huge influence on Renaissance sculptors, especially Michelangelo. The sculpture shows a Trojan priest, Laocoön, and his sons fighting with sea serpents.

Other works in the Cortile include the **Apollo del Belvedere**, a Roman copy of a fourth-century BC Greek

Laocoön group, created by Greek sculptors, in the Museo Pio-Clementino

The coffered ceiling of he Galleria delle Carte Geografiche, which is filled with beautiful 16th-century maps

bronze original, a masterpiece of classical sculpture which, like the *Laocoön*, greatly influenced Renaissance and other sculptors. The statue of the young god Apollo originally held a bow in one hand, and is thought to have held an arrow in the other. Also here is a statue of **Hermes**, another Roman copy of a Greek original, and the figure of **Perseus** by Antonio Canova, a 19th-century sculptor influenced by the sculpture of the classical world – his statue here, for example, shows the clear influence of the nearby *Apollo del Belvedere*.

Beyond the Cortile lies the **Sala degli Animali**, a truly charming collection of ancient and 18th-century sculpted animals. Moving on, you reach the Galleria delle Statue, where the highlights are the **Apollo Sauroktonos**, a magnificent Roman copy of a fourth-century BC original showing **Apollo** poised to kill a lizard, and the famed **Candelabri Barberini**, a pair of second-century lamps, which were discovered at the Villa Adriana in Tivoli (► 172). Close to the Sala degli Animali is the Sala delle Muse, which is dominated by the *Torso del Belvedere*, probably a first-century BC Greek work. The gigantic torso was much admired by Michelangelo, whose famous nudes, or *ignudi,* in the Cappella Sistina frescoes were influenced by the figure.

Statues, Tapestries and Maps

Other statues worth hunting out include the **Venere di Cnido** *(Venus of Cnidus)* in the Gabinetto delle Maschere, a copy of a famous Greek nude rejected by the islanders of Kos because it was too erotic, and purchased by the Cnidians. Also visit the **Sala a Croce Greca** to see the Sarcofago di Sant'Elena and Sarcofago di Constantina, the sarcophagi – respectively – of the mother and daughter of Emperor Constantine.

Moving on, you should at some stage walk along the long galleries on the upper of the complex's two floors: one is the Galleria dei Candelabri e degli Arazzi, which is adorned with superb tapestries, candelabra and other works. This leads on into the **Galleria delle Carte Geografiche**, a long corridor decorated with beautiful painted maps (1580–83) of the Papal States, much of Italy, and the main cities of each region.

Stanze di Raffaello

Raphael was an artist who died aged just 37 and painted relatively little. This makes the Stanze di Raffaello, or Raphael Rooms, which are almost entirely covered in frescoes by the painter, one of Italy's most treasured artistic ensembles. The four rooms were commissioned from Raphael by Pope Julius II in 1508 and completed after the painter's death in 1520 by his pupils: they include scenes inspired by Leo X, who became pope while work was in progress.

The order in which you're allowed to see the rooms varies from month to month, but if possible try to see them in the order in which they were painted. This means beginning with the **Stanza della Segnatura** (1508–11), which served as Julius' library and was the place where he applied his signature (*segnatura*) to papal bulls (edicts). The frescoes here are the rooms' finest – many critics call them an even greater achievement than the Cappella Sistina. The four main pictures provide a celebration of the triumph of Theology, Philosophy, Poetry and Justice, fusing classical, religious, artistic and philosophical themes in a complicated allegorical mixture; it is well worth buying a guide to help decipher the paintings.

Divine Inspiration

The next room to be painted was the **Stanza di Eliodoro** (1512–14), a private antechamber or waiting room. Here the paintings are a form of visual propaganda for Julius and Leo, although their professed theme is the timely intervention of Divine Providence in the defence of an endangered faith. Thus the battle scenes in *The Expulsion of Heliodorus from the Temple* – a reworking of a Biblical story – are an allusion to Julius' skill in defending the Papal States from foreign interference. Similarly, the panel ostensibly showing *Attila the Hun* turning back from Rome actually contains a portrait of the new pope, Leo X (the figure on a donkey). Note the three-part fresco showing *The Deliverance of St Peter from Prison*, the first time Raphael attempted to portray a scene set at night.

The third room chronologically is the **Stanza dell' Incendio** (1514–17), designed as a dining room for Leo X, who asked Raphael to paint a series of scenes that celebrated the achievements of two of his papal namesakes, Leo III and Leo IV. Thus the main frescoes portray the *Coronation of Charlemagne* (a ceremony conducted by Leo III in 800); the *Oath of Leo III* (when Leo denied accusations levelled at him by rivals); the *Battle of Ostia* (where Leo IV showed mercy to a defeated Saracen navy in 848, an allusion to Leo X's attempts to forge a crusade against the Turks); and the *Fire in the Borgo* (in which Leo IV – painted here as Leo X – extinguished a fire near Basilica di San Pietro by making the sign of the Cross).

Much of the Stanza dell'Incendio was painted by pupils working to designs by Raphael, as were the four principal frescoes on the life of the Emperor Constantine in the last room, the **Stanza di Costantino** (1517–24).

Before moving on from the Raphael Rooms, be sure to see the nearby **Cappella di Niccolò V**, a small chapel covered in beautiful frescoes by Fra Angelico showing scenes from the *Lives of St Stephen and St Lawrence* (1447–51).

The *Fire in the Borgo* fresco in the Stanze di Raffaello

Cappella Sistina

You will not want to miss the Cappella Sistina (Sistine Chapel), but expect crowds and considerable pressure to move on to make way for visitors behind you. This can make for a rather unsatisfactory visit, but detracts little from the majesty of Michelangelo's breathtaking frescoes.

The chapel was built for Sixtus IV between 1477 and 1481, and received its first pictorial decoration between 1480 and 1483, when the lower walls were frescoed by several of the leading artists of their day, notably Perugino, Domenico Ghirlandaio and Sandro Botticelli. A quarter of a century elapsed before Michelangelo was commissioned to fresco the chapel's ceiling, which up to that point had been adorned with a simple wash of blue covered in gold and silver stars.

Michelangelo Marvels

Michelangelo supposedly proved reluctant to accept the commission, partly because he viewed painting as a lesser art than sculpture, and partly because he was more concerned with creating a tomb for Julius (never completed). In the event the ceiling would occupy him for four years, work being completed in 1512. The frescoes – controversially restored between 1979 and 1994 – consist of nine main panels, beginning with the five principal events in the Book of Genesis: *The Separation of Light from Darkness; The Creation of the Heavenly Bodies; The Separation of Land and Sea; The Creation of Adam;* and *The Creation of Eve.* These are followed by *The Fall and Expulsion from Paradise; The Sacrifice of Noah, The Flood* and *The Drunkenness of Noah.* Scattered around the

Michelangelo's celebrated ceiling frescoes are the most famous of the many fine paintings in the Cappella Sistina

ceiling are various painted Prophets, Sibyls, Old Testament characters, and 20 *ignudi,* or nude youths. In all, the painting covers an area of 930sq m (1,110sq yards) and more than 300 individual figures.

The ceiling on its own is a masterpiece, but the chapel contains a second, and probably greater, fresco by Michelangelo, the huge **Last Judgement** (1536–41) that covers the entire wall behind the altar. Bear in mind while you admire the painting that it was painted a full 22 years after the ceiling frescoes, during which time Rome had been sacked by the forces of Emperor Charles V in 1527, an event which apparently deeply affected Michelangelo and effectively brought to an end the period of optimism of the Renaissance years.

Something of the darker forces affecting the city and the painter can be glimpsed in Michelangelo's uncompromising vision of a pitiless God venting his judgement on a cowering humanity. Those spared in this judgement are portrayed in the fresco rising to Paradise on the left, while those doomed by it are shown sinking to hell on the right. The dead rise from their graves along the lower part of the painting, while Christ stands at its centre, surrounded by the Virgin, Apostles and assorted saints. Of the 391 figures in the picture, only one is painted gazing directly at the onlooker – the famous damned soul hugging himself as he awaits his doom.

TAKING A BREAK

If you need a respite from sightseeing, visit the Musei Vaticani café or try **Non Solo Pizza** (➤ 166–167), a few blocks north of Piazza del Risorgimento.

➕ 196 B4 ✉ Viale Vaticano ☎ 06 6988 4676; 06 698 3145; http://mv.vatican.va 🕐 Mon–Sat 9–6 (last entrance 4pm), last Sunday of the month 9–2 (last entrance 12:30pm). Closed on religious and public holidays 💶 Expensive. Free last Sun of the month (➤ 155). Book tickets in advance to avoid queues online at http://biglietteriamusei.vatican.va 🚇 Ottaviano-San Pietro or Cipro-Musei Vaticani 🚌 19, 32, 49, 492, 990 to Piazza del Risorgimento

One of the Vatican Museums' elaborately decorated corridors

The beautiful
ancient
mosaics and
statues of the
Sala Rotonda

MUSEI VATICANI: INSIDE INFO

Top tips It's a 10-minute walk from San Pietro to the museum entrance;
to avoid this, take a bus or taxi to Piazza del Risorgimento.
- Entrance is **free on the last Sunday of the month**, but this means waiting time
  can be 2–3 hours. The Musei Vaticani are **open on Monday.**
- Labelling is very poor, so pick up a museum guidebook or an **audio guide**.
- Wheelchairs (free) are available by emailing accoglienza.musei@scv.va or
  by calling at the Special Permits desk in the entrance hall; you will need
  a valid identity document.
- **Binoculars** make sense for the Cappella Sistina.
- **Guided tours** of the Vatican Gardens are available (book at least one week
  ahead on 06 6988 4647 or email visiteguidatesingoli.musei@scv.va).

In more detail It's worth buying guides to the Stanze di Raffaello and
Cappella Sistina to help appreciate the allusion and meaning in the paintings.

2 Basilica di San Pietro

The Basilica di San Pietro (St Peter's) is the world's most famous church, an important place of Catholic pilgrimage, and the one sight in Rome that you simply must see, even though there are few important works of art inside.

History of the Basilica

The church is built over the shrine of St Peter, one of the Apostles and the first pope. The huge basilica you see today is not the original. St Peter himself was crucified during the persecutions of Emperor Nero somewhere between AD64 and 67, probably on the hilly slopes above the present church, and his followers then buried him in a cemetery nearby. The position of his tomb is reputedly marked by the present-day high altar, a notion supported by extensive archaeological work that has taken place around the site since 1939. Some sort of shrine to the saint probably existed by 200, but the

Piazza San Pietro provides a majestic setting for the Basilica di San Pietro

first church for which records survive was raised in 326 by Pope Sylvester I during the reign of Constantine the Great, the first Christian emperor. This church survived for well over 1,000 years. By 1452, however, its main fabric was in a precarious state, leading Nicholas V, pope at the time, to suggest the construction of a new basilica, funds for which would be collected from across the Christian world. Nicholas had 2,500 wagonloads of stone removed from the Colosseo and carried across the Tiber to prepare for construction. In the event, building only began in 1506, and would proceed – with many false starts and alterations to the original plans – for the best part of 300 years.

Basilica di San Pietro's Architects

The architect charged with designing the new church and pulling down the old one – a task that required 3,000 labourers – was Bramante. He died in 1516, and it was 1539 before Giuliano da Sangallo won a commission to complete the building. His plans proved ill fated, however, and in 1546 Pope Paul III called in Michelangelo to salvage the increasingly troubled project. The artist, then aged 72, demolished Sangallo's additions and advanced an ambitious plan for a colossal dome. Much work on this dome was accomplished by the time of Michelangelo's death in 1564, only for it to be amended in 1590 by another architect, Giacomo della Porta.

In 1605, Carlo Maderno was asked to redesign the church yet again, a scheme that involved, among other things, the construction of the present facade in 1612. Finishing touches were added by the baroque architect, Gian Lorenzo Bernini. The new church – a monument to architectural compromise – was eventually consecrated on 18 November, 1626, precisely 1,300 years after the consecration of the original basilica.

The Piazza and Basilica

Bernini was responsible not only for last-minute refinements to the church, but also for **Piazza San Pietro** (1656–67), the enormous square (340m by 240m/370 by 260 yards) that provides the Basilica di San Pietro's grand setting. The piazza's vast colonnades reach out in two half-circles, symbolizing arms stretching out to embrace visiting pilgrims. The colonnades are four columns deep and contain 284 columns – be sure to hunt out the famous pair of **stone discs**, one near each of the square's fountains. These mark the focus of each colonnade's ellipse, and the point at which the four sets of columns appear to line up as a single pillar. The statues surmounting the colonnades represent 140 saints, while the colossal 350-tonne obelisk at the centre of the piazza was brought to Rome from Egypt by Caligula in AD37. The orb at the top contains a fragment of the Holy Cross (it was thought at one time to contain the ashes of Julius Caesar).

The Facade

Note the central balcony, from which a new pope is proclaimed and where the pope proclaims sainthoods and delivers his "Urbi et Orbi" blessing on holy days. Note, too, the statues, which depict Christ, John the Baptist and 11 of the Apostles – the missing disciple is St Peter. The most celebrated of the five portals is the one on the extreme right, the **Porta Santa**, which is opened only during Holy Years, the most recent of which was the year 2000. The central doors (1433–45), cast to commemorate the Council of Florence in

The sheer scale of Bernini's ornate *baldacchino*, or altar canopy, impresses many visitors

The superb colonnaded dome of the Basilica floodlit at night

1439, survive from the original St Peter's. They are among only a handful of treasures from the old basilica, most of which were destroyed by Bramante, who earned the nickname "*ruinante*" (the destroyer). On either side of the portico stand statues of Constantine (1670) and Charlemagne (1735), to the right and left respectively.

Inside, the overwhelming impression is one of immense size: the church measures 185m (200 yards) long, 119m (390 feet) high at the dome, and can accommodate upward of 60,000 people. For many years it was the largest church in the world, losing the title only when a copy of the Basilica di San Pietro was built in Yamoussoukro, on the Ivory Coast. Just inside the entrance, look out for the series of brass line inscriptions on the marble floor which set out the world's next 14 largest churches. Look out, too, for the red porphyry disc a few metres from the entrance which marks the spot where Charlemagne was crowned Holy Roman Emperor in 800.

Fine Arts
The items of genuine artistic merit found among the swathes of marble and decorative artifice are actually few in number, and take less time to see than you might imagine. The first of these is also the greatest: Michelangelo's statue of the **Pietà**

(1498–99), which shows Mary cradling the dead Christ. Created when the sculptor was 23, it is Michelangelo's only signed work, the sculptor having reputedly added his name when he heard onlookers disputing the statue's authorship.

A Place of Worship

Farther down the church, the crossing is marked by the high altar – used only by the pope on special occasions – and a vast altar canopy, or **baldacchino** (1624–33), created by Bernini using bronze removed from the roof of the Pantheon. It was created for Urban VIII, a member of the Barberini family, hence the repeated appearance on the work of the Barberini symbol – the bee. Behind you on your right as you face the canopy is a 13th-century statue, *St Peter Enthroned*, unmissable by virtue of its right foot, which has been caressed to smoothness following a 50-day indulgence granted by Pius IX in 1857 to anyone kissing the statue after confession. The statue's authorship is disputed: it was long thought to be a fifth-century work, but was later attributed to the 13th-century Florentine sculptor Arnolfo di Cambio.

Above: The right foot of *St Peter Enthroned* has been worn smooth by the kisses of pilgrims

In the apse beyond the high altar stands Bernini's **Cattedra di San Pietro** (1656–65), a bronze canopy built to encase a throne reputedly used by St Peter (although probably dating from the ninth century). To its left and right lie two important papal tombs: Bernini's **Monument to Urban VIII** (1627–47) on the right, and Guglielmo della Porta's **Monument to Paul III** (1551–75) on the left. The latter's female figures of Justice and Prudence are said to be modelled on the Pope's sister and mother. Look also for Antonio Benci detto il Pollaiolo's **Monument to Pope Innocent VIII** (1498) – by the second main pillar of the nave on the right as you walk back toward the entrance. One of the artefacts saved from the old basilica, it shows Innocent twice – once sitting and once recumbent.

Right: Piazza San Pietro and beyond from the topmost lantern of the dome of the basilica

All else in the basilica, however, pales into insignificance compared to the views from the **dome**. The entrance is at the end of the right-hand nave, from where you can take the lift or steps to the first stage. From here, more steps lead to the higher drum and gallery, then continue up a steeper and narrower one-way staircase to the topmost lantern.

TAKING A BREAK

Taverna Angelica (➤ 167) is a good choice for a simple meal within easy striking distance of San Pietro.

🚻 196 B4 ✉ Piazza San Pietro, Città del Vaticano ☎ 06 6988 3731; 06 6988 3462; www.vatican.va 🕐 Basilica: Apr–Sep daily 7–7; Oct–Mar 7–6. Dome: Apr–Sep daily 8–6; Oct–May 8–5. Grotte: as for Basilica. Treasury: Apr–Sep daily 9–6; Oct–Mar 9–5 💶 Basilica: free. Dome, Grotte and Treasury: moderate 🚇 Ottaviano-San Pietro 🚌 40 or 62 to Via della Conciliazione, 64 to close to Piazza San Pietro or 19, 23, 32, 49, 492, 990 to Piazza del Risorgimento

BASILICA DI SAN PIETRO: INSIDE INFO

Top tips A **rigid dress code** is enforced in San Pietro, which is, of course, primarily a place of worship. Women should not wear shorts, short skirts or skimpy tops; they should also avoid displaying bare shoulders. Men should also avoid shorts and dress with decorum.

■ The one thing you should definitely do when you visit the Basilica di San Pietro is **climb the dome**, as the view of the city and surrounding countryside from the top is one of the finest in the area. Try to arrive early, as long queues develop, and pick a day when visibility is good.

In more detail There is plenty to see beneath St Peter's, where you'll find the **Sacre Grotte Vaticane**, a crypt which contains the tombs of numerous popes. The entrance is by the pillar in the church's crossing with the statues of St Peter and St Andreas.

One to miss The Treasury contains gifts made to Basilica di San Pietro over the centuries, but its best artefacts have all been moved to the Musei Vaticani.

At Your Leisure

8 Musei Vaticani

The following museums and rooms are also part of the Musei Vaticani, to which most visitors will devote less time, or simply walk through en route to the main attractions. Entry details are the same as for the main museum complex (► 154). There are still more museums not discussed below: these include the Museo Sacro (sacred art from catacombs and early Christian churches in Rome); Museo Storico (coaches and weapons); Museo Missionario Etnologico (anthropological artefacts brought to Rome by missionary and other expeditions); Museo Chiaramonti (a huge quantity of Greek and Roman sculpture); and Museo Gregoriano Profano (a collection of secular or "profane" art – mostly more Greek and Roman sculpture).

Museo Gregoriano Egizio

The Vatican's Egyptian collection was founded by Pope Pius VII and collected in this nine-room museum by Pope Gregory XVI in 1839. It contains a wide range of mummies, monumental statues, headstones, papyri and sarcophagi from the third millennium BC to the time of Christ. Many were found in and around Rome itself, having been brought to the city from Egypt, which formed part of the Roman Empire for several centuries. Highlights include the sixth-century BC statue of Udya-horres-ne in Room I and the head of a statue of Pharaoh Monthuhotep II (2100–2040BC) in Room V.

Museo Gregoriano Etrusco

This 22-room museum is excellent if your interest in the Etruscans – who dominated central Italy before the rise of Rome – is not enough to take you all the way to the much larger Etruscan collection of the Villa Giulia (► 135). Like the Villa Giulia, this museum has its fair share of dull urns and vases, but it also contains some of the greatest of all Etruscan artefacts. The most celebrated of these is the *Mars of Todi* (Room III), a large bronze statue named after the Umbrian town in which it was found. Also worth special attention are the exhibits of Room II, most of which were taken from the Regolini-Galassi Tomb (*c*.650BC), uncovered in 1836 at Cerveteri just north of Rome. The Etruscans, like the Egyptians, buried the deceased with all manner of everyday items they might need in the afterlife, thereby providing archaeologists with a graphic picture of their domestic and artistic habits.

Sala della Biga

This single marble-decked room features a Roman *biga*, or two-horsed chariot, reconstructed in 1788 from disparate and unconnected first-century elements. Part of it may once have formed a votive offering, but for years was used as an episcopal throne in the church of San Marco. Niches around the walls contain accomplished Greek and Roman statues: some date back as far as the fifth century BC.

Appartamento Borgia

This suite of apartments was built for Pope Alexander VI, a member of the notorious Borgia family, during his papacy (1492–1503). Almost a palace within a palace, it proved so sumptuous that subsequent popes chose to use it as their principal lodgings for the next hundred years. Room I, the Sala delle Sibille, is where the infamous Cesare Borgia is said to have had Alfonso of Aragon, the husband of his sister, Lucrezia Borgia, murdered. Today, the room is more remarkable for its frescoes, part of a fine series of paintings in the suite executed between 1492 and 1495 by the Umbrian artist Pinturicchio. The pictures cover a

wide variety of themes, embracing religious, humanist and mythical subjects – the best are in Room V, the Sala dei Santi. Other rooms in this complex are given over to the Collezione d'Arte Religiosa Moderna, a collection of modern religious art.

Biblioteca Apostolica Vaticana

The Vatican Library easily rates as the world's most valuable collection of books and manuscripts. Books were accumulated by the popes for centuries, but only found a permanent home in 1474 during the papacy of Sixtus IV. Material has been systematically added to the library ever since, amounting to some 100,000

Inside the sumptuous interior of the Biblioteca Apostolica Vaticana

manuscripts, 70,000 archive volumes, 800,000 printed works, 100,000 prints and maps, and around 75,000 handwritten and illustrated books. The library has been closed to tourists since 2007, functioning as an academic research library only, and its treasures are no longer on display. You can, however, admire the decorated hall that once housed the library with its gilded and frescoed vaulted ceiling and walls.

Pinacoteca Vaticana

Even on its own, the Vatican's Pinacoteca, or art gallery, would be considered one of Rome's major collections of medieval, Renaissance and other paintings. Its 18 rooms offer a chronological insight into the development of religious art, and would be richer still had Napoleon not pilfered many of their treasures at the beginning of the 19th century.

Room I opens with 11th-, 12th-and 13th-century Tuscan and Umbrian works, followed in Room II by one of the gallery's highlights – Giotto's Stefaneschi Triptych (*c.*1315). Commissioned by Cardinal Stefaneschi, it was originally intended for one of the principal altars in the old St Peter's. Among the gallery's other star attractions are two majestic paintings by Raphael in Room VIII,

An apostle in *Angeli e Apostoli Musicati* by Melozzo da Forlì, Pinacoteca Vaticana

a Transfiguration (1517–20) and the *Madonna of Foligno* (1512–13), as well as Leonardo da Vinci's unfinished *St Jerome* in Room IX. These are just four highlights among many, for the gallery possesses works by most leading Italian painters: Fra Angelico, Titian, Caravaggio, Veronese and many others.

🕒 Castel Sant'Angelo

There is no mistaking the Castel Sant'Angelo, whose dramatic round bulwarks rise on the banks of the Tiber just to the east of St Peter's. Today, the castle is a museum, but it started life in AD130 as a mausoleum for Emperor Hadrian. Its circular design – which formed the basis

FOR KIDS

Children should relish the view from the top of the dome of the **Basilica di San Pietro** (▶ 160), though they may find the climb to the top hard work (only the fittest adults should even contemplate carrying small children up the steps). **Castel Sant'Angelo** (see above), which not only looks like a "real" castle, but also has lots of spooky corridors and hidden corners, is almost guaranteed to intrigue youngsters.

In the Musei Vaticani you need to be very selective if you have children with you: try them with the **Sala degli Animali** (▶ 149), the gallery of maps (▶ 149) or the mummies of the Egyptian museum (▶ 162).

OFF THE BEATEN TRACK

For a glimpse of the inner sanctum of Vatican City (most of which is reserved for those people working or living in this tiny state), book on to one of the tours of the **Vatican Gardens** (► 155).

Outside Vatican City, the small grid of streets known as the Borgo – between Borgo Sant'Angelo and Via Crescenzio – is the least-visited enclave near St Peter's.

for all subsequent structures on the site – was copied from the Mausoleo di Augusto near the Capitoline Hill, which in turn was probably based on the design of Etruscan tombs. The mausoleum was used as a resting place for emperors until AD271, when it was incorporated into the city's defences. It then remained Rome's principal fortress for more than 1,000 years.

The strong, circular design of the Castel Sant'Angelo

On entering the castle, you walk along subterranean passages, part of the original Roman-era mausoleum, then climb up to the ramparts, which offer excellent views across the city. Immediately below, look out for the Ponte Sant'Angelo, a bridge adorned with statues of angels sculpted to a design by Bernini. The castle's various military and other exhibits are fairly dull, unlike the beautifully decorated papal apartments and libraries woven into the fortress's labyrinth of rooms.

✚ 197 E4 ✉ Lungotevere Castello 50 ☎ 06 681 9111; www.castelsantangelo.beniculturali. it ⏰ Tue–Sun 9–7:30 💶 Expensive 🚌 30, 49, 70, 87, 130, 186 and other services to Piazza Cavour and Lungotevere

Where to...
Eat and Drink

Prices
Expect to pay per person for a meal, excluding drinks and service:
€ under €30 €€ €30–€50 €€€ over €50

The area around St Peter's and the Vatican suffers from a shortage of good restaurants compared to other parts of the city. Once, the grid of streets between Via della Conciliazione and Via Crescenzio, an area known as the Borgo, was filled with artisans' workshops and traditional little eating places. Most have gone now, or have been replaced by restaurants aimed at the tourist market. A few old places remain, however, along with one restaurant – Les Étoiles (opposite) – that ranks among Rome's finest. There's a fair amount of choice if all you want is a quick snack, and an abundance of places on Via Cola di Rienzo – a street renowned for its food shops – to buy picnic supplies.

Dal Toscano €€
This lively restaurant is convenient for the Vatican Museums, being just east of the entrance on Via Germanico between Viale Ottaviano and Via Vespasiano. It's also popular with locals and families, so reservations are recommended, at least in the evenings. As the name suggests, this is not a place for Roman specialities, but rather the thick *bistecca alla fiorentina* (T-bone steaks), ribollita soups, and other staples of Tuscany.
🚩 196 C5 ⊠ Via Germanico 58–60 ☎ 06 3972 5717 ⏰ Tue–Sun 12:30–3, 7:30–11. Closed 1 week in Dec and 2 weeks in Aug

Les Étoiles €€€
This is one of the great Roman restaurants for a treat or celebration. From the moment you enter the stylish dining room and see the view of San Pietro you know you're in for something special. The Italian food and courteous service are as good as the view, and the menu changes from day to day, depending on the availability of produce and the mood of the chef. The restaurant forms part of the Atlante Star hotel, and has a roof garden and a terrace for dining outside.
🚩 197 D4 ⊠ Via dei Bastioni 1 ☎ 06 687 3233 ⏰ Daily 12–2:30, 7:30–10:30

Gran Caffè Esperia €
Right beside the river, and not far from Castel Sant'Angelo, this beautifully restored, *fin-de-siècle* café is open all day for everything from a true Roman coffee and *cornetto* (croissant) breakfast to lunchtime sandwiches and evening long drinks and cocktails. The setting is lovely, and there are tables outside.
🚩 197 F4 ⊠ Lungotevere dei Mellini 1 ☎ 06 3211 0016 ⏰ May–Sep daily 7am–midnight, Oct–Apr 7am–9:30pm

Isola della Pizza €
This long-established and much-loved local restaurant got a complete facelift in 2010, but the welcome remains as warm and the pizza just as good. There's a huge antipasto choice, pizza featuring well-sourced ingredients from all over Italy, and they also serve grills and pasta
🚩 196 C5 ⊠ Via della Scipione 45 ☎ 06 3973 3483 ⏰ Thu–Tue 12:30–3, 7:30–12

Non Solo Pizza €
Non Solo Pizza (Not Only Pizza) serves pizza by the slice (and full

pizzas after 7pm) and a selection of Roman-style deep-fried delicacies: stuffed olives, rice and cheese balls, courgette flowers and the like. It also serves a limited daily selection of inexpensive hot dishes, a good option for lunch after a visit to the Vatican Museums. The restaurant is in a side street a couple of blocks north of Piazza Risorgimento.

➕ 196 C5 ☒ Via degli Scipioni 95–97 ☎ 06 372 9470 ⏰ Tue–Sun 8:30am–9.30pm

Osteria dell'Angelo €€

You need to reserve a table at this popular restaurant on a side street just north of the busy Viale delle Milizie. The sophisticated cooking goes beyond the usual local and Italian staples, while the decoration is dominated by sporting photographs, a nod to the rugby-playing past of the owner, the eponymous Angelo. On balmy evenings you can eat outdoors.

➕ 196 B5 ☒ Via Giovanni Bettolo 32 ☎ 06 372 9470 ⏰ Tue–Fri 12:45–2.30, 8–11, Mon, Sat 8–11

Osteria Croce €

This is a reasonably convenient option for the Vatican Museums: just walk north up Via Leone IV and turn right after six blocks to find this very popular and traditional trattoria patronized mostly by Romans.

➕ 196 B5 ☒ Via Giovanni Bettoio 24 ☎ 06 372 9470 ⏰ Tue, Fri 1–2.30, 8–11, Mon, Wed–Thu, Sat 8–11

Paninoteca da Guido €

If you want a quick snack after a morning in the Vatican, you'll find a counter full of tasty ingredients at this tiny place on a street just behind the Via della Conciliazione. Choose your *panino* and it will be filled with meat, salami, cheese and salad ingredients, which you can eat on the spot – there are a few tables outside – or take away. There are also delicious pasta dishes at lunchtime and a range of snacks is available all day.

➕ 197 D4 ☒ Borgo Pio 3 ☎ 06 687 5491 ⏰ Mon–Sat 8–6

Pizzarium €

A few minutes' walk from the Vatican Museums, this takeaway is a good bet for all-day pizzas and drinks. Unlike many tourist-aimed joints, this one offers the real thing, combining slow-rise dough with imaginative toppings, which make use of local, seasonal ingredients, including fresh rocket, aubergine, home-made pesto or artichoke, as well as all the usual favourites.

➕ 196 A5 ☒ Via della Meloria 43 ☎ 06 321 1502 ⏰ Mon–Sat 12:30–2.30, 7–11

Taberna de' Gracchi €–€€

The Taberna de' Gracchi is a reliable and convenient restaurant for lunch if you have visited the Castel Sant'Angelo, for it lies just north of the Castel, close to Piazza Cola di Rienzo. The food is well cooked and good value.

➕ 197 E5 ☒ Via dei Gracchi 266–8 ☎ 06 321 3126; www.tabernagracchi.com ⏰ Tue–Sat 12:30–2.30, 7:30–10.30, Mon 7:30–10.30

Taverna Angelica €€

This, the best mid-range restaurant within easy reach of St Peter's, lies on the south side of a tiny piazza on Borgo Vittorio in the heart of the Borgo. Despite its location, it is not a typical Roman trattoria, for the modern interior is minimalist, and the cooking light, innovative and biased toward seafood. The wine list is excellent, and includes some by the glass. Tables are limited, so make a reservation.

➕ 197 D4 ☒ Piazza Amerigo Capponi 6 ☎ 06 687 4514; www.tavernaangelica.it ⏰ Dinner only: daily 7pm–midnight, plus Sun lunch 12–2:30. Closed 3 weeks in Aug

Tre Pupazzi €–€€

If you can't get into Taverna Angelica (see above), try this 400-year-old place just around the corner to the east. It is far more traditional in appearance and cuisine, and serves good fish, pizzas and pasta dishes.

➕ 197 D4 ☒ Via dei Tre Pupazzi 1 ☎ 06 686 8371 ⏰ Mon–Sat 12:30–2.30, 7:30–11

Where to...
Shop

The shops surrounding the Vatican and St Peter's mainly sell **religious souvenirs** and postcards. Borgo's grid of streets contain the occasional **artisan's workshop**, but nothing to compare with the workshops on Via dei Cappellari and around Campo dei Fiori (▶ 109–110). One exception is **Italia Garipoli** (Borgo Vittorio 91a, tel: 06 6880 2196, closed Sun), which sells linens, curtains and fabrics.

Where you will find a variety of shops is in the mainly modern streets north of Via Crescenzio, and in particular Via Cola di Rienzo, one of the busiest shopping streets in northwest Rome. The street has a wide variety of shops selling mid-range clothes, shoes and other commodities, but is especially known for its *alimentari* – food shops. One of the best known is **Castroni** (Via Cola di Rienzo 196, tel: 06 687 4383, www.castroni.com, closed Sun), which combines Italian staples (cheese, hams, olive oils and so on) with food specialities from around the world. Alternatively, visit **Franchi** (Via Cola di Rienzo 200–204, tel: 06 687 4651, closed Sun), one of Rome's most mouth-watering delicatessens, where you can buy picnic provisions or order delicious take-out sandwiches and snack lunches.

Look out for **Costantini** near Piazza Cavour 16 (tel: 06 321 3210, closed Sun, Mon morning, and Aug), an excellent wine shop to the south at Piazza Cavour 16 that also sells gourmet olive oils and pasta.

Where to...
Be Entertained

Since 1958 the **Auditorium Conciliazione** (formerly the Auditorio Pio; Via della Conciliazione 4, tel: 06 684 391, 800 904 560, www. auditoriumconciliazione.it), close to St Peter's, has staged a variety of classical music concerts. Rome's foremost classical musical association, the **Accademia Nazionale di Santa Cecilia** (tel: 06 8024 2501, www.santacecilia. it) has its own orchestra, and also organizes concerts with visiting choirs, orchestras and other ensembles. The Accademia is among many organizations that perform at Rome's spectacular **Auditorium-Parco della Musica** (▶ 142).

Superb choral and organ music can be heard in St Peter's.

Music of a different sort can be heard two blocks north of the entrance to the Vatican Museums at **Alexanderplatz** (Via Ostia 9, off Via Leone, tel: 06 3974 2171, www.alexanderplatz.it, Mon–Sat 9pm–2:30am). This is probably Rome's best venue for live jazz; you can also eat in the adjoining restaurant (reservations recommended).

Another good pub-club for hearing live jazz, blues and rock is the long-running **Fonclea** (Via Crescenzio 82a, tel: 06 689 6302, daily 7 or 8pm–2am, admission usually free except Sat). Similar music can be heard farther north at the **Four Green Fields** pub (Via C Morin 38, off Via della Giuliana, tel: 06 372 5091, daily 6pm–2am, admission generally free).

Excursions

Excursions

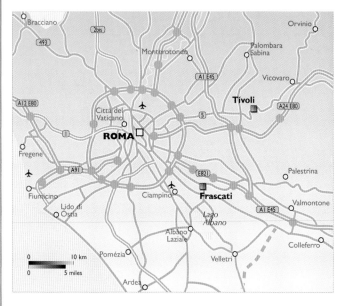

Rome is so filled with museums, ancient monuments and other sightseeing temptations that many people on a short visit prefer to stay in the city, rather than visiting the variety of towns and sights within the vicinity. However, there are two interesting excursions, which are easily made and offer an excellent counterpoint to the city and – should you need it – an escape from its often busy streets. The most popular is Tivoli, a town to the east of Rome, known for its gardens and the Villa Adriana, the ruins of Emperor Hadrian's vast private villa. The second is Frascati, a town nestled on the slopes of the Alban Hills, the volcanic peaks that rise just south of the city. Easily reached by train from Termini, the town is best known for its white wine, cooling summer breezes and lofty views over Rome.

Those with more time to spend exploring the area might also want to investigate Ostia Antica, Rome's old sea port, and today an extensive archaeological park to the west of the city. Farther up the coast to the north are Cerveteri and Tarquinia, two major Etruscan towns with large ancient necropolises containing thousands of tombs, while inland to the south lies Palestrina, known for its great pre-Roman temple. If you want a complete change, consider Orvieto, a fascinating Umbrian hill town with an outstanding cathedral, around 80 minutes from Rome by train. Contact visitor information (➤ 30) for further details or for information about companies offering guided coach tours to these sights.

Page 169: The superb Organ Fountain at the Villa d'Este in Tivoli

Tivoli

The ancient town of Tivoli – Roman Tibur – is the most popular one-day excursion from Rome. Some 36km (22 miles) from the city, it's known for two principal sights: the Villa d'Este, a Renaissance villa celebrated for its gardens, and the Villa Adriana, a vast Roman-era villa and grounds created by Emperor Hadrian. Also worth seeing are the more recent and more rugged grounds of the Villa Gregoriana.

Villa d'Este

The Villa d'Este began life as a Benedictine convent, but was converted into a country villa in 1550 for Cardinal Ippolito d'Este. The cardinal was a wealthy collector, patron of the arts and a scion of Italy's noble families – he was the son of Lucrezia Borgia. Today, following years of restoration, the villa and its extraordinary gardens are a UNESCO World Heritage Site. Stroll through the frescoed, stuccoed rooms of the villa, with its panoramic terraces and balconies, before walking into the gardens, the main reason for visiting the villa.

Lion-head spouts on the Villa d'Este's Avenue of One Hundred Fountains

First laid out as an escape from Rome's summer heat, it was **water** that inspired the gardens' design, and it cascades, spouts, falls, tumbles and trickles in myriad fountains – there are more than **500 jets**. Don't miss the **Viale delle Cento Fontane** (Avenue of One Hundred Fountains), a long walk lined with cascades and jets of water; Bernini's elegant **Fontana della Bicchierone**; and the mechanical **Organ** and **Owl Fountains**, of which the former plays music, while the latter has singing birds which fall silent when an owl appears.

Villa Gregoriana

The Villa Gregoriana is generally less crowded than the Villa d'Este and – although not particularly well maintained – is perhaps more interesting and beautiful. Centred on a pair of waterfalls and a

60m (200-foot) gorge cut by the River Aniene, it lies in the town's northeast corner about 300m (330 yards) from the Villa d'Este. The park was created in 1831 when Pope Gregory XVI built tunnels to divert the waters of the Aniene to protect Tivoli from flooding. From the ticket office follow the path signposted to the Grande Cascata, or Large Waterfall, which brings you to steps and a terrace overlooking the waterfall. Other paths nearby meander around the lush and often overgrown park, passing through the ruins of a Roman villa, among other things, and dropping down to the valley floor past ancient shrines and grottoes before a long climb up the other side of the gorge past the ruined Temple of Vesta.

Villa Adriana

Leave plenty of time for the Villa Adriana as its site covers an area equal to that of ancient Rome – making it probably the largest villa ever created in the Roman world. It was begun in AD125 and completed ten years later by Emperor Hadrian. Many of its treasures, statues and stone have long gone, but the site remains a wonderfully pretty and romantic place, and enough survives of the villa's many buildings to evoke their original grandeur.

Hadrian reproduced or adapted the designs of many of the great buildings he had visited during his travels around the Empire: the "Pecile" colonnade through which you enter, for example, reproduces the Stoa Poikile of Athens in Greece. A small museum displays finds made in the ongoing excavations, but you will get most pleasure by simply wandering the site at random. Be sure to walk along the sunken stone passageway (known as a *cryptoporticus*) while exploring the Villa Adriana. Past artists have burned their names on the ceiling with candle smoke.

To reach the Villa Adriana from Tivoli, take a taxi or catch the local CAT bus, No 4 or 4X, from the bus station in Piazza Massimo, or from the stop outside the tourist office on Largo Garibaldi.

The columns and statues that line the Canopus at the Villa Adriana are copies from the Temple of Serapis near Alexandria

TAKING A BREAK

A good restaurant choice in Tivoli is **Il Grottino della Sibilla dal** (Piazza Rivorola 21, tel: 0774 332 606, closed Mon). Out of town, on the road to the Villa Adriana, the best option is **Adriano** (Largo Marguerite Yourcenar 2, tel: 0774 382 235, daily, closed Sun pm in winter); you can eat outside in summer. Alternatively, buy food and drink from shops in Tivoli and take them to the Villa Adriana for a picnic.

The Viale delle Cento Fontane at the Villa d'Este

Villa d'Este
✉ Piazza Trento, Tivoli ☎ Toll free in Italy: 199766166; 0774 335 5850 (for disabled bookings); www.villadestetivoli.info ⏰ May–Aug daily 8:30–6:45; Sep 8:30–6:15; Oct 8:30–5:30; Nov–Jan 8:30–4; Feb 8:30–4:30; Mar 8:30–5:15; Apr 8:30–6:30 💲 Expensive

Villa Gregoriana
✉ Piazza Tempio di Vesta, Tivoli ☎ 0774 3996 7701; www.villagregoriana. it ⏰ Apr to mid-Oct Tue–Sun 10–6:30; Mar, mid-Oct to Nov Tue–Sat 10–2:30, Sun 10–4 💲 Moderate

Villa Adriana
✉ Via di Villa Adriana, Tivoli ☎ 06 3996 7900 ⏰ May–Aug daily 9–7:30; Mar, Oct 9–6:30; Apr, Sep 9–7; Nov–Jan 9–5; Feb 9–6 💲 Expensive

TIVOLI: INSIDE INFO

Getting there It is possible to take a **train** from Termini to Tivoli, but as most trains stop frequently, this is a particularly slow, albeit painless, way of getting to the town. Tivoli's station is in Viale Mazzini, approximately 400m (0.25 miles) southeast of the Villa Gregoriana.

■ **Buses** to Tivoli depart approximately every 10 to 20 minutes from the Ponte Mammolo Metro station on Line B; journey time is 50 minutes.

Top tips Tivoli's **visitor centre** lies close to the entrance to the Villa d'Este on the north side of Largo Garibaldi (tel: 0774 311 249).

■ The Villa d'Este is extremely popular, so be prepared for lots of visitors: **arrive early** to see the gardens at their least crowded. Avoid the heat of the afternoon in high summer. Allow time to explore Tivoli's attractive tangle of streets.

Hidden gem In the Villa Adriana look out for the **Teatro Marittimo**, or Maritime Theatre, a small colonnaded palace built by Hadrian on an island in an artificial lagoon. It is thought that this was the emperor's private retreat, the place to which he would retire for a siesta or to indulge his love of poetry, music and art.

Frascati

Frascati offers a cool, calm retreat from Rome's heat and hustle on hot summer days, providing a pleasant combination of good food, local wine and sweeping views of the city.

If you have time to spare, Frascati is the place to go. Trains depart from Termini approximately hourly and the journey takes about 30 minutes. You are treated to an ever-more attractive rural outlook as the train wends its way into the Colli Albani (Alban Hills), to the south of Rome. Steps from Frascati's small station lead through gardens to Piazzale (or Piazza) Marconi, the town's principal square, home to the visitor centre at No 1 (tel: 06 942 0331, www.aptprovroma. it). Above the square stands the **Villa Aldobrandini**, one of the few old buildings to survive the bombing during 1943 and 1944 that destroyed 80 per cent of old Frascati.

The villa was built for Cardinal Pietro Aldobrandini between 1598 and 1603 and is still owned by the Aldobrandini family. Though the villa itself is closed to the public, some of the grounds, which are noted for the excellent views over Rome in the hazy distance, can be visited. Look out for the gardens' Teatro dell'Acqua, a semicircular array of fountains and statues in which the central figure of Atlas is said to be a representation of Pietro Aldobrandini's uncle, Pope Clement VIII.

Frascati's other major public park is the less appealing **Villa Torlonia**, entered from close to the town hall building (the Municipio) near Piazzale Marconi. In the rest of the town, leave a short time for the rebuilt Duomo in Piazza San Pietro and the church of the Gesù (Piazza del Gesù), known for its late 17th-century paintings by Andrea dal Pozzo.

Detail of a statue seated on the terraces at Villa Aldobrandini

TAKING A BREAK

Cacciani (Via Armando Diaz 13, tel: 06 940 1991, closed Mon, also Sun pm in winter), which has an outdoor terrace for dining in summer, is the best restaurant in Frascati. For something simpler and less expensive, try **Zaraza** (Viale Regina Margherita 45, tel: 06 942 2053, closed Mon, also Sun pm Sep–May).

Villa Aldobrandini gardens
🕒 Apr–Sep Mon–Fri 9–1, 3–6; Oct–Mar 9–1, 3–5 💰 Free, though passes must be obtained from Visitor Centre at Piazza G. Marconi 1 (tel: 06 942 0331). Note that the Visitor Centre is closed Sat pm and all day Sun

Walks

1 GHETTO TO TRASTEVERE

This walk takes you to three of the city's smaller and prettier enclaves: the old Jewish Ghetto area, a lovely labyrinth of quiet streets; the Isola Tiberina, an island on the River Tiber; and the Trastevere district, an equally appealing but better-known collection of cobbled lanes, tiny squares, shops, cafés and restaurants.

DISTANCE 4.25km (2.6 miles) TIME Allow 3–4 hours START POINT Piazza del Campidoglio ✛ 199 E4
END POINT Campo dei Fiori ✛ 197 F2

1–2

Start in **Piazza del Campidoglio** (▶ 48–49) just off Piazza Venezia. With the church of Santa Maria in Aracoeli on your left, walk to the rear of the piazza and take the lane on the right of Palazzo Senatorio, the palace ahead of you. Follow the lane as it winds downhill, admiring the views of the **Foro Romano** (▶ 50–55) on your left. Turn right at the bottom on Via della Consolazione and cross Piazza della Consolazione. Bear left off the piazza down Via San Giovanni Decollato. At the end of this street on the left stands **San Giorgio in Velabro**. The church takes its name from the

Much of the Isola Tiberina is given over to a hospital

marshy area (the Velabro) by the Tiber where – according to legend – the shepherd Faustulus found Romulus and Remus, Rome's founding twins (▶ 7). The church's simple Romanesque interior – almost bare save for an apse fresco – is one of the city's finest. There are two ancient arches nearby: the one adjoining the church is **Arco degli Argentari** (Arch of the Moneychangers) erected in AD204 in honour of Emperor Septimius Severus; the other, in the short Via del Velabro in front of the church, is the **Arco di Giano**, and dates from the time of Constantine (fourth century).

2–3

Continue down Via del Velabro and Passaggio di San Giovanni Decollato, which open into the large **Piazza Bocca della Verità**. On the right, in an area of grass and trees, stand two almost perfectly preserved Roman temples: the circular Tempio di Vesta and rectangular Tempio della Fortuna Virilis (both second century BC). On the piazza's left (south) flank

stands the 12th-century church of **Santa Maria in Cosmedin**. In the portico, on the left side as you face the church, look for the round stone relief (an old Roman drain cover) known as the Bocca della Verità (Mouth of Truth). Legend claims that the mouth will clamp shut on the hands of dissemblers. The church, one of the few in the city to have escaped a baroque makeover, vies with San Clemente for the title of Rome's loveliest medieval interior.

3–4

From the area in front of the church walk northwest following the line of the Tiber on Lungotevere dei Pierleoni. Continue past Piazza Monte Savello on your right until Lungotevere dei Pierleoni becomes Lungotevere dei Cenci and you see Rome's distinctive **Sinagoga** (synagogue) ahead of you on the right. Turn right, before you pass the synagogue, on Via del Portico d'Ottavia. This takes you to the Portico d'Ottavia, a tiny fragment of a great Roman building begun in 146BC, now partly enmeshed in the eighth-century church of **Sant'Angelo in Pescheria**. Turn right (north) here on Via del Sant'Angelo in Pescheria and then left at the top of the street on Via dei Funari. This takes you to **Piazza Mattei** and the heart of Rome's old Jewish Ghetto, where Jews were segregated after 1556; the walls were torn down in 1848, but many Jewish families and businesses are still based in the area. Piazza Mattei is known for having one of the city's most charming fountains, the **Fontana delle Tartarughe**, or Fountain of the Tortoises, which was designed in 1581; it takes its name from the little bronze tortoises drinking from the fountain's upper basin.

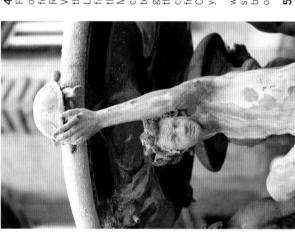

La **Fontana delle Tartarughe** in **Piazza Mattei**

4–5

From Piazza Mattei you should explore some of the surrounding side streets and piazzas for a flavour of the area. Then take Via della Reginella left (south) off the piazza, and at Via del Portico d'Ottavia turn right then left through Piazza delle Cinque Scole to rejoin Lungotevere dei Cenci. Turn left and then first right on the Ponte Fabricio which crosses the Tiber to the **Isola Tiberina** (Tiber Island). Much of the island is given over to a hospital, continuing a tradition begun in 291BC when a temple here was dedicated to Aesculapius, the god of healing. You can take the steps down to the river before looking into the 10th-century church of San Bartolomeo in the square in front of the piazza, before crossing the Ponte Cestio on the island's south side. This brings you to the **Trastevere district** (▶ 95–98).

Like the Ghetto, this is an area you may want to explore in more depth; this walk simply takes you through Trastevere's heart, but almost any random route through the web of streets is rewarding.

5–6

Beyond the Ponte Cestio cross the main, busy Lungotevere dell'Anguillara and continue

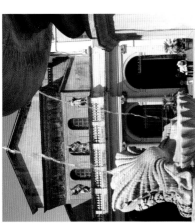

Santa Maria in Trastevere, noted for its facade

straight into Piazza in Piscinula. Go down the steps and turn right out of the piazza on Via della Lungaretta. Cross Piazza Sonnino-Viale di Trastevere and pick up the continuation of Via della Lungaretta and follow it to Piazza di Santa Maria in Trastevere and the church of **Santa Maria in Trastevere** (▲ 96). Walk out of the piazza to the right of the church

as you face it, then bear right at the rear of the church into Piazza Sant'Egidio. From the piazza follow Via della Scala until you reach Via Garibaldi. Turn right here on Via di San Dorotea, which leads to Piazza Trilussa, a small square almost on the Tiber. From here cross the Tiber on the pedestrians-only Ponte Sisto, turn left and then take the right fork into **Via Giulia**, which is framed by a pretty vine-draped archway.

6–7

Walk down Via Giulia, one of Rome's most elegant streets, noting the stone skulls decorating the facade of **Santa Maria dell'Orazione e Morte** (▲ 100) on the left at the junction with Via dei Farnesi. Via Giulia was laid out in 1508 for Pope Julius II (hence Giulia), providing what, at the time, was the city's main approach to St Peter's. In 1655 a major city prison was established at the present-day No 52.

Where Via Giulia opens out into a piazza, turn right onto Vicolo della Moretta, a short street that takes you to a junction of several more streets. If you have time, turn left here and walk a little way down Via dei Banchi Vecchi, which, like Via Giulia, is dotted with

interesting shops. Otherwise, turn right on Via del Pellegrino and then turn first right on Via dei Cappellari.

7–8

Via dei Cappellari is one of the most distinctive streets in this part of Rome, chiefly because it retains some traditional artisans' workshops, most of which are given over to furniture-making and restoration. It has a long history of artisanship, taking its name from the *cappellari*, or hatters, who were once based here. Other streets in the vicinity are named after similar trades (Via dei Baullari – the street of the trunk-makers; Via dei Chiavari – the street of the locksmiths; and Via dei Giubonnari – the street of the tailors). Continue down Via dei Cappellari, passing under the dark arch midway down and you emerge into **Campo dei Fiori** (▲ 80–81).

PLACE TO VISIT

Santa Maria in Cosmedin
✚ 199 E3 ⊠ Piazza della Bocca della Verità 18 ☎ 06 678 7759 ☺ Apr–Sep daily 9:30–6; Oct–Mar 9:30–5

2 PIAZZA VENEZIA TO PIAZZA NAVONA

This walk meanders through the heart of the medieval and Renaissance city, taking you to several key sights – notably the Fontana di Trevi (Trevi Fountain) – but also to a succession of lesser churches, streets and monuments that you might not otherwise discover on a tour of the area's major attractions.

DISTANCE 3km (1.9 miles) **TIME** Allow 2–3 hours **START POINT** Piazza Venezia ✚ 197 F3
END POINT Piazza Navona ✚ 199 E5

1–2

Start on the northern flank of **Piazza Venezia** (▲ 66) facing the Monumento a Vittorio Emanuele II. Walk out of the piazza to your left (east) along Via Cesare Battisti and turn left into Piazza dei SS Apostoli. On your right in the piazza stands the 15th-century Palazzo Colonna, home to the **Galleria Colonna**, an art gallery filled with first-rank paintings by mostly Italian masters. Alongside to the left lies the church of SS Apostoli. Behind a palace-like facade, the baroque interior is known for its huge altarpiece by Domenico Muratori, and Antonio Canova's 1789 Tomb of Clement XIV, in the north (left) aisle by the sacristy door. Continue to the end of Piazza dei SS Apostoli.

2–3

Turn right at the junction with Via del Vaccaro and first left on Via dell'Archetto. Cross Via dell'Umiltà and carry on down Via delle

The magnificent Fontana di Trevi floodlit at night

Vergini. Turn right on Via delle Muratte to emerge in the square containing the **Fontana di Trevi** (▲ 124–125). Take Via dei Crociferi from the piazza's northwest corner (to the rear left as you face the fountain) and continue straight on along Via dei Sabini to emerge on Via del Corso. Across the Corso to the right lies the open area of Piazza Colonna, named after the Colonna di Marco Aurelio at its heart. The column was raised between AD180 and 196 to celebrate the military victories of Marcus Aurelius in northern Europe. The sculpted reliefs portray episodes from the Emperor's campaigns.

3–4

Walk across Piazza Colonna and through either of the small streets off its western flank – Via della Colonna Antonina is the one on the left. Either one brings you to Piazza di Montecitorio, another large piazza, dominated by Bernini's 1650 Palazzo di Montecitorio, seat of the lower house of Italy's parliament,

the Camera dei Deputati. Take Via Uffici di Vicario west off the piazza, passing the historic Giolitti café on the left, then turn right up Via di Campo Marzio. Take the third left, Via dei Prefetti, and then turn right on Via della Lupa to emerge in **Piazza Borghese**, which takes its name from the Palazzo Borghese (closed to the public), the large palace across the street. This was the main city home of the Borghese, once one of the most powerful of Rome's leading families. Both Scipione and Paolina Borghese once lived here (➤ 128–129).

4–5

Bear left from the piazza along Via del Clementino and continue on through Piazza Nicosia and west along Via di Monte Brianzo (the river is on your right). Turn left off Via di Monte Brianzo on Via del Cancello, right on

Via dell'Orso, and then almost immediately left on Via Gigli d'Oro. You then emerge in Piazza di Sant'Apollinare with the **Palazzo Altemps** (➤ 86–89) on your right. To your left down an alley stands the church of **Sant'Agostino**

(▲ 100–101), known for Caravaggio's painting, *Madonna di Loreto* in the first chapel in the left aisle (▲ 25), Raphael's fresco, *The Prophet Isaiah* (third pillar on the left), and Jacopo Sansovino's statue, the *Madonna del Parto* (1521), venerated by expectant mothers.

5–6

Return to Piazza di Sant'Apollinare and walk south to the adjoining Piazza Cinque Lune and into **Piazza Navona** (▲ 82–85). Take Via di Sant'Agnese in Agone (which becomes Via di Tor Millina) midway down the piazza on its west side. You might pause for a drink at **Bar della Pace** (▲ 108) on the corner of Via della Pace. As you face the bar, a short distance away to its right stands **Santa Maria della Pace**, a charming (if rarely open) church begun in 1482. It contains frescoes of the Sibyls by Raphael and a cloister added in 1504 by Bramante, one of the architects of St Peter's. Return to the bar and turn right down Via della Pace and then straight on down Vicolo delle Vacche and Via della Vetrina. Turn left on **Via dei Coronari**, renowned for its antiques shops. At the end of the street continue straight down the short Vicolo del Curato to emerge on Via

del Banco di Santo Spirito. You may wish to turn right here to look at the **Ponte Sant'Angelo** and **Castel Sant'Angelo** (▲ 164–165).

6–7

If not, turn left and then first left on Via dei Banchi Nuovi. This leads eventually to **Piazza dell'Orologio**, named after the delightful clock tower or Torre dell'Orologio on the building on the piazza's far right. This forms part of the **Palazzo and Oratorio dei Filippini**, a complex largely rebuilt by Francesco Borromini after 1637. For a closer look at the Oratorio's facade, turn right (south) off the piazza down Via dei Filippini. You emerge on the busy Corso Vittorio Emanuele II in front of the 16th-century **Chiesa Nuova** ("New Church"); the Oratorio is squeezed between the palace on the left and the church facade on the right. Look inside the Chiesa Nuova to admire Pietro da Cortona's frescoes and the decoration (1664) of the vault, apse and dome, and three paintings by Peter Paul Rubens (1608) in the presbytery around the high altar. Return to Piazza dell'Orologio and turn right to follow Via del Governo Vecchio – a more interesting walk than Corso Vittorio Emanuele II – to Piazza di Pasquino and back to Piazza Navona.

TAKING A BREAK

Try the trendy, ever-popular Bar della Pace (▲ 108) or the equally hip, but quieter Bar del Fico (▲ 111). Alternatively, there are plenty of cafés from which to choose in Piazza Navona.

PLACES TO VISIT

Galleria Colonna
➕ 200 A5 ⊠ Via della Pilotta 17 ☎ 06 678 4350 ◉ Sat 9–1, or by request 💷 Expensive

Sant'Agostino
➕ 194 A1 ⊠ Piazza di Sant'Agostino ☎ 06 6880 1962 ◉ Daily 7:30–12:30, 4–6:30

Santa Maria della Pace
➕ 197 F3 ⊠ Vicolo dell'Arco della Pace 5 ☎ 06 686 1156 ◉ Mon, Wed, Sat 9–12

Chiesa Nuova
➕ 197 E3 ⊠ Piazza della Chiesa Nuova ☎ 06 687 5289 ◉ Daily 7:30–12, 4 or 4:30–7

3 PIAZZA DI SPAGNA TO PIAZZA DEL POPOLO

This short walk offers memorable views over the city from above Piazza di Spagna and concludes in Piazza del Popolo, the northernmost square of the "old" Rome. It also gives you the chance to explore the Giardino del Pincio (Pincio Gardens), on the fringes of the Villa Borghese, the city's principal park. The walk can easily be extended to take in the park.

DISTANCE 1.25km (0.75 miles) **TIME** Allow 1–2 hours **START POINT** Piazza di Spagna ⊞ 194 C3
END POINT Piazza del Popolo ⊞ 194 A3

1–2

Start in Piazza di Spagna (▶ 126–127), allowing time to look at the shops here and in the surrounding streets. Admire the **Fontana della Barcaccia** at the foot of the Spanish Steps; decide if you wish to visit the **Keats-Shelley Museum** to the right of the steps as you face them (▶ 134). Climb to the top of the Spanish Steps. Turn to admire the view over the piazza below and spend a few moments inside the church of **Trinità dei Monti** at the top of the steps. It is best known for its frescoed chapels and for two faded 16th-century paintings by Daniele da Volterra. The obelisk

in front of the church was raised here in 1788, but was brought to Rome in the second or third century AD, when its hieroglyphics were carved in emulation of those on a similar obelisk in Piazza del Popolo.

2–3

From the piazza in front of Trinità dei Monti turn left as you face the church. This takes you into **Viale Trinità dei Monti**, a street that hugs the side of the hill and offers fine views over the city's rooftops toward the dome of St Peter's in the middle distance. After the street kinks slightly to the left, you pass the **Villa Medici** on your right, bought by Napoleon in 1801 and home to the French Academy since 1803. It was built in about 1540 for a Tuscan cardinal, and purchased in 1576 by Ferdinando de' Medici, a member of the famous Florentine family. Much of the family's sculpture collection was kept here before being returned to Florence. The scientist Galileo was a famous if reluctant occupant

Carved stone head in the Villa Medici gardens

of the villa, having been kept here by the Inquisition between 1630 and 1633. The villa is open only rarely, but hosts occasional exhibitions. The magnificent gardens are open daily throughout the year and are well worth seeing (tel: 06 67 611, www.villamedici.it).

3–4

Viale Trinità dei Monti ends at the junction with Viale Mickiewicz (or Viale Mickev) and Viale Gabriele d'Annunzio. Turn right on the

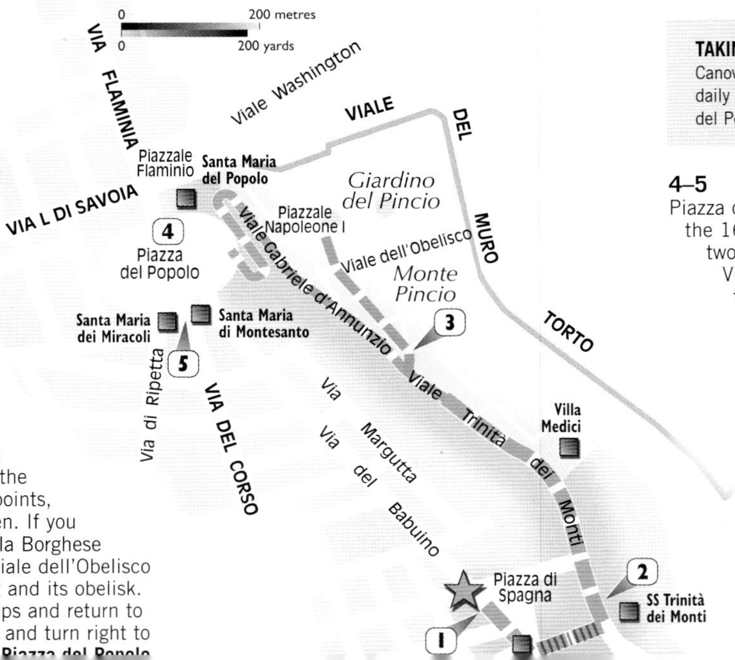

TAKING A BREAK

Canova (Piazza del Popolo 16, tel: 06 361 2231, daily 7:30am–10:30pm or later), in the Piazza del Popolo, is a lively place for a drink.

4–5

Piazza del Popolo's appearance dates from the 16th century, but long before that two Roman roads, the Via Cassia and Via Flaminia, entered the city here, following the line of the present Via del Corso to the Capitoline Hill and Roman and Imperial fora (▶ 48–49, 50–55, 68–69). Today, the square is dominated by the obelisk of Pharaoh Rameses II, brought from Egypt by Emperor Augustus. On the square's northern flank stands Santa Maria del Popolo (▶ 103–104), while on its southern edge rise the 17th-century churches of Santa Maria dei Miracoli and Santa Maria di Montesanto. From here you can return to central Rome either down Via del Corso or Via di Ripetta, if you want to visit Ara Pacis (▶ 102).

former to climb to the **Pincio**, gardens laid out between 1809 and 1814 on the Pincian Hill. The area has a long history as an open space, having formed ancient Rome's Collis Hortulorum, a series of gardens belonging to the emperors and several of the city's aristocratic families. Turn left where the Viale doglegs right to become Viale Belvedere and make for Piazzale Napoleone I, the best of several good viewpoints, before exploring the garden. If you wish to push on to the Villa Borghese for a longer walk, follow Viale dell'Obelisco east from Piazza Bucarest and return to Piazzale Napoleone I. Otherwise retrace your steps and return to Viale Gabriele d'Annunzio and turn right to follow this street down to **Piazza del Popolo.**

Practicalities

BEFORE YOU GO

WHAT YOU NEED

		UK	Germany	USA	Canada	Australia	Ireland	Netherlands	Spain
● Required	Some countries require a passport to remain valid for a minimum period (usually at least six months) beyond the date of entry – check before you travel.								
○ Suggested									
▲ Not required									
△ Not applicable									
Passport		●	●	●	●	●	●	●	●
Visa (regulations can change – check before you travel)		▲	▲	▲	▲	▲	▲	▲	▲
Onward or Return Ticket		○	○	●	●	●	●	○	○
Health Inoculations		▲	▲	▲	▲	▲	▲	▲	▲
Health Documentation (► 190)		▲	▲	▲	▲	▲	▲	▲	▲
Travel Insurance		○	○	○	○	○	○	○	○
Driver's Licence (national)		●	●	●	●	●	●	●	●
Car Insurance Certificate		●	●	●	●	●	●	●	●
Car Registration Document		●	●	●	●	●	●	●	●

WHEN TO GO

High season ▭   Low season ▭

JAN	FEB	MAR	APR	MAY	JUN	JUL	AUG	SEP	OCT	NOV	DEC
7°C	8°C	12°C	14°C	18°C	25°C	28°C	32°C	23°C	18°C	13°C	9°C
45°C	46°F	54°F	57°F	64°F	77°F	82°F	90°F	73°F	64°F	55°F	48°F

☼ Sun   ⛅ Sunshine and showers   🌧 Wet   ☁ Cloud

Temperatures are the **average daily maximum** for each month. Average daily minimum temperatures are approximately 6 to 10°C (10–18°F) lower. Temperatures of over 35°C (95°F) are likely in July and August, making the city extremely hot and uncomfortable. Consequently, August is low season because many businesses and sights close to allow the locals to leave the city for cooler areas.

The best times of the year for good weather are May, June, July, August and September. Thunderstorms are possible in summer and through September and October. Winters (January and February) are short and cold, but snow is extremely rare. Spring starts in March, but March and April can be humid and sometimes very rainy. Autumn weather is mixed, but often produces crisp or warm days with clear skies.

GETTING ADVANCE INFORMATION

Websites
- Official tourism board of the City of Rome: www.romaturismo.it
- www.060608.it

- Museum online reservations: www.ticketeria.it
- Official Vatican site for all aspects of the Holy See: www.vatican.va

In Italy
The website (www.060608. it) has replaced the main tourist office in Italy

GETTING THERE

By Air Rome has two main airports: Leonardo da Vinci (better known as Fiumicino) and Ciampino. Most UK and other European and international carriers fly to Fiumicino. Low-cost and charter airlines usually fly to Ciampino. There are many non-stop flights to Rome from London (Heathrow, Gatwick and Stansted) as well as regional airports in the UK, most major European cities and many US and Canadian cities. Flights from Melbourne and Sydney make one stop, usually in Bangkok; from other cities in Australia and New Zealand, the best connections are in Hong Kong or Singapore.

Ticket prices tend to be highest at Easter, Christmas and in summer. Best prices are obtained the further you reserve in advance but check airlines, travel agents, newspapers and the internet for special offers. Non-direct flights via hub airports such as Heathrow or Frankfurt may offer substantial savings. Short stays are generally expensive unless a Saturday night stay is included. City-break packages include flights and accommodation.

Airport taxes are included in ticket prices and no fee is payable at either Rome airport.

Approximate flying times to Rome: New Zealand (24 hours), east coast of Australia (21 hours), western US (11 hours), eastern US and Canada (8–10 hours); London (2 hours), Frankfurt (1 hour).

By Rail Ticket prices are usually the same or more than equivalent air fares. Numerous fast and overnight services operate to Rome from most European capitals, with connections from major towns. Rome has several stations, but most international services stop at Stazione Termini or Roma Tiburtina.

TIME

Rome is one hour ahead of GMT in winter, one hour ahead of BST in summer, six hours ahead of New York and nine hours ahead of Los Angeles. Clocks are advanced one hour in March and turned back one hour in October.

CURRENCY AND FOREIGN EXCHANGE

Currency Italy is one of the majority of European Union countries to use a single currency, the euro (€). Coins are issued in denominations of 1, 2, 5, 10, 20 and 50 cents and €1 and €2. Notes are issued in denominations of €5, €10, €20, €50, €100, €200 and €500.

Exchange Most major **travellers' cheques** – the best way to carry money – can be changed at exchange kiosks *(cambio)* at the airports, at Termini railway station and in exchange offices near major tourist sights. Many banks also have exchange desks.

Credit cards Most credit cards *(carta di credito)* are accepted in larger hotels, restaurants and shops, but cash is often preferred in smaller establishments. Credit cards can also be used to obtain cash from ATM cash dispensers, although this can be expensive – most credit cards charge a fee for this. Contact your card issuer before you leave home to find out which machines in Rome accept your card and confirm the dates you will be in Italy. Failure to do this may mean your credit card is refused.

In the UK
ENIT
1 Princes Street
London W1R 8AY
☎ 020 7408 1254

In the US
ENIT
630 Fifth Avenue
Suite 1565
New York NY 10111
☎ 212/245 5618

In Australia
Italian Consulate
Level 24,
44 Market Square
Sydney NSW 2000
☎ (02) 9262 1677

WHEN YOU ARE THERE

NATIONAL HOLIDAYS

1 Jan	New Year's Day
6 Jan	Epiphany
Mar/Apr	Easter Monday
25 Apr	Liberation Day
1 May	Labour Day
29 Jun	St Peter and St Paul Day
15 Aug	Assumption of the Virgin
1 Nov	All Saints' Day
8 Dec	Feast of the Immaculate Conception
25 Dec	Christmas Day
26 Dec	St Stephen's Day

ELECTRICITY

Current is 220 volts AC, 50 cycles. Plugs are two-round-pin continental types; UK and North American visitors will require an adaptor. North American visitors should check whether 110/120-volt AC appliances require a voltage transformer.

OPENING HOURS

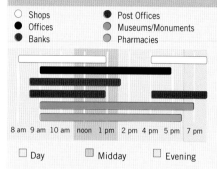

○ Shops
● Offices
◐ Banks
● Post Offices
◑ Museums/Monuments
◔ Pharmacies

8 am 9 am 10 am noon 1 pm 2 pm 4 pm 5 pm 7 pm

☐ Day   ☐ Midday   ☐ Evening

Shops Usually Tue–Sat 8–1, 4–8, Mon 4–8.
Restaurants Usually 12:30–3, 7:30–10:30; many close Sun evening and Mon lunchtime.
Museums Hours vary: usually Tue–Sat 9–7, Sun 9–1.
Churches Daily 7–12, 4:30–7pm; closed during services.
Banks Major branches open weekdays and also Sat.
Post offices Usually Mon–Fri 8:15–2, Sat 8:15–12 or 2pm.

TIPS/GRATUITIES

Tipping is not expected for all services and rates are lower than those elsewhere. As a general guide:

Pizzerias	Nearest €
Trattorias	€1–€3
Smart restaurant	10 per cent or discretion
Bar service	€0.10–€0.25
Tour guides	Discretion
Taxis	Round up to nearest €0.50
Porters	€0.50–€1 per bag
Chambermaids	€0.50–€1 a day

ROMAN QUEUES

Roman queues seem chaotic, but queue-jumpers will not be tolerated by the locals, so when standing in line in bars and restaurants, shops and when using public transport, it's a case of drawing a fine line between surging forward and giving as good as you get, or hanging back and getting nowhere.

TIME DIFFERENCES

GMT	Rome	USA New York	Germany	Rest of Italy	Australia Sydney
12 noon	1pm	7am	1pm	1pm	10pm

STAYING IN TOUCH

Post Rome's central post office
(*ufficio postale*) is at Piazza
San Silvestro 18–20. Stamps
(*francobolli*) are bought from
post offices and bars. Mail
boxes are red (slots for city mail
and other destinations), or blue
for the more efficient *posta
prioritaria* (priority post).

Public telephones Telecom Italia (TI) payphones are on
streets and in bars, tobacconists and restaurants. Most
take coins or a phone card (*una scheda telefonica*),
bought from post offices, shops or bars. Tear the
corner off the card before use.

To dial numbers in Rome while there, dial the 06 code
then the number. Cheap rate is Mon–Sat 10pm–8am.
Hotels usually add a surcharge to calls from rooms.
Dial 170 to make reverse
charge calls. Dial 12 for
operator or directory enquiries.

International Dialling Codes
Dial 00 followed by

UK:	44
USA / Canada:	1
Irish Republic:	353
Australia:	61
Germany:	49

Mobile providers and services in the UK, Australia
and NZ mobiles work in Italy, but not the US. The
main providers are Tim (www.tim.it), Vodafone (www.
vodafone.it) and Wind (www.wind.it); all have outlets
throughout Rome, but check call rates with your
provider before travelling.

WiFi and internet Much of Rome is covered by wireless
hot spots sponsored by the city council. Once you
open your browser you'll need to register, using your
mobile phone number, then log on; access is free
(www.romawireless.com). In addition, many hotels
have built-in dataports, and even budget places will
allow you to plug into their phone systems. Download
speeds are excellent. There are numerous internet
cafés; try EasyEverything (Via Barberini 2, 8am–2am
daily, €2 per hour, 250 terminals).

PERSONAL SAFETY

Rome is generally safe and
mugging is rare. However,
pickpocketing is rife in the
main tourist areas, so take
precautions:

- Carry money and valuables
  with care. Men should
  never put wallets in back
  pockets, and women
  should wear bags across
  their bodies, and keep a
  hand on top in crowded
  buses.
- Keep cameras looped
  around your wrist or on a
  strap across your body.
- Keep bags and cameras
  away from the kerb to foil
  motorcycle theft.
- Take particular care
  of children working as
  thieves, who will often try
  to distract your attention;
  they work in pairs.
- At night avoid parks and
  the streets around Termini,
  Trastevere and the Campo
  dei Fiori.
- If you are a victim of crime,
  you must make a *denuncia*
  (statement), and obtain a
  copy, at a police station
  in order to claim on your
  insurance.

Police assistance:
☎ 112 from any phone

POLICE 112 OR 113

FIRE 115

AMBULANCE 118

HEALTH

 Insurance Citizens of EU countries receive free or reduced-cost emergency medical treatment with relevant documentation (European Health Insurance Card), but private medical insurance is still advised and essential for all other visitors.

 Doctors Ask at your hotel for details of English-speaking doctors.
Dental Services Travel insurance should cover dental treatment, which is expensive.

 Weather Minor health worries include too much sun, dehydration or mosquito bites: drink plenty of fluids, and wear sunscreen and a hat in summer. Insect repellent may be useful if you have to sleep in rooms with windows open in summer.

 Drugs Prescription and other medicines are available from a pharmacy *(una farmacia)*, indicated by a green cross. Opening hours are usually Mon–Sat 8:30–1 and 4–8, but a rota system ensures that some are always open. Two 24-hour pharmacies are: Piram (Via Nazionale 228, tel: 06 488 0754); Farmacia della Stazione (Piazza dei Cinquecento-corner Via Cavour, tel: 06 488 0019).

 Safe Water Tap water is safe. So, too, is water from public drinking fountains unless marked "*Acqua Non Potabile*".

CONCESSIONS

Young People/Senior Citizens Young visitors and students aged under 18 from EU countries are entitled to free entrance or reduced rates to most galleries. Similar concessions are available to senior citizens over 65. A passport will be required as proof of age.
Roma Pass This 3-day pass gives entrance to two museums or archaeological sites, reductions on museum entries, travel on public transport, a city map and discounts on music, theatre and entertainment tickets, and tours. It costs €25; available from Tourist Information Points (► 30) and at www.romapass.it.

TRAVELLING WITH A DISABILITY

Rome is a difficult city for those with disabilities, especially if you use a wheelchair. Streets are narrow, busy, often cobbled and usually filled with badly parked cars. There are few pavements or dropped kerbs. Transport, museums, hotels and other public spaces are improving, but much remains to be done.
For information, contact the Consorzio Cooperative Integrate (CO.IN), Via Enrico Giglioli 54a, tel: 06 712 7001, www.coinsociale.it or the "COINtel" information service, tel: 800 271 027 (toll free).

CHILDREN

Most hotels, restaurants and bars welcome children, but few have baby-changing facilities. Be extremely careful on Rome's busy streets.

TOILETS

Best facilities are in hotels and museums; Rome has few public toilets. Bars usually have toilets. Ask for *il bagno* or *il gabinetto*.

LOST PROPERTY

Airport 06 6595 3343
Buses 06 581 6040
Metro 06 487 4309 (Line A); 06 5753 2264/5 (Line B)

EMBASSIES AND HIGH COMMISSIONS

UK	USA	Ireland	Australia	New Zealand
☎ 06 4220 0001	☎ 06 46 741	☎ 06 697 9121	☎ 06 852 721	☎ 06 441 7171

SURVIVAL PHRASES

yes/no **sì/non**
please **per favore**
thank you **grazie**
You're welcome **Di niente/prego**
I'm sorry **Mi dispiace**
Goodbye **Arrivederci**
Good morning **Buongiorno**
Goodnight **Buona sera**
How are you? **Come sta?**
How much? **Quanto costa?**
I would like... **Vorrei...**
open **aperto**
closed **chiuso**
today **oggi**
tomorrow **domani**
Monday **lunedì**
Tuesday **martedì**
Wednesday **mercoledì**
Thursday **giovedì**
Friday **venerdì**
Saturday **sabato**
Sunday **domenica**

DIRECTIONS

I'm lost **Mi sono perso/a**
Where is...? **Dove si trova...?**
  the station **la stazione**
  the telephone **il telefono**
  the bank **la banca**
  the toilet **il bagno**
Turn left **Volti a sinistra**
Turn right **Volti a destra**
Go straight on **Vada dritto**
At the corner **All'angolo**
the street **la strada**
the building **il edificio**
the traffic light **il semaforo**
the crossroads **l'incrocio**
the signs for... **le indicazione per...**

IF YOU NEED HELP

Help! **Aiuto!**
Could you help me, please? **Mi potrebbe aiutare?**
Do you speak English? **Parla inglese?**
I don't understand **Non capisco**
Please could you call a doctor quickly? **Mi chiami presto un medico, per favore**

RESTAURANT

I'd like to book a table **Vorrei prenotare un tavolo**
A table for two please **Un tavolo per due, per favore**
Could we see the menu, please? **Ci porta la lista, per favore?**
What's this? **Cosa è questo?**
A bottle of/a glass of... **Un bottiglia di/un bicchiere di...**
Could I have the bill? **Ci porta il conto**

ACCOMMODATION

Do you have a single/double room? **Ha una camera singola/doppia?**
with/without bath/toilet/shower **con/senza vasca/gabinetto/doccia**
Does that include breakfast? **E'inclusa la prima colazione?**
Does that include dinner? **E'inclusa la cena?**
Do you have room service? **C'è il servizio in camera?**
Could I see the room? **E' possibile vedere la camera?**
I'll take this room **Prendo questa**
Thanks for your hospitality **Grazie per l'ospitalità**

NUMBERS

0	**zero**	12	**dodici**	40	**quaranta**	400	**quattrocento**
1	**uno**	13	**tredici**	50	**cinquanta**	500	**cinquecento**
2	**due**	14	**quattordici**	60	**sessanta**	600	**seicento**
3	**tre**	15	**quindici**	70	**settanta**	700	**settecento**
4	**quattro**	16	**sedici**	80	**ottanta**	800	**ottocento**
5	**cinque**	17	**diciassette**	90	**novanta**	900	**novecento**
6	**sei**	18	**diciotto**	100	**cento**	1000	**mille**
7	**sette**	19	**diciannove**	101	**cento uno**	2000	**duemila**
8	**otto**	20	**venti**	110	**centodieci**	10,000	**diecimila**
9	**nove**	21	**ventuno**	120	**centoventi**		
10	**dieci**	22	**ventidue**	200	**duecento**		
11	**undici**	30	**trenta**	300	**trecento**		

MENU READER

acciuga anchovy
acqua water
affettati sliced
  cured meats
affumicato
  smoked
aglio garlic
agnello lamb
anatra duck
antipasti hors
  d'oeuvres
arista roast pork
arrosto roast
asparagi
  asparagus
birra beer
bistecca steak
bollito boiled meat
braciola minute
  steak
brasato braised
brodo broth
bruschetta toasted
  bread with garlic or
  tomato topping
budino pudding
burro butter
cacciagione game
cacciatora, alla
  rich tomato sauce
  with mushrooms
caffè corretto/
  macchiato coffee
  with liqueur/spirit,
  or with a drop of
  milk
caffè freddo iced
  coffee
caffè lungo weak
  coffee
caffè latte milky
  coffee
caffè ristretto
  strong coffee
calamaro squid
cappero caper
carciofo artichoke
carota carrot
carne meat
carpa carp

casalingho home-
  made
cassata Sicilian
  fruit ice cream
cavolfiore
  cauliflower
cavolo cabbage
ceci chickpeas
cervello brains
cervo venison
cetriolino gherkin
cetriolo cucumber
cicoria chicory
cinghiale boar
cioccolata
  chocolate
cipolla onion
coda di bue oxtail
coniglio rabbit
contorni vegetables
coperto cover
  charge
cornetto croissant
coscia leg of meat
cotolette cutlets
cozze mussels
crema custard
crostini canapé
  with savoury
  toppings or
  croutons
crudo raw
digestivo after-
  dinner liqueur
dolci cakes/
  desserts
erbe aromatiche
  herbs
fagioli beans
fagiolini green
  beans
faraona guinea fowl
farcito stuffed
fegato liver
finocchio fennel
formaggio cheese
forno, al baked
frittata omelette
fritto fried
frizzante fizzy

frulatto whisked
frutti di mare
  seafood
frutta fruit
funghi mushrooms
gamberetto shrimp
gelato ice cream
ghiaccio ice
gnocchi potato
  dumplings
granchio crab
gran(o)turco corn
griglia, alla grilled
imbottito stuffed
insalata salad
IVA VAT
latte milk
lepre hare
lumache snails
manzo beef
merluzzo cod
miele honey
minestra soup
molluschi shellfish
olio oil
oliva olive
ostrica oyster
pancetta bacon
pane bread
panna cream
parmigiano
  Parmesan
passata sieved or
  creamed
pastasciutta dried
  pasta
pasta sfoglia puff
  pastry
patate fritte chips
pecora mutton
pecorino sheep's
  milk cheese
peperoncino chilli
peperone red/
  green pepper
pesce fish
petto breast
piccione pigeon
piselli peas
pollame fowl

pollo chicken
polpetta meatball
porto port wine
prezzemolo parsley
primo piatto first
  course
prosciutto cured
  ham
ragù meat sauce
ripieno stuffed
riso rice
salsa sauce
salsiccia sausage
saltimbocca veal
  with prosciutto and
  sage
secco dry
secondo piatto
  main course
senape mustard
servizio compreso
  service charge
  included
sogliola sole
spuntini snacks
succo di frutta
  fruit juice
sugo sauce
tonno tuna
uova strapazzate
  scambled egg
uovo affogato/in
  carnica poached
  egg
uovo al tegamo/
  fritto fried egg
uovo alla coque
  soft-boiled egg
uovo alla sodo
  hard-boiled egg
vino bianco white
  wine
vino rosso red wine
vino rosato rosé
  wine
verdure vegetables
vitello veal
zucchero sugar
zucchino courgette
zuppa soup

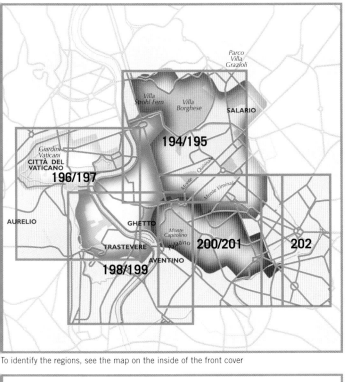

Parco
Villa
Grazioli

Villa
Strohl Fern

Villa
Borghese

SALARIO

194/195

Giardini
Vaticani
**CITTÀ DEL
VATICANO**

196/197

Monte Quirinale

Monte Viminale

AURELIO

GHETTO

Monte
Capitolino

200/201

202

TRASTEVERE

Palatino

AVENTINO

198/199

To identify the regions, see the map on the inside of the front cover

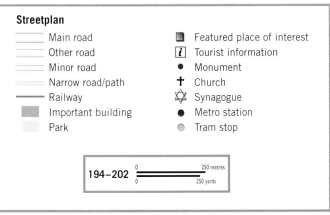

Streetplan

Main road	🔲 Featured place of interest
Other road	ℹ️ Tourist information
Minor road	● Monument
Narrow road/path	✝ Church
Railway	✡ Synagogue
Important building	● Metro station
Park	◎ Tram stop

194–202
0 — 250 metres
0 — 250 yards

Streetplan

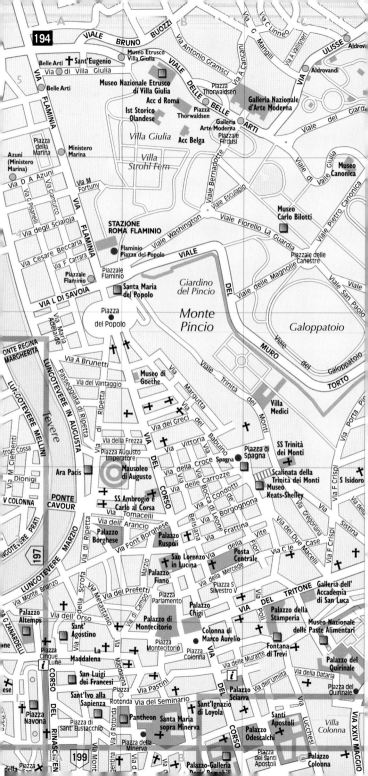

VIALE BRUNO BUOZZI

Via Antonio Gramsci

Via C Linneo

Via A Cancani

Via A Vallisneri

VIALE ULISSE

Aldrov

VIA

Aldrovandi

Museo Etrusco
Villa Giulia

Belle Arti · Sant'Eugenio

Via di Villa Giulia

VIALE DELLE BELLE

Museo Nazionale Etrusco
di Villa Giulia

Acc d Roma

Piazza
Thorwaldsen

Galleria Nazionale
d'Arte Moderna

Belle Arti

Ist Storico
Olandese

Piazza
Thorwaldsen

ARTI

Viale del Giard

FLAMINIA

Villa Giulia

Galleria
Arte Moderna

Acc Belga

Piazzale
Firdusi

Museo
Canonica

Piazza
della Marina

Ministero
Marina

Villa
Strohl Fern

Viale di Villa Giulia

Via D A Azuni

Via M
Fortuny

Viale Bernadotte

Museo
Carlo Bilotti

Azuni
(Ministero
Marina)

Via C Pianelli

Via degli Scialoja

Via Cesare Beccaria

Via F Carrara

STAZIONE
ROMA FLAMINIO

Viale Esculapio

Via Pietro Canonica

Viale Fiorello La Guardia

Piazzale delle
Canestre

FLAMINIA

Flaminio
Piazza del Popolo

Viale Washington

VIALE

Piazzale delle
Magnolie

Viale San Paolo

Piazzale
Flaminio

Santa Maria
del Popolo

Giardino
del Pincio

DEL

Viale delle Magnolie

VIA L DI SAVOIA

Via Maria Adelaide

Piazza
del Popolo

Monte
Pincio

Galoppatoio

MURO

Galoppatoio

ONTE REGINA
MARGHERITA

Via A Brunetti

Viale Trinità

TORTO

LUNGOTEVERE IN AUGUSTA

Passeggiata di Ripetta

Museo di
Goethe

Via Margutta

dei

Viale

del

Villa
Medici

Tevere

Via di Ripetta

Via del Vantaggio

Via della Frezza

Via dei Greci

Via del Babuino

Monti

Via Clementino

SS Trinità
dei Monti

Via M Cossa

Via Augusto
Imperatore

Vittoria

Piazza di
Spagna

Via F Crispi

S Isidoro

Ara Pacis

Mausoleo
di Augusto

Via della Croce

Piazza di
Spagna

Scalinata della
Trinità dei Monti
Museo
Keats-Shelley

V COLONNA

PONTE
CAVOUR

SS Ambrogio e
Carlo al Corso

Via delle Carrozze

Via della Mercede

Via delle Muratte

Via Crespicina

Sistina

Via dei Due Case

Via F Crispi

NCOTEVERE PRATI

LUNGOTEVERE MARZIO

Via di Ripetta

Via dell' Arancio

Via
Tomacelli

Via della Bocca di Leone

Via Bongognona

Via Frattina

Via delle Vite

Via della Fontanella di Borghese

Via del Corso

Galleria dell'
Accademia
di San Luca

Via Monte Branzio

Palazzo
Borghese

Palazzo
Ruspoli

San Lorenzo
in Lucina

Posta
Centrale

Via Fior

DEL TRITONE

Palazzo della
Stamperia

Museo Nazionale
delle Paste Alimentari

Palazzo
Altemps

Via dell' Orso

Palazzo
Fiano

Piazza
Parlamento

Piazza S
Silvestro V

VIA

DEL

Via Poli

Fontana
di Trevi

Palazzo del
Quirinale

C ZANARDELLI

Sant'
Agostino

La
Maddalena

Via del Prefetti

Via dei Metastasio

Palazzo di
Montecitorio

Palazzo
Chigi

Colonna di
Marco Aurelio

Palazzo
Colonna

Via della Dataria

Piazza del
Quirinale

Piazza
Cinque
Lune

San-Luigi
dei Francesi

Via della Maddalena

Via del Seminario

Piazza
Montecitorio

Piazza
Colonna

Via dell'Umiltà

Palazzo
Sciarra

Piazza
Navona

Sant'Ivo alla
Sapienza

Piazza
Rotonda

Pantheon

Sant'Ignazio
di Loyola

CORSO

Santi
Apostoli

Villa
Colonna

Piazza di
Sant'Eustacchio

Santa Maria
sopra Minerva

Palazzo
Odescalchi

VIA XXIV MAGGIO

RINASCIMEN

Piazza della
Minerva

CORSO

DEL

Piazza
dei Santi
Apostoli

Palazzo
Colonna

della

Piazza

Palazzo-Galleria

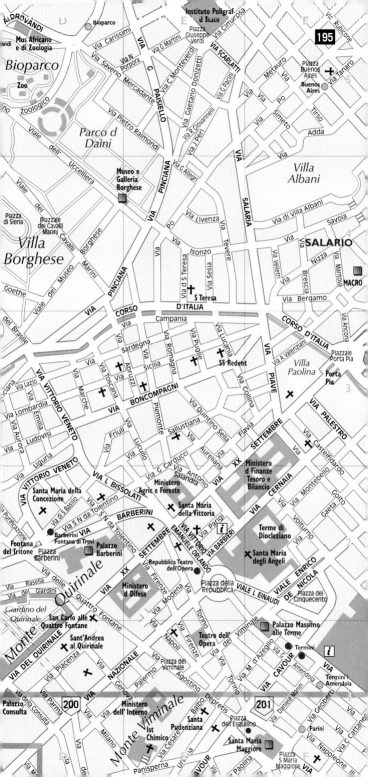

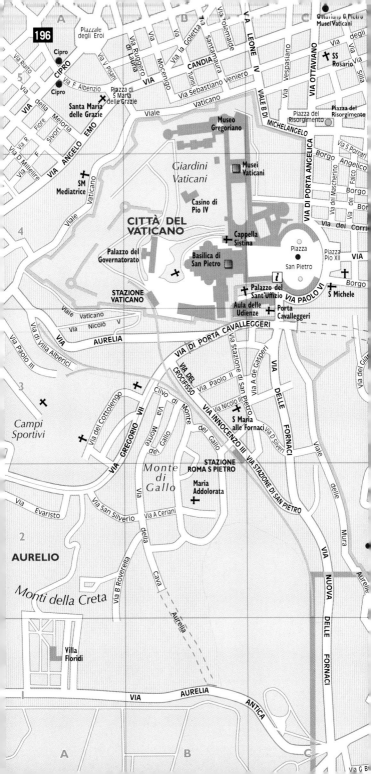

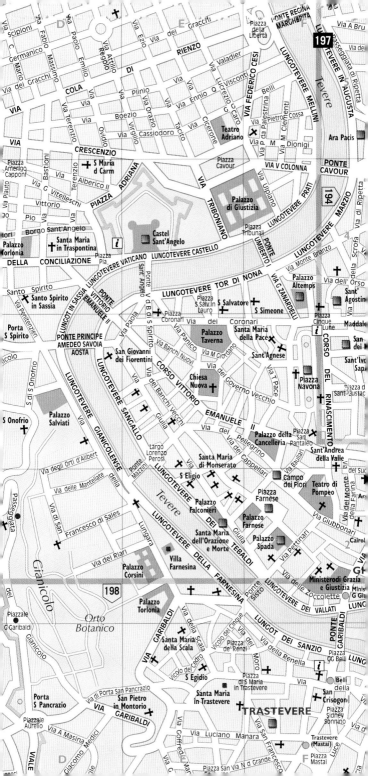

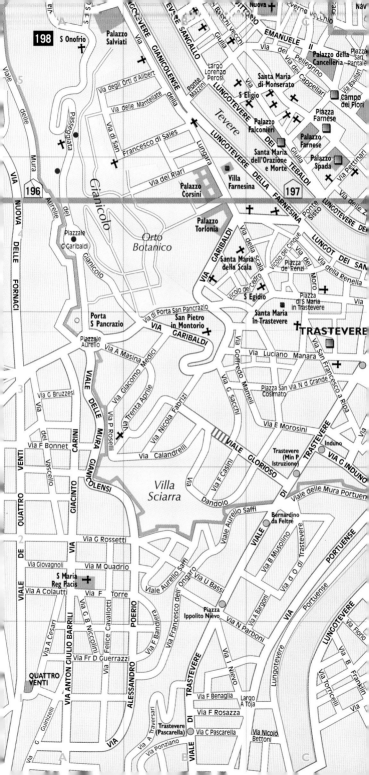

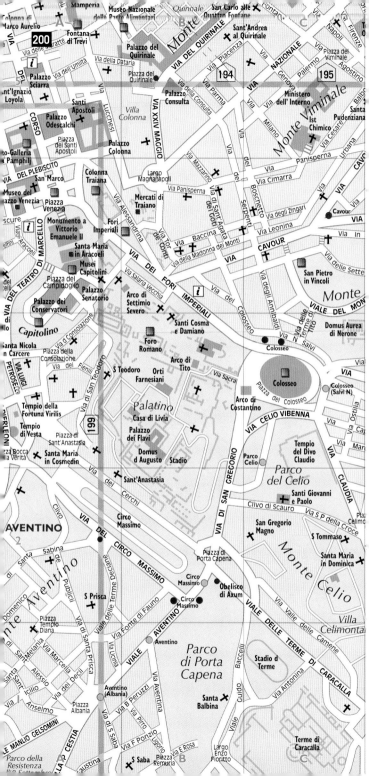

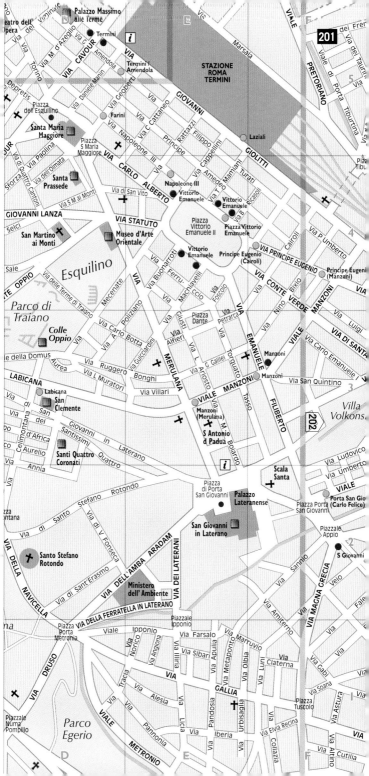

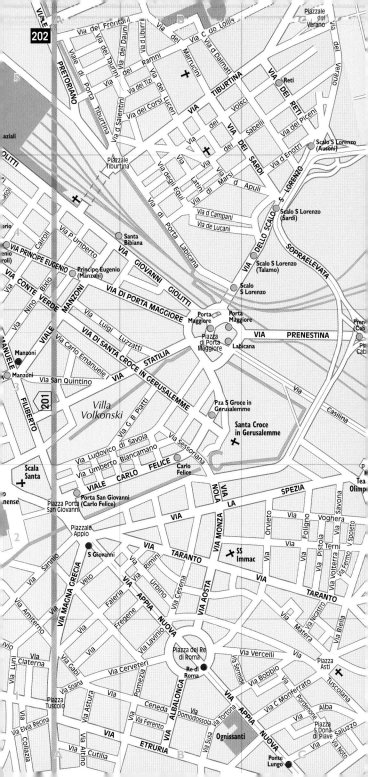

Rome

The Automobile Association wishes to thank the following photographers and libraries for their assistance with the preparation of this book.

Abbreviations for the picture credits are as follows – (t) top; (b) bottom; (c) centre; (l) left; (r) right; (AA) AA World Travel Library.

2t AA/Mockford & Bonetti; 2ct AA/Mockford & Bonetti; 2cb AA/S McBride; 2b AA/S McBride; 3t AA/Mockford & Bonetti; 3ct AA/Mockford & Bonetti; 3cb AA/Mockford & Bonetti; 3b AA/Mockford & Bonetti; 5l AA/Mockford & Bonetti; 5c AA/Mockford & Bonetti; 5r AA/Mockford & Bonetti; 6/7 AA/Mockford & Bonetti; 8 AA/J Holmes; 10 AA/Mockford & Bonetti; 11 AA/Mockford & Bonetti; 12 AA/T Souter; 13 AA/Mockford & Bonetti; 14 AA/Mockford & Bonetti; 15 AA/Mockford & Bonetti; 16 AA/C Sawyer; 17 AA/P Wilson; 18 AA/Mockford & Bonetti; 19l AA/S McBride; 19c AA/Mockford & Bonetti; 19r AA/P Wilson; 20 AA/Mockford & Bonetti; 21 AA/J Holmes; 22l Wirelmage/Getty Images; 22r AA/C Sawyer; 23l AA/Mockford & Bonetti; 23r AA/Mockford & Bonetti; 24 AA/Mockford & Bonetti; 25 AA/Mockford & Bonetti; 26 AA/Mockford & Bonetti; 27l AA/Mockford & Bonetti; 27c AA/S McBride; 27r AA/Mockford & Bonetti; 43l AA/S McBride; 43c AA/Mockford & Bonetti; 43r AA/J Holmes; 45 AA/Mockford & Bonetti; 46 AA/Mockford & Bonetti; 47 AA/Mockford & Bonetti; 48 AA/A Kouprianoff; 49 AA/Mockford & Bonetti; 50/51 AA/Mockford & Bonetti; 51 AA/Mockford & Bonetti; 52 AA/Mockford & Bonetti; 53 AA/Mockford & Bonetti; 54 AA/Mockford & Bonetti; 55 AA/Mockford & Bonetti; 56/57 AA/Mockford & Bonetti; 58 AA/Mockford & Bonetti; 59 AA/Mockford & Bonetti; 60 AA/Mockford & Bonetti; 61 AA/Mockford & Bonetti; 62 AA/Mockford & Bonetti; 63 AA/Mockford & Bonetti; 64 AA/J Holmes; 65 AA/S McBride; 66 AA/S McBride; 67 AA/Mockford & Bonetti; 69 AA/D Miterdiri; 70 AA/Mockford & Bonetti; 71 AA/Mockford & Bonetti; 75l AA/S McBride; 75c AA/D Miterdiri; 75r AA/Mockford & Bonetti; 76 AA/Mockford & Bonetti; 78 AA/Mockford & Bonetti; 79 AA/Mockford & Bonetti; 80/81 AA/C Sawyer; 81 AA/A Kouprianoff; 82/83 AA/S McBride; 84 AA/Mockford & Bonetti; 86 AA/Mockford & Bonetti; 87 AA/Mockford & Bonetti; 88 AA/Mockford & Bonetti; 89 AA/Mockford & Bonetti; 90/91 AA/Mockford & Bonetti; 92 AA/Mockford & Bonetti; 93 AA/Mockford & Bonetti; 94 AA/Mockford & Bonetti; 95 AA/Mockford & Bonetti; 96 AA/Mockford & Bonetti; 97 AA/Mockford & Bonetti; 98t AA/J Holmes; 98b AA/Mockford & Bonetti; 100 AA/Mockford & Bonetti; 101 AA/Mockford & Bonetti; 102 AA/Mockford & Bonetti; 103 AA/F-A Bartholdi; 104 AA/J Holmes; 106 AA/J Holmes; 113l AA/Mockford & Bonetti; 113c AA/D Miterdiri; 113r AA/Mockford & Bonetti; 114 AA/P Wilson; 116 AA/P Wilson; 117t AA/Mockford & Bonetti; 117b AA/D Miterdiri; 118 AA/Mockford & Bonetti; 119 AA/Mockford & Bonetti; 120 AA/Mockford & Bonetti; 121 AA/Mockford & Bonetti; 122 AA/Mockford & Bonetti; 123 AA/Mockford & Bonetti; 124 AA/Mockford & Bonetti; 125 AA/Mockford & Bonetti; 126/127 AA/Mockford & Bonetti; 128 AA/D Miterdiri; 129 AA/D Miterdiri; 130/131 AA/D Miterdiri; 132 AA/D Miterdiri; 134 AA/J Holmes; 135 AA/Mockford & Bonetti; 143l AA/Mockford & Bonetti; 143c AA/Mockford & Bonetti; 143r AA/Mockford & Bonetti; 146 AA/Mockford & Bonetti; 147t AA/Mockford & Bonetti; 147b AA/Mockford & Bonetti; 148 AA/Mockford & Bonetti; 149 AA/Mockford & Bonetti; 150 AA/S McBride; 152/153 AA/S McBride; 154 AA/S McBride; 155 AA/Mockford & Bonetti; 156/157 AA/Mockford & Bonetti; 157t AA/Mockford & Bonetti; 158 AA/Mockford & Bonetti; 159 AA/Mockford & Bonetti; 160 AA/S McBride; 161 AA/J Holmes; 163 AA/Mockford & Bonetti; 164 AA/Mockford & Bonetti; 165 AA/Mockford & Bonetti; 169l AA/Mockford & Bonetti; 169c AA/Mockford & Bonetti; 169r AA/S McBride; 171 AA/Mockford & Bonetti; 172 AA/Mockford & Bonetti; 173 AA/Mockford & Bonetti; 174 AA/S McBride; 175l AA/Mockford & Bonetti; 175c AA/Mockford & Bonetti; 175r AA/Mockford & Bonetti; 176 AA/Mockford & Bonetti; 178 AA/Mockford & Bonetti; 179 AA/Mockford & Bonetti; 180 AA/Mockford & Bonetti; 183 AA/Mockford & Bonetti; 185l AA/S McBride; 185c AA/Mockford & Bonetti; 185r AA/Mockford & Bonetti; 189t AA/Mockford & Bonetti; 189c AA/Mockford & Bonetti; 189b AA/Mockford & Bonetti

Every effort has been made to trace the copyright holders, and we apologise in advance for any unintentional omissions or errors. We would be happy to apply the corrections in a following edition of this publication.

SPIRALGUIDES

Questionnaire

Dear Traveler

Your comments, opinions and recommendations are very important to us. So please help us to improve our travel guides by taking a few minutes to complete this simple questionnaire.

Send to: Spiral Guides, MailStop 64, 1000 AAA Drive, Heathrow, FL 32746–5063

Your recommendations...
We always encourage readers' recommendations for restaurants, nightlife or shopping – if your recommendation is added to the next edition of the guide, we will send you a FREE AAA Spiral Guide of your choice. Please state below the establishment name, location and your reasons for recommending it.

Please send me AAA Spiral
(see list of titles inside the back cover)

About this guide...
Which title did you buy?

_____ AAA Spiral

Where did you buy it? _____

When? m m / y y

Why did you choose a AAA Spiral Guide? _____

Did this guide meet your expectations?

Exceeded ☐   Met all ☐   Met most ☐   Fell below ☐

Please give your reasons _____

continued on next page...

Were there any aspects of this guide that you particularly liked?

Is there anything we could have done better?

About you...

Name (Mr/Mrs/Ms)

Address

Zip

Daytime tel nos.

Which age group are you in?

Under 25 ☐   25–34 ☐   35–44 ☐   45–54 ☐   55–64 ☐   65+ ☐

How many trips do you make a year?

Less than one ☐   One ☐   Two ☐   Three or more ☐

Are you a AAA member? Yes ☐   No ☐

Name of AAA club

About your trip...

When did you book? _m_ _m_ / _y_ _y_   When did you travel? _m_ _m_ / _y_ _y_

How long did you stay?

Was it for business or leisure?

Did you buy any other travel guides for your trip?   Yes ☐   No ☐

If yes, which ones?

Thank you for taking the time to complete this questionnaire.